Love Yourself, Love Your Life

AP Filosa, Psy. D.

Licensed Clinical Psychologist aka Anne F. Creekmore Psy. D.

Copyright © 2024 AP Filosa, Psy. D.
All rights reserved
First Edition

NEWMAN SPRINGS PUBLISHING
320 Broad Street
Red Bank, NJ 07701

First originally published by Newman Springs Publishing 2024

ISBN 978-1-63692-752-7 (Paperback)
ISBN 978-1-63692-753-4 (Digital)

Printed in the United States of America

Contents

Acknowledgments v
Introduction vii

Chapter 1   The Self-fulfilling Prophecy 1
Chapter 2   Feel Your Feelings 15
Chapter 3   Heal Emotional Wounds of the Past 25
Chapter 4   Open Up to Help 33
Chapter 5   Words—Your Magical, Mystical Wand 54
Chapter 6   Speak Your Truth 81
Chapter 7   Create Healthy Relationships 92
Chapter 8   Be a Whole, Fulfilled Person 128
Chapter 9   Raise the Human Race 138
Chapter 10 Shine the Light 154

Glossary 157
References and Resources 163
Information for the Helping Professional—the Clinical Psychotherapeutic Model 167
Index 169

ACKNOWLEDGMENTS

I have so many acknowledgments and words of thanks. I wish to thank my wonderful family: the Filosas—especially Rob, Shirley, Lou, Katie, and Tammy; the Hymeses—especially Matt; my great supporter, Eric Siena; and my awesome children—Elise Creekmore, for her typing, suggestions, and editing, and Trey Creekmore, for the freedom and direction to accomplish this. Thanks for helping me in so many ways with this book and this writing process support, insights, inspiration, even oppositional opinions which helped me grow and be able to understand the work through the eyes and needs of others, as well as all your hands-on help, including typing, reading, editing, financial patronage, etc.

I want to also express appreciation to support people in my life who have shared their knowledge with me that provide information for the book as well as for giving their time and energy generously to read, discuss, and edit the book and help get the book published—Reverend Dwight and Thelma Smith; George Nixon, LPC; Beth Johnson; Joe Burcham; and Robin Zieger, PhD (see chapter 9).

I wish to thank Edna Hepler (notice the twist on "helper") whose partnership with me to type, edit, and format—with a dash of writing thrown in—was a godsend when my morale was low because the hard drive crashed and part of the original book was lost.

I also express gratitude to Patricia Tucker Dodson for her help with the book cover design, and thanks to Devin T. Dodson for his awesome computer graphics. Thanks to the staff at Morris Publishing, especially Gerald Bergstrom, art director, for his extra help and graphics—dynamite logo. Much thanks to Ann Cherry and Mike Shiflett for being my original promotion team, who are generous and gifted in their areas.

I wish to thank Oprah Winfrey and her staff for all her shows, particularly those imparting a spiritual message, such as *The Secret*. By bringing these concepts to the public's attention, she has given me the courage to come forth with my ideas, which expand on the law of attraction. It is my hope that my book's message will bring love and healing to the world, following the path that Oprah has so courageously forged and achieved, in my opinion.

INTRODUCTION

*You can transform your life. You can be happy and fulfilled. You are what you believe.
Your thoughts, your words, your beliefs*—your consciousness creates.

This book teaches you how to use your power, which, like electricity, can be used positively to fry a meal for a man to eat or negatively to fry a man—electrocution. Your power can be controlled by you for your good—rather than causing mishaps innocently as happens in our world.

Over the ages, great masters of religion, spirituality, philosophy, and healing have guided us to better lives. Masters have tried to teach us that there's no need to suffer even in the appearance of pain. They have demonstrated to us how to connect to the divine to be in blissful oneness with the higher power as you perceive it—and to even perform miracles.

As a licensed clinical psychologist, I have worked decades successfully and helped people with all kinds of needs and perspectives, using a clinical model I developed, based on interpretation and integration of the major schools of thought of the human behavior sciences—psychology and other helping professions—as well as concepts from some of the great masters in theology, philosophy, and spirituality to provide a framework to help people transform their lives to joy and fulfillment.

In a down-to-earth language with entertaining stories, poems, workbook instructions, and exercises, this book supplies you with incredible knowledge and skills. I have helped many clients successfully with this model. Measurable benefits are provided to readers whether or not they have spiritual or religious beliefs because the concepts and tools in this model for well-being, such as positive thinking, can be used with great effectiveness without accepting the underpinnings of any conscious religious beliefs. Awareness of the scientifically based spiritual laws strengthens and makes skills, such as positive thinking, last.

This book is for anyone who has ever suffered and who wishes to enhance their well-being.

We will teach how to heal all the aspects of your life—for you to be the true joyful light being that is your essence:

* The Self-fulfilling Prophecy
* Feel Your Feelings
* Heal Emotional Wounds of the Past
* Open Up to Help
* Words—Your Magical, Mystical Wand
* Speak Your Truth
* Create Healthy Relationships
* Be a Whole, Fulfilled Person
* Raise the Human Race
* Shine the Light

My hope is to reach people at many levels:

* Teach the individual self-help concepts and tools so you can heal, be happy and fulfilled, and dramatically improve your life and eliminate suffering.
* Educate the public about psychology and other resources to aid them to be more informed consumers who understand the role of the psychotherapy process so they can appreciate it and benefit from it.
* Encourage a paradigm shift, formally known as thinking outside the box, that will help raise our human consciousness. I hope to even enlighten fellow helping professionals to understand and incorporate the positive underpinnings as to why psychotherapy works and to get on board with scientists and other great minds who are investigating using light energy in their fields—namely, that we are made of light energy that follows certain laws that if we utilize them, then we can manifest our desires and create our lives and, as a human race, reach a critical mass of divinity.

Look, the prison door is open. Learn to love yourself and love your life!

Also, I have included a glossary, which presents new ideas to help you understand and benefit from the book. Words may be defined differently than you have been used to. Feel free now to skim the glossary located after chapter 10.

It would be helpful to keep a journal notebook with you as you read. Begin to write your feelings, thoughts, and responses to exercises. Journaling speeds your progress and helps you dig deeper as well as remember and integrate what you learn.

For more information about the process and the author, visit us at www.psychologistsinvirginia.com.

Chapter 1

The Self-fulfilling Prophecy

All my thoughts are positive and self-enhancing. My feelings are good and happy. My relationships are healthy, loving, harmonious, peaceful, and mutual. I have radiant health. I'm guided to right action at all times. I live in serenity, prosperity, and abundance. I'm healed and healthy in mind, body, and spirit.

What is a self-fulfilling prophecy?

Prophecy is forecasting the future. In psychology, a self-fulfilling prophecy refers to when we have certain thoughts and/or attitudes about our lives and ourselves, which in turn create our feelings and intensifies the thought. These intense beliefs cause us to behave in certain ways and make certain choices and thus create our life outcomes. How do you believe your life would be if you said the above affirmation (in italics) throughout your day?

Exercise: Now, say the affirmation to yourself. Can you feel a difference in your emotions and your body? Do you feel more relaxed and positive? Can you see how your calmness and confidence might enhance your ability to handle experiences as you come about them during the day?

Diagram of the self-fulfilling prophecy

    Thoughts cluster into beliefs and attitudes, which affect and combine with
    ↓
    our emotions, or feelings, which intensify our thinking and choices, which
    ↓
    manifest in the physical: our lives, our behaviors, our life situations, our lifestyles, which include
    ↓
    relationships, work, finances, health, etc.

The importance of positive self-talk and positive self-statements

It's not what happens to us but what we think about and say to ourselves about what happens that determines how we feel. Our interpretation of events tells us how to react.

For example, when I was a child, I was shy. Perhaps this originated because my parents didn't like my dramatic nature of emotional expression. They constantly reprimanded me to stop expressing myself with "Who are you, Sarah Bernhardt?" a famous actress of their time. As I grew older, I replayed these tapes in my mind after interpersonal scenarios. After I left situations, I would criticize what I'd said and done. Naturally, over time, I chose to interact and expose myself less and less. My shyness grew. That is, until I became a clinical psychologist and learned the power of self-talk. I realized that my social anxiety did not stem from anything bad happening in my real-life situations. No one actually said or did anything nasty to me, *but me*. I realized I avoided social situations not because they were difficult but because I beat myself up verbally! Once I stopped my negative self-statements, my shyness diminished. Social situations became fun.

Let us take another example. Let us compare two different reactions to the same test results, if you are a student, or a performance evaluation, if you are an employee. Two people get the same written feedback. The test results or job evaluation contains some negative feedback or comments. One person with positive self-worth says to himself or herself: "This is a fluke," "I'm a really good student or worker," "I just need to study or present myself better," or "I'll try harder." The next test grade or evaluation is likely to show improvement. The person has encouraged himself or herself through positive self-talk. Conversely, a different individual with belief and feelings of low self-worth interprets the critical test or evaluation negatively and says: "I'm a failure," "They don't like me," "I'm going to fail the grade or lose my job," "I'm not good," "People don't like me," "My teacher or boss doesn't like me," "I don't belong here," "I can't do this," or something else to that effect. This creates a depressed, sad, disappointed, or irritated feeling from negative thinking.

In the first case, the person felt supported, motivated, and complimented to try harder. And in the latter case, the feelings engendered were discouragement and depression; and the consequent behavioral reaction was to either become so anxious that he or she couldn't think straight to perform well or to give up, not try, and thereby fail.

These feelings and thoughts combine to create how the person reacts to the evaluation. Usually, when a person thinks that he or she is not acceptable, put down, or considered a loser in a situation, he or she doesn't try very hard because he or she doesn't feel able to change the situation. Or there is anxiety, so mistakes are made and performance is poor. Both outcomes are impaired performance at school or work.

If you say such negative things to yourself, you're not empowering yourself to create a better situation. You perceive yourself as helpless; you probably will not improve in your performance. You'll do worse and have a negative outcome.

Exercise: Put the book down. And for the next ten minutes, go about your business and notice what, if anything, your inner voice says to yourself. As you work on some tasks, go watch television or whatever you do. You'll notice that you are making some commentary about what's going on, about what you're seeing and doing. This doesn't mean that you are crazy. You're human; we are different from animals. We think and can speak. We don't just act in an instinctual fashion. We have the capacity to observe or comment on ourselves to analyze what's going on in our lives and to verbalize experiences. Was this a surprise to you? Then this is a good start. If you were aware of this before, this is also good.

We think and talk silently to ourselves, sometimes even aloud, and that is okay too. We observe our situations and ourselves. We also talk about ourselves, not just what's going on around us. We call these comments in psychology "self-statements." Our self-statements create a lot about our life experience, as was demonstrated in the previous example. Our self-statements, not the actual situation—our interpretation of our life experiences—provide the core of our existence.

Self-statements are thoughts about us—and like thoughts attract each other and crystallize and combine into beliefs and attitudes about ourselves, particularly our self-esteem and self-worthiness, such as beliefs of being successful, good, and lovable versus feelings of being bad, unlovable, and unsuccessful. We may or may not be aware of our beliefs or thought of self-worthiness.

Exercise: Go about your business or task for another ten minutes and notice what comments you silently, or perhaps even aloud, make to yourself. If you make a mistake while you're doing something, what did you say? Do you say to yourself, "That was stupid"? Or do you say to yourself: "No big deal," "Stuff happens," or, better, "I'm going to make lemonade out of a lemon"? What did your self-statements say about your beliefs about yourself? Were your comments encouraging and reflective of good self-worth? This is an opportunity to talk to yourself differently. Some good will come out of it.

Exercise: Test your understanding of this concept with this real-life example. A man regularly attended, enjoyed, and benefited from Adult Children of Alcoholics and Al-Anon meetings. However, after one meeting, a woman who had monopolized the sharing time of the meeting approached him and said, "You were awfully quiet tonight." Perhaps she was wondering if she had talked too much, but he began to obsess over his perceived inadequacy. Question: If he says to himself something such as, "People are looking down on me because I don't know how to express myself," what are his feelings and reactions likely to be? If it were you, would you attend more or fewer meetings? How could one differently interpret the woman's comment in a non-self-defeating manner? (A clue is in the description of what happened—she did all the talking! Don't take what others say personally. They're usually talking about themselves and their own stuff.) What could this man have thought to support himself and his positive efforts toward self-growth so he doesn't shy away from future support groups and continues to grow at his own pace?

This is based on an inspiring, true event:

View

In this little area,
I make my home.
My blindness a barrier
To my desire to roam.

Yet I can see,
Oh, blinding brilliant light
Like a shining beacon
In the dark black night.

I chose this chained body
That my spirit can soar
And warm like a toddy
On a crisp, cool fall morn.

My love and I travel
On a dismal dawn,
Yet my senses unravel
The Beauty beyond.

"Oh, listen," I cry,
"To the rustling leaves.
They scamper and fly
With delight in the breeze."

Aghast, he scans the car lot,
And he shares a news flash,
"Dear, this is just Wal-Mart,
And it's littered with trash."

I say, "I like my view,"
And we laugh with glee,
For in his heart, he knew.
Truly, I can see.

Through our hearts,
We can see
Divine Sparks
Of Truth and Beauty.

Through our hearts,
We can see
Divine Sparks
Of Reality.

—A. Filosa, PsyD

The process of change

Likewise, when we want to improve our lives, we follow three steps so that we can arrive at our goal of joy and fulfillment. One, we must know ourselves (know our underlying thoughts, beliefs, and attitudes and their origins). This way, we know where we are—our starting point—and our desired goal. Two, we must accept this and not fool ourselves by coping or defending ourselves against our inner reality (explanation below). Then, three, we must figure out the actions necessary to get to where we want to go, such as positive self-talk or affirmations that create positive life outcomes for us.

The process of change to improve our lives involves three steps:

1. awareness
2. acceptance
3. action

Let's relate these to a car trip:

1. Awareness. To get anywhere, we have to know or be aware of where we are in the first place, our place of origin as well as our point of destination or goal.
2. Acceptance. We have to accept where we are. Only then can we figure out how to go from point A to point B, our destination. No map can help us unless we accept reality and know or are aware of our starting point and ending.
3. Action. Finally, we have to get into the car and actually drive there; we have to take action.

Thinking positively is crucial

The true measure of a man's mental health [and happiness] is his ability to see good everywhere.

—Ralph Waldo Emerson

Change can be introduced at any of the above levels in the self-fulfilling prophecy chain: thoughts, feelings, or physical life manifestations. In the most effective type of psychotherapy, cognitive therapy, the therapist directs the client to become aware of or recognize his or her thoughts or cognitions. This is done in order to change negative thoughts, particularly negative self-statements (statements about oneself), to positive self-enhancing ones, thereby improving general emotional well-being and sense of control over one's life and consequently enhancing one's confidence, self-esteem, and motivation to take care of oneself and improve one's life. Problem-solving life situations become much easier once the client realizes his or her responsibility or control.

Positive thinking works because we—as part of the universe—are a pulsating light energy field balancing off each other and affecting each other. There is a tremendous amount of research supporting the observer effect—that our consciousness influences matter. This will be discussed at greater length later on in the book.

Given that the first cause of our lives is "sponsoring thoughts" (Louise Hay, *Heal Your Life*), logically change is best aimed at this level. This is necessary and sufficient for change to occur. On the other hand, if our negative thoughts do not change, our life problems will return inevitably in some other negative form even if we try to change the life situation.

Psychotherapy research supports that cognitive (thought) change leads to stable, proper brain chemistry, increased serotonin, and a positive mood. Cognitive therapy works as well for depression as psychiatric antidepressant drugs. It has been shown to work effectively, in general, with mental or emotional disorders, even psychoses (when the person accepts the hallucinations as hallucinations and tells them to go back or away).

Focusing on our physical reality, we often direct our efforts toward changing our physical experience, situations, other people, status, etc. Power struggling to change the physical, however, without the awareness of the basis of life—namely, our thoughts—is a waste of time. Changing aspects of physical reality can be helpful only if we change the underlying thought pattern. It can be helpful on a permanent basis when we change the underlying negative thinking. For example, if unhappy at work, we can change jobs. But if we do not change our attitude, we will manifest, in some way, the same restlessness, dissatisfaction. We can divorce our spouse, but unless we recognize the underlying thought pattern, such as trust issues with people, we will continue to hold beliefs that we are unlovable or treated unfairly. We will continue to create interpersonal suffering and unhappy partnerships. We may learn some new tricks to make our situation look better by appearance. However, we will create problems in future partnerships or situations unless the underlying negative thoughts are changed.

Our lives are the physical manifestation of our core thinking and beliefs about our world and us. We believe we are good, and our lives will reflect this. We doubt ourselves, and apparent suffering results.

Origins of negative thinking patterns

Many of these thought patterns originate from childhood experiences. We are constantly replaying tapes about what our parents and other significant people in our lives said and did to us about our world and us. Experiences that created pain and negativity in us—traumas, losses, neglects, abuses, even smaller-magnitude disappointments, criticisms, rejections, and fears—had to be tolerated when we were children; a child cannot get in a car and escape family troubles or go vent to a counselor. To cope, we developed defense mechanisms or "blind spots" to survive, ways of numbing ourselves and adapting to the discomfort. For example, individuals who were brutally traumatized may have mentally escaped through multiple personalities or psychosis. Since few escape at least some degree of family dysfunction, we can safely assume that all of us have defense mechanisms that would allow us to avoid the intensity of our emotional pain related to uncomfortable childhood situations. Usually, our defense mechanisms develop in our childhood to survive certain dysfunctional family situations that we had no way out of but to try to tolerate and cope with it.

The difficulty ensues when we persist in using these coping mechanisms of childhood later on in life to our detriment. We do this because our blind spots are invisible, being psychological. We often are unaware of and cannot make the necessary adjustments to release them even though they cripple us. They may bind or chafe as old shoes would. For example, take the individual whose trust was shattered as a child through sexual abuse and continues as an adult to have multiple personalities when there is no longer any abuse to escape. As a child, he or she could not drive to a therapist's office and complain. He or she was stuck at home, so he or she learned to mentally, creatively withdraw from abusive incidents. In dissociative disorders, this is called going away or switching into alters (alternative personality or mood states).

Let me give you an analogy about defenses from a real-life example. When my son was about six months old, he was sitting on the floor in his little carrier seat watching *Barney*, his favorite popular children's TV show. Upstairs, putting away linens, I heard him screech. Then he quickly stopped. I hurriedly rushed down the steps. To my surprise, my baby son was still contentedly watching his show—only from the funny-looking, awkward position of holding himself up by one arm. As the carrier seat had fallen over sideways, he had prevented his fall by holding himself up in a sideways push-up. He resumed his viewing of the purple dinosaur by simply cocking his head to right his viewing capacity—hence, the instant quiet of his cry and, perhaps, the beginnings of a soft TV addiction!

To draw an analogy, let us assume that his carrier seat was defective, he fell over regularly, and he had to constantly protect himself like this. But let us add that I could not see him in his awkward position. Let us add that because I am drawing an analogy between a physical situation and a development of an emotional pattern, and we cannot actually see inner psychological processes of emotions, so we need to pretend we cannot see this situation. If this situation repeated itself enough, he would assume this posture regularly to watch TV until it became a habit. This illustrates how we can become crippled psychologically and emotionally in awkward, although appropriate, positions to the original situation. We ourselves do not see such as problematic but rather as a helpful coping strategy to a dysfunctional situation. Furthermore, others, even our parents, are oblivious to the distorted state since our emotions and thinking are invisible and they were not privy to the original development, so they don't know why we are acting that distorted way. Others recognize the oddness or inappropriateness of the behavior, but no one knows why or what had become second nature to us or our comfort zone or habit.

Only when we, as adults, let go of our defenses and allow ourselves to face the painful feelings associated with the original dysfunctional scenarios we tried to cope with can we confront our life proactively, rather than seeing ourselves as victims. In the case of my son, he would first need to brave his fear and cease straining to hold himself up whereupon he would find out he did not fall. Once we become aware of our defense mechanisms and stop using them, we learn more appropriate strategies on how to get our needs met and create our lives the way we would like them to be instead of reacting as if we are still trapped in the old defective situation. We can become aware of how our underlying negative beliefs, about the world and ourselves, come from experiences. These cause us to overreact to aspects in our current situation. When aspects of our current situation remind us of past traumatic situations, we react defensively as we did in the past to protect ourselves, as my son did when he flung out his arm to hold himself up. If this had happened repeatedly and no one had known to rescue him, he might have developed a habit in later life every time he felt a little off-balance to lean sideways and support himself with one arm. This posture would surely have seemed odd to others but would have felt comfortable and necessary to his well-being. He would be inappropriately defensive or extreme, acting in a self-defeating way, only with understandably good reason if you understood this development of the behavior or coping mechanism. Moreover, backfiring ironically, defenses usually create what we fear will happen. No doubt, our fictional baby would have developed a chronic physical imbalance, some nasty side effects (and nasty looks), from straining sideways chronically.

The first step in the process of change is awareness

Step 1, *awareness*. Become aware of negative thinking. Consider subconscious thoughts, beliefs, or attitudes that are non-self-enhancing—any thoughts not consistent with believing in yourself as prosperous, lovable, successful, happy, or whatever else your heart desires. Any problem that we have in our physical reality is a result of a problem in our thought pattern.

It may be easy to identify our negative self-statement. With some turning inward, one recognizes saying negative things to oneself—statements so rude only an enemy might make them and certainly not friendly or encouraging words. For example, would you tell a friend who was afraid to try something new that he or she is a loser, would probably fail, or everybody would probably reject them anyway? No. That would not be acting like a friend—more like an enemy. Yet people do this to themselves all the time.

For example, a client recently moved to this area and was feeling depressed and lonely, unable to adjust to the new location. How her negative self-statements impaired her ability to transcend her isolation and develop fulfilling activities in the area became clear. She shared that she was becoming tearful while filling out an application to volunteer at a museum because she evaluated her work experiences as inadequate. She expected to be rejected for a volunteer position. Her thought that she was not good enough made her so fearful of rejection that she could not bear to complete the application, let alone send it in. Hence, her fear resulted in exactly what she was afraid of—continued isolation.

Have you ever said anything like that to yourself when you consider doing something new? Have you ever heard or seen your role models and significant others say or display nastiness or negativity to you or others? This may also clue you to the negative thinking you have internalized (audiotapes you may be replaying unconsciously in your head to yourself) which may impair the quality of your life. Know that if you have any life problems at all, you are thinking or accepting some negative thoughts related to and underlying the difficulties.

Defense mechanisms are tricky, and sometimes we need extra help to realize when we are using them. Other people, friends, and therapists can help us. However, if we continue to use ways to avoid our painful feelings such that we do not deal with the fact that we are unhappy in our lives, we may never be motivated to understand ourselves and change thought patterns to improve our lives. These defense mechanisms interfere with our lives because we are having negative thoughts causing our problems. We may not remember or credit much importance to events, such as trauma and loss, which cause us to have low self-worth and mistrustful attitudes about our world. The pain and hurt underlying disparaging attitudes which shape our existence remain unrecognized.

I heard somewhere that, first, we are cameras, and then we become projectors. As infants, we are like the blank screen of unused film. Then our life experiences imprint on us such that we are much like a video camera recording life happenings in an audio-visual form. We internalize our experiences in our memories, feelings, and thinking patterns. What happens to us begins to shape what we think and feel about our world and ourselves. We replay the tapes repeatedly, and since we are doing this while we are experiencing our lives simultaneously, the tapes become confused with our reality. The tapes interfere with and weaken our perception of reality, much like if we were to wear special cloudy colored glasses or like if we were schizophrenic—see and hear things that are not there but are actually hallucinations. This is how and when we become projectors. These are projections of the baggage of tapes we have experienced and hence interpreted in our daily life experiences based on old home movies. Our dark sides are our blind spots and haze our thinking and perceptions of the moment. We live in a fantasy camp.

Psychological defense mechanisms can interfere with our awareness that we are thinking negatively. These are outdated coping mechanisms we learned growing up to survive dysfunctional families or lifestyles. Refusing to see the obvious, "everyday living insanity" is doing the same thing repeatedly but expecting a different result.

Defense mechanisms

The following is a list, by no means exhaustive, of possible defense mechanisms reflecting our projector state of mind. Even though one of the defenses is called projection technically and means blaming someone else for our problems, all defenses are actually projections of our old, past internalized issues and result in distortions of perceptions of our current experiences:

Denial (Don't Even kNow IAm Lying). For example, an alcoholic—who has received a DWI (driving while intoxicated) is on the verge of divorce, can't manage his money, and is known by all as a "drunk"— denies that his drinking has anything to do with his life problems, including the DWI. Until he stops denying that he has a drinking problem, he will not take responsibility to control his drinking nor be able to see how his life problems relate to his heavy drinking. Nor will he identify what upsetting situations, his underlying negative ideas, and feelings that he is avoiding or trying to cope with through his addiction. Can he rectify his problems in living unless he faces and deals with them maturely rather than avoiding them? The more he avoids, the more they build up.

Identification with a lost object (incorporating an aspect of someone who you have lost—into your own personality). For example, a woman's aunt dies. She inherits some of her clothes. Red was the aunt's favorite color. The woman begins wearing red all the time. For another instance, children who are sexually abused will often feel shame; they have internalized the perpetrator's fear of being caught.

Immature defenses (fantasy avoidance, addictions, or acting out behaviors). One can be an alcoholic, workaholic, foodaholic, sexaholic, emotionsaholic, or TVaholic—there are soft addictions like TV. In other words, any mental preoccupation can sap one's energy and focus from taking care of yourself and being responsible. This causes the avoidance of painful feelings, getting your mind off your troubles through escapism. Avoidance of your life dissatisfactions and stressors creates more trouble because you do not deal maturely with your feelings to resolve your life problems—until one hits rock bottom and experiences painful negative consequences and is forced to face the issues.

Intellectualization (avoiding feelings through overthinking or overanalyzing). We do not experience our feelings, such as grief or sadness, because when a feeling is triggered, we automatically begin obsessing and trying to understand the upsetting situation intellectually, which keeps us from experiencing painful feelings.

Introjection (internalizing other people's stuff or responsibilities). One feels guilty for something that is someone else's responsibility. For example, mothers often feel guilty when family members experience troubles they brought on themselves. For another example, spouses of alcoholics often feel guilty for their partners' drinking.

Minimization (downplaying the importance of a negative behavior). This is like repression in that an individual does not take responsibility for one's actions. One minimizes one's negative behavior, as with all defense mechanisms; therefore, you cannot look at yourself or your behavior or accept it. An example is an alcoholic who drinks all day and says he cannot be an alcoholic because he only drinks beer. Minimizing is that beer has less alcoholic content than liquor.

Projection (blaming others, or something else, for our problems). An example is an alcoholic who claims he would never drink if his wife would stop nagging him. How likely is he to stop drinking? And how likely is she to stop nagging?

Projective identification (one projects out onto other people and the environment one's own negative feelings). For examples, a person who has a lot of rage believes others are out to get him or her or the sneaky person projects his or her own sneakiness and consequently mistrusts and sees others' actions in a suspicious manner.

Rationalization (making excuses for why we do things a certain way). For an example of rationalization, a person with intimacy problems says, "I have to work this hard because we need the money to survive as a couple," even though the couple may be on the verge of divorce because they have no time together. This sets up having to pay for double living expenses like separate residences when they divorce! The fear of intimacy sets up an intimacy barrier. Work is just an excuse.

This also illustrates important aspects of how defense mechanisms backfire or set the person up for the exact original painful experience—repeating or reenacting itself. The defense mechanisms actually push buttons in people so they treat us in a manner similarly to the original painful experience. Ideally, we can reexperience and heal from it. More on healing these past wounds later (see chapter 5). In the above example, the person sets himself up for rejection and prevents intimacy, confirming the original fear of the precariousness of love stemming from a sense of unlovability and/or untrustworthiness of people from parental neglects and/or abandonment.

Repression (blocking out memories or isolating feelings from memories). We believe everything is okay because we blocked out, at least partially, memory of the trauma or grief experience. The whole memory, part of the memory, or only the feeling may be isolated from the event.

Here is an example: When I was ten years old, we moved from New York to Virginia because my father needed to get a job. That meant leaving my whole, close-knit family in New York. Because my parents did not have a lot of money, we did not go back to visit, except for a funeral for my grandfather, which we children could not attend because we were sick. Moving away from my family was a major loss. At the same time, my best girlfriend's mother and my two grandfathers (with whom I had been close) all died in the same year. This created a catastrophic grief for me with so many losses that I blocked out the painful feelings about it. I knew about the events, but I did not have awareness of my grief, which was too painful. This coping, or defense mechanism of isolating the feeling from the memory, was encouraged by my family. They discouraged displays of grief—and never allowed us to mourn to release sad feelings nor showing me by role modeling how to grieve, release feelings, get comfort, etc. Interestingly, I would say to myself periodically, "Gee, I hope I never lose anyone close to me to death. Since I have never had to do it, I don't know if I could handle it." I was so in denial that, even though I remembered the deaths and losses, I felt numb and I never connected or experienced my grief. Instead, I became overprotective of loved ones, such as my children, fearing their demise around every corner—anticipatory loss. Actually, I feared the emergence of my buried repressed grief.

In my case, repressed grief was an intergenerational problem. My father lost his father as a young child. When we moved from New York and left his family, this also brought up the grief of his father's death. His defense mechanism of denial and repression prevented him from experiencing his grief and role modeled for me how not to grieve.

Exercise: Look at the list of defense mechanisms. Do you think you might use any of these? If you feel comfortable, ask a supportive, trusted friend or helping professional to evaluate you as well.

For example, recently, a man moved in with a woman. As he was fixing up his study, she made the innocent comment that his office had such strong overhead lighting he would not even need a lamp for lighting. He became enraged, shouting, "Are you going to try to run my life?" He had felt overcontrolled as a child and was constantly replaying these tapes unconsciously in buried, seething resentment as he went through life. He frequently misinterpreted interpersonal circumstances as if he was being controlled. He was projecting out onto his reality his old home movies. He was being a projector rather than a camera and actually was doing what he perceived her to be doing—trying to overcontrol the situation. For if he did not even allow her to make simple remarks that could somehow suggest a desire to control, he was in fact commanding control of her basic right to freedom of speech!

Unfortunately, the more emotionally intimate we become to others, the freer we feel to express ourselves immediately and vehemently, when one would think the opposite would be preferred—e.g., that we would want to be nicest and most polite to the ones we love the most. That same caring yet sensitive man, for instance, became enraged and jealous when a fellow Alanon member mentioned to him that he was going to an event with his new sponsor, who turned out to be the same sponsor he had. However, because he did not feel the same lack of reserve he did with his partner, he did not lash into automatic projection mode. Instead, he spent a fitful night wondering why the information that his friend also shared his sponsor bothered him. He realized it was because he himself had not been using his sponsor at all, and it reminded him of his own lack of self-care and growth in the twelve-step program. Now that's being a camera!

Homework: Ask yourself, "Am I a camera or a projector?" the next time you become angry or upset.

The second step in the process of change is acceptance

Step 2, *acceptance*. Once we become aware and know where we are (point A), then we can set our sights on joy and fulfillment, our goal (point B), and plan how we can arrive at our destination. In other words, if we get into a car and aren't aware of our starting point, no map can help us arrive at a destination. We can only take action to change to become our best selves and live our most fulfilling lives when we become aware of our true deep beliefs about ourselves and the world and our consequent feelings. We must recognize our defense mechanisms, know, and accept who we are.

Defense mechanisms interfere with solving our real-life problems because we do not accept where we are or who we are and that our negative thoughts are overpicturing into our behaviors and our negative life experiences—the negative thoughts that are causing our problems. We might not even realize, or remember, events such as a trauma or loss that caused us to have very low self-worth. Take the individuals who face their addictions and enter a twelve-step recovery programs or support groups. As they wean from their escapist defenses and abstain from their addiction, underlying issues and personal pain that caused them to drink emerges and come up for healing—buried traumas and losses growing up, perhaps their own abusive, neglectful, alcoholic parents. This brings us to the root of problems in living—the negative core beliefs about our world and our negative self-statements, thinking and those erroneous tapes, and ourselves filled with negativity that we keep bombarding ourselves with—terrorizing ourselves that we must shut off! Getting at the root cause of the problem is like removing a weed from the lawn at its root instead of just mowing over it, which keeps it coming back.

The third step in the process of change is action

Step 3, *action*. This involves moving out of our comfort zone—releasing the defense mechanisms—stopping the addictions that interfere with our true awareness, taking responsibility for ourselves and our self-imposed misery as well as recognizing our responsibility for our lives and the relationship between our negative thinking and life problems. This involves being willing to change.

Exercise: Part A. As you did in a previous exercise, for the next ten or fifteen minutes, go about your business and observe without judgment what you are saying to yourself. Having an ongoing inner dialogue, which we know reflects our own thinking, is not crazy but rather reflects our humanness. Different from the animal that behaves instinctively in a unified manner, we humans possess the capacity to be or behave while simultaneously observing, analyzing, and evaluating ourselves. As you do tasks or relax over the next fifteen minutes, note what you say to yourself. If you make a mistake, do you speak supportively with encouragement or do you cut yourself down with an insult? In other words, do your self-statements encourage you to feel good or in some way cause you to have negative feelings, like guilt, worry, or dissatisfaction?

Part B. After you complete the above exercise, try a corrective approach. For the next ten or fifteen minutes, speak only in a complimentary way to yourself. See and state that everything you do and everything that is happening to you is good. You are wonderful, and the entire events that are happening to you are blessings. How do you feel?

Challenge exercise: Do this exercise for the rest of the day and every day for the rest of your life!

Helpful hint: Use "thought stopping." Whenever you make a self or other depreciating comment, stop. Say the opposite. One therapist even advocated that his clients wear rubber bands on their wrists so they can snap them lightly to get their attention when they said something negative to themselves! Gentle please.

Thoughts are your empowerment and key to creating a fulfilling life

I am good, and I have and deserve good.

Happiness is earned through the perfect control of your emotional nature. There cannot be happiness when there is fear, apprehension, or dread. Where do our feelings come from? Where do the feelings of love or fear originate? They come from our thoughts. Our power to control our lives does not come from focusing on manipulating external life stressors, situations, or people. We do not gain true power through money, interpersonal power, job success, or any other traditionally assumed forms of happiness. The American dream of a good job, family, nice house, a good income, etc., as many of us have found out, is not a guarantee to personal happiness. Happiness stems from within. The appearance of external abundance, such as the American dream, does not necessarily equate with inner happiness. Research has shown that we adapt to material stuff after a while and need more stuff to make us happy. The power struggle and the striving for control over external situations are wrong. What looks good on the surface does not necessarily feel good inside.

This is so because our true empowerment or our feeling good come from control and discipline of our consciousness and our thoughts to be positive. This is so because thoughts create and fulfill our inner hearts' desires. As Gary Zukav states in his best seller, *Seat of the Soul*, it is our intention (our thoughts and accompanying emotions) that shape the direction our lives will take.

The foundation or core of our life situation lies within our deepest feelings and thoughts. These thoughts create feelings and together overpicture in our physical reality. Our lives manifest or demonstrate what we are thinking. It is not so much what happens to us that determines how we feel but what we think about what happens or how we interpret events.

For example, a client of mine who wanted to be an art therapist suddenly realized that working with children might be a satisfying specialty area for her. She was at a church service when the speaker shared that her son had an aggressive cancer. Inspired, my client was drawn to speak words of courage and appreciation to the speaker after the service. The woman hugged and thanked her.

Afterward, however, although nothing negative had happened in the situation, my client began criticizing herself, "Who was she to be bold? What did she know?" and so on, to the point that she felt bad about a beautiful experience she had initiated. Sometimes we act right yet still think wrong.

This client was also having extreme difficulty completing an application to get into graduate school because of all her self-hate and self-criticism. She loathed herself while others recognized her talent. She constantly reprimanded herself, "Not for me," and could not make career progress. Instead, she would take an isolated academic course and volunteer work, rather than enrolling in an actual art therapy program (her dream) which would enable her to get into a self-respecting career.

How to train your thoughts to be healthy

1. Thought stop: Stop. Observe or listen to your thinking. What are you saying to yourself internally? Pay special attention to your self-statements—comments you make about yourself.
2. Are they positive or negative? Identify and isolate the negative self-statements—nasty things you might think about an enemy, not what you would say to a friend, any statement that makes you feel bad, upset, discouraged, unhappy, etc.
3. Dig deeper and identify negative core beliefs—beliefs that you are not worthy, lovable, good, deserving, etc.

Examples of negative core beliefs are:

* I am worthless.
* I am not good enough.
* I am unlovable. People don't like or care about me. If people like me or care about me, something must be wrong with them. If people knew me, they would not like me or approve of me.
* Life is a struggle. Life is not worth living.
* I have to constantly prove myself to others.
* I am empty. I have nothing good inside me, and I have nothing to give.
* I am stupid, incompetent, a failure, a loser.
* I cannot be me. I cannot express. I have to please people to get acceptance.
* I need to make you feel bad so you do not realize how bad I am (the best defense is a good offense).

And any other verbally or mentally abusive thoughts about yourself.

4. One, replace the negative thought about yourself with a better, positive one, usually the opposite. For example, change the negative thought "I'm stupid" to a replacement positive thought "I'm smart." Two, argue to convince yourself of the truth of the positive. For example, I have a good GPA. I am in graduate school, or I got the best score on the test this week. Three, act as if this new thought is true—that you believe thoroughly in yourself.
5. Afterward, compliment yourself for thinking positively. You are transforming your life. Good job! Good work! You are likely to repeat this positive affirming process if you reward yourself after you do it.

This coming week's homework

1. Check your internal voice messages.
2. Ask yourself, "Am I leaving myself friendly or mean messages? Do I feel better or worse after what I say to myself? Do my thoughts and self-statements bring me up or down?
3. "Thought stop" the downers. Ignore the negative self-statements. Stop the thought. Do not go there. Tell yourself no.
4. Replace the negative thought or self-statement with a positive one that brings you up, makes you feel good about yourself and hopeful about your life.
5. Compliment yourself for taking the time and energy to work the program to learn to love yourself and create a happy, fulfilling life.
6. Formulate a positive affirmation based on the new thought. Repeat it to yourself throughout the day. Examples: I am good. I am lovable. I am competent. Your positive affirmations.
7. Identify your negative defensive patterns, like projection or blame. "Fear—Face Everything and Recover" (Alcoholics Anonymous (AA) motto).
8. Note: Liberally use yet don't hide behind positive defensives, like humor and sublimation (channeling painful feelings, like anger or despair, into creative outlets or hobbies and constructive causes—for example, express your pain through an artistic or humanitarian endeavor).

Chapter 2

Feel Your Feelings

Feel your way to a beautiful feeling. Aah, I feel joy.

Your feelings are your guides to understand and love yourself

Feeling and dealing with your emotions is crucial because (1) thoughts without emotion have no power because the thoughts' passion and intensity create the self-fulfilling prophecy and (2) feelings provide clues to your deepest underlying thoughts, your beliefs and attitudes, which subconsciously or unconsciously direct your life. Awareness of the underlying causes—painful feelings or issues, like childhood traumas—is needed to understand one's core negative beliefs or attitudes which, because of emotional damage done, may be self-limiting. Your core beliefs have to be positive so you can accept positive stuff into your life.

The theory of cognitive dissonance holds that a person cannot believe two competing ideas at the same time. One has to go. For example, a chemist blending tobacco for cigarettes cannot hold two competing thoughts, like "I am a good person" and "Smoking kills people." Therefore, to maintain the sense of being a good person, he has to deny that smoking damages people, buying into the idea that smoking disease research is purely correlational and that smoking is not causative of health problems. Likewise, if you have experiences of being rejected or not cared for properly in childhood, you may hold the unconscious belief that you are not good or lovable, and thus, it may be difficult for you to truly engage in positive thinking, positive self-talk, and healthy, loving relationship until you let go of this underlying limiting belief.

Wouldn't it be nice to feel our power of intent to the extent that the biblical character Daniel did in the den of lions? Daniel knew he was one with the omnipotent power of God and that the lions could not hurt him. One with the source—God flowing through and around him—he put forth his desire, and he was safe. He *thought* of the lions as wonderful, awesome creatures with whom he could harmoniously commune, and so he did. As we come to accept our thoughts as our power, we can rely on changing our thoughts as the source to create new and better lives.

Imagine your thoughts are like a glass of water that is filled with murky mud. If you take a pitcher of clear, clean water and keep pouring it into the muddy glass, the mud will overflow out, and clear water will replace it. If you keep doing this, eventually you will have a glass of clean, pure, fresh water. Wouldn't it be nice to flush out your own negativity and replace it with clear, healthy, positive thoughts and feelings? As our thoughts change, we are moved, or guided, to change ourselves to do things differently. As our thought pattern changes, this manifests in the physical overpicturing of our minds' true joyful desires.

For example, as I affirm that my relationships are healthy, functional, supportive, loving, and peaceful, I find myself immediately walking away if anyone expresses negativity. This is not in my world. My world is peaceful and harmonious. I deny the existence of negativity, and so it is. My actions change, corresponding to my beliefs. What does this have to do with feelings? My feelings guided me to what I needed to do to make happen what I believed I deserved. When I felt angry, which is hurt underneath, I was guided to manifest my beliefs of harmony to withdraw from the situation. Feeling my anger sparked me to walk away from the situation to take care of and love myself.

Feelings provide us with clues to our thoughts and unconscious feelings, beliefs, and attitudes. As was stated earlier, we may use psychological defense mechanisms that interfere with knowing our thoughts or feelings. As we take time to experience and become aware of our feelings, we can trace them back to our often self-limiting or negative thoughts. In the example, when a person received critical comments from others on a performance evaluation and reacted negatively, the feelings could be traced back to the belief that they were a failure or loser at heart. Without acknowledging the feelings of disappointment or rejection, you cannot trace back to the original self-limiting belief. Feeling your feelings is important because it allows you to become aware of your thoughts and change them. If you use defense mechanisms, rather than feel your feelings, you are not motivated or able to correct your thoughts. If you admit you feel bad about yourself and your life, instead of blaming others, you can access the root cause of your problems, namely, your negative thinking.

Love and fear: the basic emotions

We have many feelings and emotions. These feelings are all variations of four basic emotions: happy, sad, scared, and mad. According to psychological research, even four-year-old children can identify the four basic feelings. They actually can be condensed into two basic feelings: love or happiness and fear, which includes sadness or anticipatory loss. Fear includes sadness because fear of loss is at its root. For example, when we feel disappointed, we can take it to a deeper level, which involves a fear of losing something crucial to us. If we feel hurt by a loved one, at the bottom is fear; we cannot survive in some way without this person. They may abandon us, and we are going to reexperience an old loss or abandonment or, most likely, fear that we will experience our own deeply buried grief over someone or something we've already lost, which we have been avoiding.

Exercise: Think about some recent emotions or typical emotions you have experienced frequently. Label them—for example, "depressed," "jealous," "thrilled," etc. Now evaluate them and decide whether they are an expression of love or fear. Example: "thrilled—love" or "depressed—fear" (sad type).

Turn to the next page for a feelings chart to check your answers. You will notice that on the left side are emotions related to love and on the right side are feelings related to the opposite of love—fear. At the top surface of fear is anger—a superficial defense mechanism against the underlying feelings. You will notice fear broken into its two genuine expressions: fear and sad.

Anger is the mask that men wear to hide their feelings. Do not stay stuck in anger. Ask yourself, "What's below the anger? Sad or afraid?" Then focus on healing the sad or afraid feelings.

Feel Your Feelings

THE FEELINGS CHART

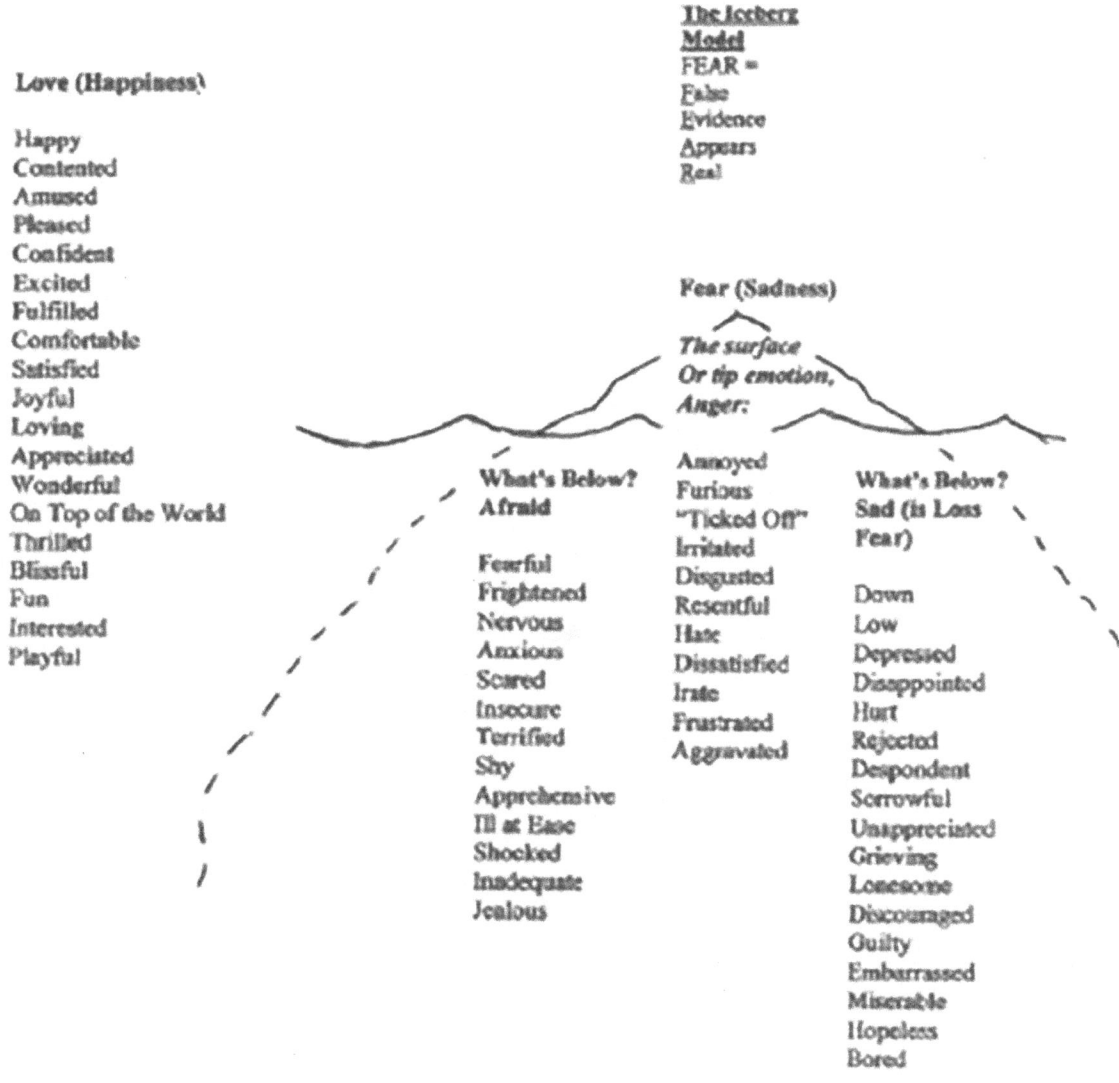

Understanding anger as a signal or red flag to take care of your emotional well-being—like hunger signals to take care of your physical well-being

Anger is considered a surface emotion, an initial defensive reaction to something bothersome or frustrating. It is a desirable instinctual signal, like hunger, that we need to do something to take care of ourselves. As hunger signals that our bodies are starving and we need to feed ourselves to survive physically, anger often signals that we need to do something to preserve our emotional well-being. It also gives an adrenaline rush that energizes us to do the job at hand.

Beyond these functions, however, anger does not require its own focus to be healed. In fact, anger cannot be healed or resolved unto itself unless we look deeper to discover the underlying emotion of fear (sadness) and deal with, resolve, or heal this. If we remain focused on our anger, we are stuck in pain. This is why anger is not truly an emotion unto itself. It is a cover-up or signal to other emotions. If we stay focused on the anger, as we all probably know, all we do is get more and more angry and create trouble in our lives through losing our temper.

What is anger? The iceberg analogy—it is what is down below that counts

Under the tip of the iceberg, mountains of ice run deep under the water. Anger is like that tip of the iceberg that we are able to see. Usually, people can come to understand that under the tip of the iceberg, there is more ice and that if they continue, like a boat at ramming speed pretending that there is only a slice of ice floating on top of the water, they are going to painfully crash and sink—like the people did when the ocean liner, *Titanic*, which scraped the side of the berg just below the waterline. Focusing on one's anger is about as painful as allowing an ocean liner to go head-on onto an iceberg. Anger is like a floating piece of ice with great depths below, which we cannot plow through. The real emotions run deep.

Anger is a superficial emotion. However, it is one that almost everyone is familiar with. In my experience as a therapist, I have found that most people, when asked about how they feel about a problem in their life, first describe some aspect of anger, such as annoyance, irritation, or frustration.

Feelings or emotions are our guides to our emotional survival. As hunger is a signal to our physical survival, feelings are our guides to our emotional personal survival. Recognizing our feelings is essential to changing our lives because we need this signal to clue us into our thoughts and to let us know that we need to change something. Without experiencing negative feelings, we would not know that we have a problem. This is why addictions that preoccupy our minds and pacify or distract us from our feelings are so dangerous. Emotional health deteriorates greatly if we are addicted and preoccupied with obtaining outside power, such as through work, drugs, alcohol, gambling, religious, cleanliness (obsessive-compulsive disorder or OCD), or hypersexuality. We are not aware that we are not surviving emotionally. This will be talked more about in the chapter on becoming a whole person (see chapter 8).

Venting—the misunderstood expression of anger

Feelings are not the same as behavior. With this in mind, is immediate venting at the person you are frustrated with a healthy response? No, because lashing out at others, in temper, can only be damaging to others and destructive to oneself; it prevents us from understanding our self and our needs. It is like staying focused on being hungry rather than knowing how to follow hunger as a signal to do what is necessary to survive—to eat. Harriet Lerner, PhD, in her best-selling book, *The Dance of Anger*, explains anger as a guide to clarify the self. The goal is to acknowledge the deeper feelings below the anger to the real emotions, fear or sadness, to experience these feelings fully and to let them lead you to a solution that leaves you with a beautiful feeling of love and happiness.

Unfortunately, many of our parents did not validate underlying emotions or encourage us to feel our feelings freely, look deeper, and respect them. Many people often stay angry (emotionally hungry) for their needs to be met and their own emotional well-being to be restored. Even in therapy, it can be difficult to help people see below their anger. Blaming someone or something (the defense of projection), they fear the pain and do not want to look at the underlying painful sadness and fear. They prefer the energizing effect anger can give. This is unfortunate. If one could understand that looking internally and sticking with the process would eventually bring the relief desired, this motivation would help you overcome the difficulty.

In this light, the psychological movement of the past to help us get in touch with our feelings has been misconstrued by the masses to mean to go ahead and vent, "Let it all hang out." Not so. Primal screaming was a form of therapy carried out in a therapist's office to allow the release of emotions in a safe setting. This is much different from yelling at your spouse because you had a bad day at the office. Carol Tarvis described this well in *Anger, The Misunderstood Emotion*.

How do we not overdo? How can we turn inward, be still, and experience our feelings? How can we figure out how to use them and take ourselves to a place of beautiful feeling? How do we not overheat and lash out our rage? Have you heard of the phrase "dry drunk"? These people do not necessarily drink alcohol but act as immaturely and impulsively, letting it all hang out as alcoholics do while drinking. If you like, fast-forward to the chapter on communication and how to control one's temper so you can be still enough to go within, self-acknowledge feelings, and begin to use them effectively. In chapter 6, there is a section "Ways to Cool Down or Chill," when you feel other people or situations are driving you crazy. You can control your temper. Use anger as a signal to figure out what's bothering you and as an energy to take care of yourself—in other words, to use the frustration and figure out how to take yourself to a better scenario that meets your needs.

Resistance to feeling our feelings

We avoid our feelings because they are painful. It's human nature to avoid pain. The defense mechanisms described in chapter 1 are the ways we try not to feel our discomfort or inner pain. We also ignore our feelings because we have been taught to be externally focused to not take our emotions, our needs, and ourselves seriously. In America, this is especially true. In Europe, for example, you would not see someone frantically driving to work while talking simultaneously on a cell phone and shoveling in fast food and coffee as they rush to produce, produce, and produce for the company.

This training to ignore our feelings and needs starts early in childhood: "Don't cry," "Don't be a sissy," "Be a big boy or girl." In other words, do not pay attention to your feelings or needs. As adults, we need to undo this training and allow ourselves to experience our fear or sadness. We need to take ourselves seriously. Our feelings are guides to clarify our self and will lead to life-enhancing choices.

Focusing inward: using your feelings as a guide to clarifying yourself and your needs

First, we need to feel our feelings and then take steps to analyze our feelings to figure out our needs and develop solutions that can make us feel better. Communicating our anger to others is only one possible solution. How to share your feelings effectively is explained in chapter 6, "Speak Your Truth." For now, think in terms of not expressing your emotions. The only appropriate self-expression is to discuss your feelings with a supportive friend or helping professional to better understand yourself using your anger as a guide to clarify yourself.

Focusing*

What do I want?

1. Think about what feels uncomfortable or yucky in your life *right now*. (You can imagine your problems as boxes sitting on the floor. Label the boxes. Examples might be "her temper," "my job," "no time for myself." Which box is the biggest and heaviest?)
2. Ask yourself, "How do I feel? What is my strongest feeling?" (Get a visual image, if possible.) "Why does this bother me so much?" (It is a very personal individual question.) "What are my *painful* feelings, and which is the worst painful feeling, and why?"
3. Ask yourself, "What will make this better? What will make me feel better or right?" You should get a comfortable and relaxed body response. You should not have any negative feelings (like guilt or resentment). It should be a possible solution that can occur in reality. Ask yourself, "Do I feel good in my body? Do I have mixed feelings? Can this happen?"
4. Carry out the solution. Be brave.
5. Affirm yourself. Tell yourself you are proud of yourself—that you are good and have rights to feel good.

* This soul-searching will change your life. The techniques (steps 1 to 3) were originated by Eugene T. Gendlin, PhD, from the book *Focusing*.

Until now, we think about what we should do, what is expected of us, or what is available. In other words, the focus is on externals, meeting others' expectations or standards or reacting to what we believe we can have. This is giving our power away. Often, our perceptions are limited by dysfunctional family backgrounds, which did not teach us our full rights or to respect our feelings and needs. Thus, we learned to treat ourselves similarly. We underestimate our rights and ignore ourselves and needs. Our focus is not internal enough on what we want, what would truly meet our needs, or feel right for us. We perceive unclearly our real needs. How often, when we make a decision about something, do we ask ourselves the all-important question, "What do I want?" Until now, we are more likely to ask something like "What should I do?" "What can I do?" or "What are my options?" These questions are narrow and self-limiting. How needlessly focused on the external have you been? How little have you settled for? "What do I want?" (the sky is the limit) is the question you need to continually ask yourself and bravely risk following through on.

At first, you may feel like a toddler trying to run a marathon. Like every skill, focusing inward takes practice. You must do this continually and use the focusing steps until you get the hang of it because it is a process that is, at first, difficult.

Exercise: First, cross your arms across your chest the way you normally would. Feel comfortable? Try crossing your arms across your chest in the opposite manner. Awkward? Uncomfortable? This moves you uncomfortably out of your comfort zone.

Using the focusing process will feel strange at first. The process of beginning to focus on yourself will take some time and discipline to get comfortable and for it to become second nature. Remember to feel your feelings, even painful ones, to figure out the solution that brings you relief and into a beautiful and loving state. These simple questions will help you get in touch with yourself as you use your feelings as guides to meet your needs.

The following is an example of a therapy session, to illustrate the focusing process.

Step 1:
Therapist: Think about what feels yucky in your life right now. Think about the problems that are bothering you right now. Imagine them concretely, if you will, as boxes in a room sitting on the floor for you to view. Label them clearly.
Client: One box might be called "my husband's drinking." Another might be "my guilt feelings and low self-esteem." Another might be "my father's criticism." Another might be "my lack of free time for self," etc.
Therapist: Now ask yourself which box is the heaviest if you had to actually carry it. Which feels the yuckiest to you? Really feel these feelings. Take your time. This is how your feelings will guide you to what you need to focus on.
Client: My husband's drinking.

Step 2:
Therapist: Experience your feelings. Visualize an image to describe them. A picture is worth a thousand words. This means be still with yourself and feel how you experience these emotions. Try to visualize the feelings. For example, if it is anxiety, you might visualize being caught in a tornado or on a roller coaster. If you are sad, you might feel like you are in a deep, dark pit. Remember to go beneath the tip of the iceberg to see what is below, then decide whether you feel more sad, scared, or a combination.
Client: I feel terrified. I feel like I am on a never-ending treadmill of land mines to avoid.
Therapist: Ask yourself why does this bother you so much. What is it about this problem that is a problem? For example, a woman came to the doctor very scared. He knew she had cancer but did not assume he understood the source of her fear. He might have automatically assumed she was afraid of dying. However, he listened and found out that what was truly bothering her at that moment was the fear of losing hair from chemotherapy. The solution to her problem was to order a wig in case this happened. As a result, she was not so frightened. This illustrates how what bothers us can be highly individual and personal, so it may take some thinking on your part to figure out why you are so bothered.
Client: His argumentativeness or blaming behavior and my need to walk on eggshells.

Step 3:
Therapist: Ask yourself what would make this better. What will make you feel better or right?
Client: To not be abused.

You should get a relieved, relaxed bodily response to this question if you answered it correctly. You know you have reached the right solution or decision when what you think causes you to feel good in your body—meaning comfortable, relaxed, relieved, and good. The answer is not a "yes but"—not something that makes you feel guilty, angry, anxious, sad, or any other negative emotion at the same time even if it brings some good feelings. You cannot feel truly better and bad at the same time. The solution may involve approaching someone and letting them know your needs. However, on this quest, you may encounter situations or people unwilling to change what would make you feel better. Remember, you only can change yourself, not others. A solution exists that feels good, no matter what others do. As you know, your consciousness can change anything over time as well as there is an immediate answer, which makes you feel better right now in the present.

Whether the person agrees and changes or doesn't, you can take your power and meet your need. For example, in this case, this woman feels hurt about an argument with her husband—his verbal aggression.

What would make it better is if he apologized. Yet he usually won't do this. So what could make this better for her? She needs to learn to avoid emotional violence. Growing up in her family, verbal and emotional aggression occurred frequently, which hurt her. Hence, she tended to attract this in her life to master it. You have probably heard about women whose fathers are alcoholics, and they often ironically marry alcoholics. This is to give the opportunity to master a situation and to bring up the situation for healing. Through the process of focusing inward, she might express her hurt to her husband without any result or apology. What really made her feel better was to walk away and stay away from that person.

Step 4: As a person changes, the family system changes. Because he did not want to lose his wife, he changed and went to AA. She had moved out—consistent with her belief that she has beautiful, peaceful, harmonious, loving relationships and nothing to the contrary was acknowledged. It was not any direct rejection of the person but simply an acknowledgment of the beautiful life that she led.

You may surprise yourself as to which one is making you feel the worst. You have to dig deep and break it down into simple solutions to simple problems. Another client of mine, a woman, was trying to adopt her grandson. She was anxious to get him out of foster care and dismayed that she had to apply for a license, which would take some time. The worst thing bothering her was wanting him back as quickly as possible because they were drugging him. Was it possible to get him back right away and not jeopardize the adoption? Yes—the worst thing that bothered her was that she was required to make phone calls to clarify whether obtaining the license was necessary in private adoption. She was afraid to talk to authority figures for fear of messing up the situation by saying something wrong. Calling was not a good solution; she was still anxious. It does not bring relaxation to the body. What ultimately felt good was to think through and write down exactly what she wanted to say before she spoke to an authority figure. Then she felt good to go ahead, stand up, and take charge. Sometimes there are simple solutions to simple problems. Since the worst thing bothering her was that she felt anxious about talking to authority, she needed to simply take the time to collect her thoughts and write them down before she made the phone call. This is a simple solution to a simple problem. If you break the problem down into its parts, it eliminates the overwhelming feeling. You can handle it. Once you break it down into what specifically is bothering you—and what would be the simple solution to fix it—you experience a great deal of relief.

The focusing exercise was a painstaking process for me at first even though I am a person who loves to think and do mental things as a rule. It became much easier over time to do this. Dr. Gendlin's book, *Focusing*, is excellent and goes in-depth about this process. In addition, if you need help, check the website for Eugene Gendlin's *Focusing*. There used to be partners available nationally who can help you through learning the focusing process.

All good therapists probably do this in some form with their clients. The process is well worth teaching clients to do for themselves as well. At some point, I usually provide a handout to clients and teach them how to work on it as homework and encourage them to borrow the book *Focusing* and consider buying it to provide information that is more detailed.

Let's take the woman in the previous example being emotionally abused by her partner. She would ask herself those focusing-inward questions to get at her hurt and fear below her anger in order to figure out what she needed to do to make herself feel better.

Step 1: Identify what bothers her the most—being belittled or scolded or verbally abused by her partner—by laying out the various problems bothering her, including boredom with children routine in the evening, not enough time for friends, etc. And still, the biggest one is verbal aggression.

Step 2: Why does this bother her? What is her feeling (below anger)? The underlying feeling is hurt, rejection, disappointment, and—probably if she takes it to the deepest level—fear of losing the person. His temper suggests to her he would like to leave, which is threatening.

Step 3: What will make her feel better? If her partner realizes he is expressing himself too forcefully and tones it down when she expresses her feelings of hurt and fear.

This takes care of that fear to some extent. Yet there is still some hurt or loss from past stuff and fear that, if his temper continues to erupt, this could lead to the relationship dissolving. That is not truly a feel-good, relaxed feeling. So what is a truly feel-good, relaxed feeling? Trace back the relationship problem to an internal problem, an inner-thought problem, "I am feeling unlovable." This is the attitude or belief that one is not going to be treated properly or that one is not truly loved, which probably stems from childhood issues. Change the thought to "I am lovable" or that "I have healthy, peaceful, calm, loving, supportive relationships." It is complete once in the present reality. She is guided to recognize that she does not participate in anything that is negative. To walk away from somebody and not get involved in it, to not take it personally, and to keep her space free of negativity. At the same time, painful feelings persist that relate to childhood issues of rejection, verbal aggression, or fear of abandonment. So it feels good to release that, to cry, to talk about it, and heal (which is the topic of the next chapter, "Heal Emotional Wounds of the Past").

Step 4: Take action. Be brave. From now on, she walks away if she feels belittled. She cries and lets her feelings of sadness out, including the grief over past issues where she was treated poorly, so that is released and healed. She goes through a healing process to heal her past emotional wounds. (The topic "inner child work" is addressed more thoroughly in the next chapter).

Step 5: She affirms herself for following through. She pats herself on the back and tells herself that she is proud for thinking positively about relationships, for creating her experience of positive relationships, and for being willing to heal her own wounds and to cry. This makes her more likely to repeat the process to receive the rewards for the positive feedback she is giving herself. In other words, by making positive statements encouraging herself to take care of herself and to feel good about setting limits in a self-fulfilling prophecy manner, she's more likely to repeat the behavior in a healthy self-caring way in the future.

The adage "Don't worry, be happy" involves feeling your feelings, even—especially—the painful ones so you work the program to let it guide you to what brings you joy and relief.

Summary: How to use your negative feelings to take you to a beautiful place—a focusing-inward technique

Focusing*

What do I want?

1. Think about what feels uncomfortable or yucky in your life *right now*. (You can imagine your problems as boxes sitting on the floor. Label the boxes. Examples might be "her temper," "my job," "no time for myself." Which box is the biggest and heaviest?)
2. Ask yourself, "How do I feel? What is my strongest feeling?" (Get a visual image, if possible.) "Why does this bother me so much?" (It is a very personal individual question). "What are my *painful* feelings, and which is the worst painful feeling, and why?"
3. Ask yourself, "What will make this better? What will make me feel better or right?" You should get a comfortable and relaxed body response. You should not have any negative feelings (like guilt or resentment). It should be a possible solution that can occur in reality.
   Ask yourself, "Do I feel good in my body? Do I have mixed feelings? Can this happen?"
4. Carry out the solution. Be brave.
5. Affirm yourself. Tell yourself you are proud of yourself—that you are good and have rights to feel good.

* This soul-searching will change your life. The techniques (steps 1 to 3) were originated by Eugene T. Gendlin, PhD., from the book *Focusing*.

Chapter 3

Heal Emotional Wounds of the Past

I am now willing to love and approve of myself as beautiful, magnificent, awesome, loving, and lovable. There is no suffering. There is only divine opportunity to love yourself even more.

Distinguishing past from present emotional pain

Why do we keep repeating history? For example, we might have a father who was an alcoholic or emotionally disturbed, so we marry a man who is an alcoholic or emotionally disturbed and, in doing this, forget the pain that we suffered with as a child. To break the cycle, we have to acknowledge it, claim it, heal it, and let it go.

When we are in the process of nurturing our feelings, focusing inward on our pain to find a solution that brings us a beautiful feeling, we find in interpersonal problems that 90 percent of our feelings stem from old wounds. Only 10 percent of our feelings are related to the current situation. John Gray—who wrote *Men Are from Mars, Women Are from Venus*, a best-selling book on male-female relationships—noted this percentage in his in-depth work with couples. When we take time to focus inward, we find it is less what is happening currently than what it triggers, or reminds us of, from our past that creates our intense reaction.

For example, an insightful client of mine harbored hurt because his father had not been involved with him. During a session, he complained that his wife was going to bed early when he would come home every night from his bowling league. He had some empathy and ability to put himself into another person's shoes and realized that she had to get up early for work the next morning—and she was pregnant and exhausted, a point which had not occurred to him. When probed, he recognized his abandonment feelings stemmed from the lack of a relationship with his father. He did not lash out at his wife because she was going to bed early—carrying his unborn child—yet, rather through counseling, was able to look inward and understand the source of the intensity of this feeling. He was overreacting to the given situation, which was a trigger causing him to reexperience old childhood wounds, painful feelings of past abandonment by his father. The solution was to access underlying feelings of abandonment—and his belief of himself as unlovable. These negative feelings affected his marriage so much that they were considering breaking up because he was so angry with her for not "being there" for him.

How do you heal from childhood trauma?

Have you ever had an incident that triggered an intensely horrible feeling, like you fell into a deep pit of agony and spent hours venting, obsessing, and stressing out, trying to get over what happened? That is a hole in the soul, a past emotional wound that has been triggered. How do you heal from the pain you have experienced from your childhood? First, you have to be aware of your painful feelings and how they affect you. Many people consciously believe and state that they have had "wonderful," "perfect," "happy," and/or "normal" childhoods when they definitely did not. They tend to use defense mechanisms to block the pain. In my client's case above, he protected himself from feeling grief about his father's abandonment through several defense mechanisms. First was the use of mind-altering chemicals (he would escape into pot). Second, he went bowling every night. He kept himself constantly busy so he would not feel his feelings. If he was not around, he could not be abandoned. He joked that the only advantage to punctuality was that no one was there to appreciate it. Third, he projected his responsibility for the marital problems onto his wife. He had to let go of his psychological defenses and face his deep insecurities for change to occur.

Unfortunately, most of us have had dysfunctional family systems in some way or another. How can we become aware of our psychological defenses and maladaptive learning that developed in our dysfunctional family systems growing up?

Our psychological defenses are invisible, which makes them more difficult to deal with. I have heard parents say that they wished their child had a broken leg versus a more invisible kind of mental problem, like attention deficit disorder (ADD). At least, that way, others would be able to see and make accommodations for it; others do not understand the invisible impairment. Therefore, they may not react in a positive or helpful way with their child.

Remember the story about my son when he was sitting on the floor and his carrier seat toppled over? He propped himself up on his arm so he could continue watching TV. This was to illustrate how we do this at the psychological level—invisibly. We don't know we are doing it, and others don't know we're doing it. That is why defense mechanisms are called blind spots. That is why it has often been beneficial to seek help with this part of your growing process from a helping professional, like a psychologist, or to be in a group, such as a community support group such as Adult Children of Alcoholics, in order to have support and feedback in terms of observing oneself and learning.

Button pushing in relationships—the triggers to bring up past wounds for healing

The first step is to identify the invisible maladaptive learning patterns. Ask yourself, "Am I mad because of *now* or because of something from the *past*? What are my buttons and triggers? How do they affect me?"

The goal is not to let other peoples' issues personally offend or further harm you in any way. How do I become "a hollow bone for spirit to pass through"? How do I remove these buttons so there are no buttons to be pushed anymore, so I have no wounds to be licked, so I have no blocks to my happiness, so that my spirit, my divine spark, the truth of who I am, can flow freely and easily through me and guide me to my happiness?

The first step is to feel your feelings and identify your maladaptive learning pattern or bad habits. This involves the focusing process. When you get to the feeling level, ask yourself, "Am I mad underneath, scared, or sad about something now or about something that had happened from my past?" As you get in touch and visualize the feelings, ask yourself when in the past you felt similarly this way. What memories and associations come up? Once you become aware and can make this major distinction, you can begin your healing process. Talking immediately to the person who triggered your feelings engages a power struggle for external power. In other words, it is a waste of time. Until you can clarify why you feel so intensely and how much of it relates to the past, you are barking up the wrong tree. Professional help or support groups can help with this and give you a chance to vent without doing any damage to others or relationships as well as give you time to be still and analyze the feelings.

This is like learning to ride a bicycle. Originally, most of us receive some kind of assistance as we learn—training wheels at least. With our parents' encouragement and belief in us—and their steadying hands to keep us balanced—we felt we could do it. Likewise, wise professional help steadies us as we learn to balance our emotional handlebars and be able to ride the bike of life, ultimately on our own. However, we must have the courage to go out on our own. Do not enter therapy to be fixed. This works no better than expecting our parents to actually ride the bike for us! Ultimately, you have to possess the courage to execute all the complex motions and to risk falling. Without courage to pedal on your own, change will not occur. You will remain stuck on your vehicle with no real way to move or explore. Remember the freedom you felt after learning to ride and could strike out on your own in wide-open spaces? Therapy can provide the same—independence, joy, freedom.

Becoming whole—no more holes in the soul

How do we heal from past painful feelings? How do we heal our buttons? First, we acknowledge that our relationships are the vehicles for our healing and that, when we do experience some intense feelings and reactions, we need to be grateful to our "triggers"—those people who bring up our pain for us so we can reexperience it, feel it, own it, learn from it, and let it go. We feel our pain to gain. An example is my client who was abandoned by his father. He needed to work through his intense feelings of rejection. This was by crying, hitting pillows, and sharing the trauma with a supportive therapist.

Also, ask yourself, "How do I empower myself right now? How do I love myself even more at this time?" It is at these moments that we have the opportunity to learn, to grow, and to love ourselves more than at any other time. When things are the worst, this is the opportunity to love yourself even more and learn to consistently protect yourself from having these feelings ever again—no matter what happens or what anybody else does to you.

Be still and quiet with yourself and feel your feelings. Ask yourself, "What have I learned from this experience that helps me realize that I need not take anyone's stuff personally ever again?" As the feelings are intense, some private expression of release is needed. For example, one could cut wood when feeling this mad. Beat on pillows. Regular exercise is very good to keep your physical tension down so it becomes bearable.

Crying is a wonderful outlet. Your tears are wonderful. Feel free to feel your sadness. You need to grieve. It is just a feeling; it will pass, and you will feel much better afterward. According to research, sad tears, as opposed to happy ones, release up to ninety toxins from the body compared to about ten toxins from happy ones. You are physically and emotionally cleansed through crying, which is why people report feeling better after a good cry.

Apart from some nonharmful release—"nonharmful" in the sense that it does not prevent you from feeling your feelings and does not cause outside problems because you have not lashed out at somebody and caused trouble—it can be helpful to remember that the goal is to turn the painful, uncomfortable feeling into a beautiful, relaxed, relieved feeling. Remember where you are going—the light at the end of the tunnel. Through this process, keep telling yourself this so you can stick with it.

When using the focusing process, remember to understand that anger is a normal secondary emotion—a defense for other deeper emotions. Anger is good. Anger tells us we need to "eat some food," so to speak. In other words, anger tells us to nourish, love, or nurture ourselves emotionally. Just like with hunger, we need to eat. At the time we are feeling our emotional pain, we need to nourish ourselves emotionally.

Anger, the guide to clarifying oneself, is a signal that something is bothering us in our lives and that we need to look deeper into ourselves and discover the feelings below—fear and sadness—in order to figure out solutions. To help ourselves, we cannot really heal the anger; it is more of a protective defense. Therefore, we need to recognize the underlying feelings. We cannot do this by immediately reacting and lashing out in anger. We must talk and think about our feelings and then feel them. The goal is to go from yucky feelings to beautiful ones and to change our thoughts correspondingly so that we do not recreate or reenact past negative events in the future for ourselves.

This cannot happen if we are arguing. Venting lets a little steam out at the time, but the underlying tension will not be healed. It will emerge again, perhaps yuckier still, having harmed others or our relationship with the sidetracking behavior and may even reenact the past. This was happening in the case of the man ready to divorce his wife because of his unconscious pain over his father's abandonment. He defended against this pain and reenacted his own isolation. Until he went into therapy, he was setting up a future reenactment for his own unborn child to not have a father in the home because he projected out his own rejecting behavior onto his wife and accused her of abandoning him—and was ready to leave her.

Ask yourself the questions, "What am I feeling below the anger, and who am I really feeling this way about?" Distinguish between past and current rage and the past and current sadness and fear under it. If the feeling is very intense and out of proportion to the situation, it probably stems from a past situation triggered by the current situation, which resembles it in some way. If one expresses oneself right away to change the current situation, it would not be dealing with feelings appropriately. This would just be venting. Expressing is not feeling. Healing can't occur until the feelings have been analyzed or processed first. Heal the past feelings by owning and releasing them and—most importantly—by loving yourself!

How to love yourself at the moment

This phase involves healing your wounded inner child. What is the inner child? Transactional analysis provides us with a way of understanding ourselves and our personality system better. You have a "parent," "child," and "adult" within yourself. The adult is the rational, objective part. The parent is the overseeing caretaker (possibly critical), nurturer part. The child is the innocent, earliest part of yourself, which may have been wounded through family interactions and events growing up. The goal is to get in touch with this inner child, to heal any hurt or wounds and to allow the playful, innocent, loving child that you were meant to be to emerge.

When you are upset, imagine that the little you—and call the little you by your name "Little So-and-So"—is sitting next to you. Get in touch with the time when you were little and you felt this intense pain bothering you now. Imagine the little you now sitting with the big you who is rationally thinking and has nurturing, parental qualities. Talk to the little you as you would to a crying, hurt child. Provide comfort, reassurance, and love. Remind the little you that the trauma is over. Soothe the little you. Tell the little you that everything is okay. Remind the little you that he or she is loved. In other words, act like the nurturing parent—the soothing best friend that you wish you had during the traumatic event(s). Adopt this approach to love yourself whenever you are upset. Provide soothing and nurturing. Ask the little you what he or she would like to make things better. Like with a young child, it may even be a trip to the ice cream shop or some time to play, whatever works to soothe; an adult pleasure may hit the spot. You can use the focusing process to figure out what makes you feel better and do it.

As children, we may not have been validated, reassured, soothed, and comforted when we needed it. Instead, we felt abandoned, neglected, and rejected. We may continue to treat ourselves like this even when we are adults. Until we know better, when something bad has happened, we may have ignored our pain and put ourselves down. Our parents may have said things, like "Don't cry. That is for babies," "You don't have anything to be upset about," and so on. You are changing this thought pattern now. You are not only revisiting the past and providing that nurturing that should have occurred then, but you are also changing the thought pattern to including that your feelings are important. Affirm that your feelings are important and that, if you feel hurt, you deserve nurturing. Do good things for you at this time. Love yourself.

The opportunity for self-love peaks at the moment of pain. This is the teachable moment when you can learn in a gentle and loving way from this experience. Remember, there is only success and/or learning success. You are revisiting this painful trauma. So allow your adult self to tell the little you a better perspective on the situation. Do not let the little you walk away from the situation feeling bad or taking anything personally from it as you did in the past.

For example, a client related that, at the age of seven, he walked into his parents' bedroom while they were having sex. It looked like fun, and he wanted to join in. He had no idea what was going on. However, his father got up quickly, pulled his shorts on, shot him a hostile look, and left the room. The client was crushed. Innocently, he wanted to be part of the group and felt left out by his father's reaction. As an adult, he still remembered this incident with pain, bound up in memories of his father being withdrawn and rejecting him in general. After all these years, he had never gotten over it.

Through therapy, he revisited the experience. Quite likely, he had been told, "Stay outside playing." How would he feel, as an adult, if someone walked in when he was having sex? Would he have been appreciative or disappointed? Would he have shown it through some anger on the surface? Would it have been appropriate for his father to say, "Come on, son, let's have a ménage à trois." No. In other words, his father was reacting how anyone probably would, and the child probably could have considered himself lucky to not have been punished for having walked in the middle of that. Of course, it would have helped if his parents had explained and helped him feel better at the time. He would not have to do it forty years later in psychotherapy. He lived with the pain all those years.

Because he revisited this experience, he recognized that he had not done anything wrong and that his father was disappointed—as an adult man, he understood not being able to complete his sexual act—and uncomfortable with his son seeing the situation. He did not know how to talk to his son about it. Little Matt was able to be comforted by Big Matt. He retold to Little Matt what really happened and that he was not being rejected. He reminded him this event was over and that he was okay now. He hugged and told himself that he was a member of the family and was loved and explained that the issue of privacy had been awkward for his parents to be able to handle. It would not have been appropriate for him to be able to join in with them. Thus, he helped heal the wound about not having the relationship he desired with his dad.

For another example, a client felt disappointed because of his father's criticisms. When he role-played his own nurturing parenting part of himself reaching out to his wounded little child self—and utilized the focusing-inward process as well—his little child revealed that the worst for him was that he was being treated unfairly constantly and he did not know how to prevent it or protect himself. His adult self was able to validate his little self's worthiness and right to not experience verbal and emotional abuse and helped the little self problem-solve and figure out to walk away from negative interactions and protect himself and still maintain and realize that his self-respect was totally independent of pleasing anybody else. After the inner child work, this man was able to carve out some time to pursue his dream, a new career avenue that he had previously believed he did not have time for. He stopped pleasing everybody else all the time.

Exercise for inner child work

1. Think about a current situation bothering you. Feel your feelings. Ask yourself when you felt similarly in the past. What association or memories come up?
2. Think about this traumatic incident or loss. Pretend that the little you—the innocent little wounded or hurt child—is sitting next to you. Take the role of the comforting, soothing parent. Talk to your inner child and find out what's wrong. Provide information and an adult perspective to help the child feel better. Also provide soothing comfort to help the little you. Love yourself. Let your child express his or her needs. Take turns, moving from one seat to the other. Be open to what happens. Continue the role play until you have helped your inner child feel completely better.
3. Afterward, take this opportunity to love yourself even more. Do something special for your innocent little you.

The little you remembers the experience with its feelings of powerlessness, intimidation, and not knowing how to respond. The little you—as an adult now—creates a sense of equality and can replay the experience from a place of equal power and the knowing to respond healthily.

Grief work

Grief is mourning the loss of a loved one or something dear. This includes mourning the loss of the dreams of how your childhood should have been—the loss of love, attention, care, protection that you should have received—grief over the pain and damage that you have incurred from dysfunctional situations.

Grief hits you in ocean waves, bubbling up, often when you don't expect it. You may suddenly feel sad and not know why, or you may attribute your sadness to something superficial. Normal grief may feel so intense that you feel like you are going crazy.

Grief is a series of phases that are sequential but may go back and forth—one step forward, two steps back—as follows:

1. denial—disbelief, numbness, shock, this is not really happening
2. bargaining—the idea that you can get this person or thing to come back if you are really good or do something good in some way
3. anger or guilt (which is anger turned inward)—resentment at any source, including doctors, the person who died, self, God, others, your parents, your spouse—a sign is that you may lash out wildly
4. sadness—crying, depression, releasing the grief
5. acceptance of the loss—rebuilding of life, emergence of loving, warm memories and closeness to the person in spirit or heart, feeling one has learned important lessons from the loss

Contrary to popular belief—and the almighty American work schedule—grief is not worked through in a couple of days. It may last up to a year or two when a person close to you dies—or longer, a lifetime with a spouse, and what feels like many lifetimes with the loss of a child.

If a person avoids feelings of grief, they build up and eventually develop into an emotional disorder. For example, anxiety is like a boiling pot with the lid shaking. The shaky lid is the experience of anxiety. Underneath the anxiety is the boiling water—the brokenhearted raging tears, the grief—pushing to come out.

If you feel sad for someone else and are crying, make this an opportunity to do some grieving for yourself and your losses. In other words, you have primed the pump. The tears are already flowing, so think about your losses and let out some feelings about your losses. Any unresolved grief from past losses will tumble out with current grief and intensify it—so clean your slate.

Eye movement desensitization and reprocessing, hypnosis, emotional freedom therapy, and tennis rackets

As a person realizes he or she did not have the perfect childhood they thought they had—recovers memories and feelings of pain—then talking, venting, and abreacting (releasing feelings) is the way to heal. This can be done through talking about the events and feelings in therapy and with support of others.

EMDR (eye movement desensitization and reprocessing) is a fairly recent psychotherapy technique used to help people who have survived disasters and catastrophes. However, it works well with any kind of trauma. Symptoms such as flashbacks, sleep problems, paranoia, and dissociation are all part of posttraumatic stress disorder. The client is asked to reexperience many aspects of the trauma while the psychotherapist neurologically reprocesses the brain. The client follows the therapist's finger movements or listens to tapping while disclosing the traumatic event. This has the effect of neurologically reprocessing the event in the person's brain, whereby the intense horror is erased. The person can remember the incident without the accompanying painful feelings.

Hypnosis reaches your unconscious, your deeper intuitive self that knows you are whole, complete, and perfect. It suspends your conscious, subconscious, or deeply buried unconscious negative, limiting beliefs. It allows you to express your truth and best potential.

Hypnosis can be used to regress to previous painful experiences and release and heal from them. Hypnosis can also provide easy, quick symptom relief for problems, such as anxiety, depression, phobias, procrastination, jealousy, lack of confidence (personally or socially), sleep disturbances, smoking, weight, physical complaints, and many others.

People don't realize they often go in and out of a trance every day. For example, when you are driving and suddenly look up and realize that you have gone further than you thought, you have been in a trance. You have zoned out and tuned in to your inner reality. If you can do this, you can be hypnotized. Hypnosis is actually a voluntary process of relaxing yourself. In hypnosis, one tunes out all the external arguments—your conscious limiting beliefs—against you achieving your goal. You are tuned in to your deeper unconscious and able to take in and absorb your goals—the positive suggestions you and your therapist have decided on prior to the hypnosis session.

EFT (emotional freedom therapy) is taught by paraprofessionals to people who want a take-home technique to reprogram themselves. EFT is a series of tapping on energy meridians on the body—also known as acupressure points. Acupressure is like acupuncture without the needles. While tapping the points, we speak the pattern that we desire to change as it now is. Then we start over, tapping the same point but affirming the replacement, healthy thought pattern. This involves learning a tapping process while thinking certain positive suggestions to get over problems.

Attachment theory has generated a model for working with children and adults who have had poor attachments (or bonding) experiences in early childhood. The theory defines poor attachment as a reaction to lack of affection, closeness, safety, and inappropriate bonding (parents' needs being met instead of the child's). These reactions range from anxious attachments on the child's part to reaction attachment (disengagement from others emotionally). As a child grows up, the attachment experience becomes obvious in the adult's interpersonal relationship style. Therapy that addresses the issues of attachment as the fundamental problem may utilize a range of approaches, including the cognitive therapy and inner child work to foster the security the child should have developed in early bonding with the parent.

Psychotherapists—in addition to listening, supporting, and comforting clients by helping them release their pain—also may give homework to clients to do some releasing work. For example, a person may use an old tennis racket to beat up some old phone books while imagining the event and the person(s) who traumatized them to release the pain.

How you heal from past trauma

> Distinguish past from present pain. Develop insight. When upset, ask yourself, "When did I feel similarly in the past? What associations or memories are being triggered by the current upsetting event? Does the current situation warrant this intensity, or do I feel this intensely because it is bringing up past emotional wounds?"
>
> Love and soothe yourself. Cry and release the pain. Learn to see things differently. Refer to inner child work exercise in this chapter.
>
> Enlist the aid of a good therapist, such as a licensed clinical psychologist, to help heal the wounds. Ask if he or she does cognitive therapy. Make sure they can provide at least one of the following effectively: EMDR, hypnosis, EFT, short-term psychodynamic therapy, attachment theory-based therapy, and trauma or grief resolutions.
>
> Remember that positive consciousness creates your life. Claim that these past events no longer have power over you and that you can lead a full, happy life now. Forgiveness of others is really something you do for yourself. The anger and pain you feel inside harms you—and may not even be known to the perpetrator of your pain—so forgive others and yourself, for you.

Chapter 4

Open Up to Help

I am good, and I deserve and have good things.

We must believe we are worthy of all that is good. Being a hard worker includes working hard at taking care of us, not neglecting ourselves or dismissing ourselves as if we are not worth the trouble. We need to open up to help. What is the point of worrying? If you are unable to achieve what you need yourself, then seek support from outside sources rather than neglecting the need. How often do therapists hear from individuals with alcohol problems that they cannot afford to take time off from work to detox at a hospital and get treatment? The alcoholics' refusal ends up causing his or her marriage, job, health, money, driver's license, and more in the long run. Forget the immediate bills. What about life itself?

Sometimes to become truly independent, we need to admit when we need help and then take action to get it. We need to allow ourselves to depend temporarily in order to become independent ultimately. For example, we take out an educational loan so we can work toward a more fulfilling and better-paying career. Likewise, a woman with no financial resources may depend on outside help, like Medicaid, so that she can raise fatherless children healthily. The point is there are options there to help. We need to recognize the importance and practicality of finding help when we have the need, rather than coping alone.

Good self-esteem, making yourself a priority as well as the ability to focus inward and understand your needs is essential. We were not put on earth to suffer. As Jesus, the great way shower, said, "Ask and thou shall receive" and "The kingdom of heaven is within you." Open yourself to the surprises of universal abundance. When your mind and heart are open, answers and assistance are available.

For example, I remember desiring a wooden fence when my children were small. I was talking with my mother, who revealed that I had an insurance policy my parents had purchased at my birth, which accrued interest. The dividends amounted to exactly what I needed for the fence! This is one of many instances where I had been rewarded unexpectedly because of my openness to help. "God helps those who help themselves." In other words, I had to take the action to find the help, bolstered by an optimistic attitude that help would be forthcoming.

How psychotherapy works. Is a person a TV set?

A gentle voice to echo your own so yours sings strongly and beautifully alone.

Sometimes we need a voice to echo our own. Sometimes our voice has been discounted for so long, overwhelmed by outside stressors, demands, and others' expectations, that we can barely perceive our own voice. Sometimes our support systems are so nonexistent that when our tiny voice squeaks, it is immediately squished and stilled; we feel isolated and unbearably dissatisfied without knowing how to change things for the better. We buy into a "learned helplessness," pessimistic, depressed belief system that says our situations cannot be changed. This happens, for example, when we are in dysfunctional relationships that are abusive, neglectful, or toxic. This can happen when we take on too many external demands and stressors: too much work, too many children, too many projects, too many people to please. We try keeping busy so that we do not recognize how dissatisfied we might be with life's current situations or to keep from feeling unresolved pain from traumas or losses in our childhood. If we are achieving, doing, and pleasing others, then we possess a semblance of self-esteem even though we are truly not satisfied inside.

A vicious cycle, the more we neglect our feelings and needs, the more unhappy we are at an inside level, the more isolated we become, and consequently the worse our life situations become because we ignore our feelings instead of taking ourselves seriously and loving ourselves enough to confront problems and make them better. The American dream perpetuates this focus on external achievement—being on the go and ignoring true inner needs, like being drunk for a really long time, living in a fantasy world—such that when you finally do face yourself, such as in therapy, the experience can be soberingly painful.

For another analogy, if you ignore an ulcer by continuing about your "busyness," the problem persists, the pain intensifies, and the holes in your stomach grow larger until a major medical crisis occurs and you are forced to face a small problem that has turned into a monster in circumstances that are terrifying. One can thus cause almost a life breakdown from a small issue, such as the horror of internal bleeding and major surgery, whereas if it had been faced originally, a simple change in how to process life—diet, stress reduction, supplements, and/or medication—would have worked wonders.

Effective psychotherapy facilitates this vital focusing-inward process—the getting in touch with your feelings and needs—and provides the support and encouragement to take yourself seriously. Then you can begin the process of creating a lifestyle based on self-respect and good self-esteem and meeting your needs.

Individual therapy assists you to understand the origins in childhood and other past experiences of current dysfunction and provides the space and support for you to release these powerful painful feelings about traumas, losses, neglect, abuse, etc., which is essential because people avoid their feelings and consequently avoid themselves in general for fear of experiencing their inner fear, pain, and grief. Individual therapy with an accepting therapist may give a person their first experience of what it is like to be in a healthy, respectful, loving relationship with oneself and then with everyone else. The mistrust and fear of closeness—originated from issues—diminishes and allows people to be open to healthy, intimate relationships in their lives and to relate to oneself in a caring, healthy manner.

The only thing we have to fear is fear itself, and there is no need to fear your inner pain. It is just a feeling, and it will pass. Yet the avoidance of our feelings paves the path to more pain. Look at the long view—the big picture—not the immediate short view. Resistance to being in therapy and facing yourself and your issues needs to be worked through to prevent disaster. The past traumas are all over, unless we recreate them because we have not worked through our maladaptive learning—our negative beliefs, attitudes, and expectations.

When we feel helpless, isolated, unhappy, and dissatisfied, turning to an experienced psychotherapist who will listen to your inner voice and echo it until it is strong enough to sing on its own can be immeasurably helpful. As one German client told me, there really is no stigma to being in counseling. As he put it, "In Germany, everyone has a family physician. In America, everyone has a psychologist."

How therapy does and does not work

Many people do not understand how psychotherapy works. Their expectations are too high and inappropriate. The most important contribution of psychotherapy—with a warm, caring, empathetic therapist—is assistance to change one's negative thoughts or cognitions to positive ones.

Remember, however, that your thoughts are invisible. A psychotherapist cannot fix you. A joint venture, therapy is a journey the therapist and client travel together. When people complain that therapy is too costly and time-consuming, they need to understand that it is invisible work. Your motivation, openness, and honesty with your therapist are crucial to how far you progress and how fast. If one has not trusted anyone before in his or her life, building the relationship may take time to occur.

Let's look at this analogy. Let's pretend a client is a TV set. It would be a different matter. The TV repair person is not visually handicapped the way helping professionals are because they cannot see the client's inner psyche when doing psychotherapy. The TV repair person can go directly to the TV and look directly into the set and twist, unscrew, and remove wires and parts. Furthermore, the TV has no feeling. It does not hurt when probed. It doesn't cry in pain. It is not angry at the intrusion.

Not so with people. People come to therapy but understandably do not relish the exposure involved. They would prefer to be fixed without their parts being touched. This means that the therapist must proceed slowly, gently, and supportively to keep the person in therapy and willing to tolerate this program. Moreover, each person's wiring is unique and invisible. Unlike the TV, the person has to explain to the repair person where it hurts, what happened to cause it, and whether or not the repair people's interventions are making a dent to improve it. The inner workings of our fictional TV set (client) are invisible. The therapist must work by memory and communication, admirably supported by years of graduate education and clinical experience. Is it any wonder that good psychotherapy takes more than a few weeks long? It's not as if you drop yourself off and just pick yourself up like a fixed TV from a repair shop. Yet sometimes people expect quick fixes from psychotherapy rather than recognizing the respectful process that it is. Do you remember the joke, "How many psychologists does it take to change a light bulb? Just one. But it takes a long time, and the light bulb really has to want to change!"

Sometimes people drop out of therapy prematurely. They mistake their own painful feelings that talking about their lives brings up as attributable simply to dissatisfaction with the therapy—rather than owning the pain as a natural part of the "getting better" process. Sometimes you feel good after a therapy session. And other times, despite the therapist's gentleness, a wire is cut and replaced, and that may hurt temporarily. If a person was ripped apart like a TV, they probably wouldn't come back. Psychotherapy is that process of remaking yourself, and people often drop out because of discomfort or false belief that it should be quick and easy.

I am not encouraging clients to discount their feelings if they don't feel their therapist is "getting them" or they have some real reasons for dissatisfaction, such as if the therapist is trying to abuse them or violate their confidentiality by telling others their secrets. Finding a competent, ethical therapist is necessary. You should feel increasing trust with your therapist and the ability to become open and honest. Initially, focus will be on helping resolve life stressors, building your self-esteem, and encouraging you to follow through with taking care of yourself. Putting out the brush fires in your life—stabilizing your life and helping you problem-solve your crises and stressors in relationships, work, finances, etc.—could take a year. As time goes on, your therapist helps you see connections between current life dissatisfactions and unresolved feelings about past events. People unconsciously seek out the familiar, even if it is painful; often, your current problem situation parallels or repeats your childhood dysfunctional situations. Getting insight into this and healing from the past will help you not repeat the mistakes in the future. The focus is to help you get out of the alligator pit and then to make sure that you do not fall into it again—equipped with your newfound insight, love of you, and healthy ways of relating.

Employee Assistance Program (EAP)

If you are distressed, you can sometimes turn to your human resources department at your job for a referral for free counseling services. Most large companies offer these referral services to their employees.

Twelve-step support groups

Twelve-step support groups provide help to you from people in similar situations as yours. You can learn from people who have been there and made it out.

These are community-based support groups, and they are free! Unless you wish to make a donation. They are designed to help people who come from dysfunctional family" situations who have had to develop maladaptive coping strategies, soft or hard addictions, numb the pain and fill their inner emotional voids.

There are many types of groups: Overeaters Anonymous (OA) for compulsive eaters or for persons with eating disorders, Alcoholics Anonymous (AA), Narcotics Anonymous (NA) for substance abusers, Al-Anon and Adult Children of Alcoholics (ACOA) for persons involved with or who have been involved with or affected by alcoholics and substance abusers, Codependents Anonymous (CoDA) for relationship dependency and enablers, Sex and Love Addicts Anonymous (SLAA), Emotions Anonymous (EA), etc.

You can locate an ongoing group in your area through the Internet or phone directory information. Large groups, like AA and Al-Anon or ACOA, have several groups going on daily. They usually have a phone tree where you can press a number and find out when and where the groups are, or you can just request a written schedule of meetings.

They help you withdraw from addictive behaviors and face and release past pain to develop a healthy self-image—reestablish your original innocent inner child belief in the goodness of your essence so you can live a happy, full life. To reiterate, they are ongoing and free. People may attend as many groups as they like a week and usually pick a home-based or favorite group to attend regularly. Group members take turn speaking if they desire to share, but they do not have to. I knew one man who listened for three years before speaking. You can learn a lot from just being there. Often, people, including this man who never spoke until after meetings, make great friends and fulfilling hobbies to replace negative relationships and addictive behaviors with the person's real, joyful passions.

These groups provide group support and a specific step-by-step process to work through your issues. You can work the steps at your pace. For example, one person took several years to work on step 1.

Maladaptive learnings of childhood do not go away in a snap; they are deep-seated. For example, a woman came to therapy for depression with suicidal thoughts. She was assisting her aunt, a substance abuser and caretaking her four children—all of whom lived with her. Codependent and overwhelmed, she learned through psychotherapy that her codependency stemmed back to when she was five years old when she would spend weekends with her alcoholic grandmother trying to stop her from drinking. "Only one, Grandma, please!" These long-term, ongoing support services give you the time and care to heal. These support services are a useful adjunct to psychotherapy.

Movement

Open up to a partnership that gets you exercising. Movement is the key to keeping your mind and body alive and well. Researchers have shown that regular aerobic exercise three times a week increases serotonin (positive mood) and endorphins (natural painkillers), thereby enhancing positive mood and reducing depression and somatic complaints (aches and pains). Thirty minutes a day releases a neurotransmitter that increases your metabolic rate and burns your calories a lot quicker, so it helps with weight loss.

Be open to help. Join a club or class or collaborate with a person to keep you going. Some kind of partnership with accountability will help you keep moving.

When I encourage you to find your passion physically, a sport of some kind, I emphasize the word "passion"—not something you feel forced to do.

Exercise: Think back for a moment in your childhood when you felt high on life. What activity were you doing? Use this memory to guide you to your sport. For me, it was third grade class square dancing. Although I never took dancing lessons as a child, I remembered that high feeling. And it led me as an adult to take dance, and now I have an upcoming advanced jazz dance recital with twenty-year-old classmates who think it is wonderful that I took up jazz in my thirties.

Discover inner peace—fulfill your spiritual needs

The true measure of a man's mental health (and happiness) is his ability to see good everywhere.

—Ralph Waldo Emerson

Spirituality is a genuine experience, which can be part of yet extends beyond specific religions. Until you experience spirituality, you cannot comprehend it. The spiritual experience is like chocolate; you must taste it because someone cannot describe it to you. It is well worth experiencing your spirituality. You know how wonderful chocolate is!

What is spirituality? Spirituality is being aware of your spiritual core or essence. It is recognition that you are not just a material body. It is your recognition that there is more to life than just meets the eye. It is your acceptance of what all the major world religions teach or suspect—that you are an eternal spirit who is connected to the ultimate source or power, God by all his many names.

The spirit life or metaphysical world exists, and you can choose to deal with it or not. That brings me to a story about a manifestation that supports my thesis that thoughts create. A helicopter pilot, who had become a security guard at a beach resort we visited annually, shared how in his helicopter travels he would look down on the swimmers in the ocean and see sharks swimming all about them close by, although unbeknownst to the swimmers. Spirit life metaphysical reality is like these sharks teeming about us that we can choose to acknowledge. After I found out about the preponderance of sharks in the ocean water, I was concerned about my two small children playing in the water. I put out my word, my intention, my desire that my children's experiences in the ocean would be awesome and beautiful—and "even the sharks would be friendly." Shortly thereafter, my son and his little friend had to run to the shore as two sharks passed five feet ahead of them! Something unheard of in the area or in general, if you know about sharks and their solitary nature, and a good example of a bad example: watch what you wish for!

Spirituality is not institutionalized religion with doctrines, dogma, and rules, although certainly, spirituality may involve belonging to a particular religion so that you have some group of like-minded people to associate with and so that you can grow in your philosophy and be accountable to share and practice beliefs.

I believe that for any of your healthy life changes to stick, you need to find your spiritual core, your connection to a higher power as you see it, to find your sacred space. This is the glue for your life changes to stick—a special place inside you of peace and goodness where you transcend everyday life experiences and connect to the larger divine or divine presence or higher power, if you will. It is a state of receiving fullness and goodness in life and trusting that things are progressing perfectly despite outward appearance of disruptive or even tragic life circumstances to the contrary. Bask in the sacred place in your heart and soul where you experience a sense of oneness with God, where you feel safe from harm, and where you feel strength, power, well-being, and total belief that you are good and worthy of love and goodness. This dispels the negative beliefs you have learned. You need this core to manifest a wonderful life.

To be happy, discover your spiritual self, believe that you are good and worthy of a better life, and have faith that good things are supposed to be. If you feel unworthy and guilty, how can you feel good and have a good life? If you see the world as haphazard or cruel, why bother to try to change or improve your life? To change your life, pursue the development of your spiritual source of peace and harmony. Each person's journey is an individual one. Each person's understanding of his or her higher power is unique as each of us is seeing through the special filter of our own personal experiences, generation or era, culture, family, background, temperament, intelligence, and so on. Each of us thus expresses God in a unique way, much like each snowflake christens a new fallen snow with its spectacular distinctive crystal beauty.

Resistance to spirituality or participation in religious organizations

Some people resist their own spirituality for good reasons. I did. About twenty years ago, I had difficulty accepting "the ocean of God" for a variety of reasons. I, like many people, had been hurt by experiences with organized religion in the past. Some people have had religion imposed on them as children and were turned off and even traumatized or damaged by their religion, their parents, or religious authority figures. I was raised a Catholic when much guilt was induced in us. This was pre-Vatican II when the popes' perceptual filters, through which God was described, were strict and harsh.

In *The Prophet*, Kahil Gibran's poetry describes religious law and our image of God as like the sun in whose glory we bask and are nourished. Yet he notes that unfortunately sometimes our religious leaders misconstrue their own shadow cast from their own backs to the sun as the sun itself. Men interpret what God is as a function of the filter of the times and their specific individual perceptions based on their own background, needs, culture, and even political demands—assuming and insisting to others that they were basking full face in the glorious sunshine rays of God.

I believe such a shadow was cast pre-Vatican II council. As a child, I learned there were two kinds of sins, mortal and venial, and only a few (how many?) venial sins could add up to a mortal sin. Mortal sins were punishable by eternal damnation lest you die without confession and forgiveness first. Scary! I lived in constant fear that I might not make it to confession before my transgressions overloaded. For example, maybe I had thought nasty thoughts about my family and munched down on a bologna sandwich before I realized it was fish-only Friday. I was doomed if I did not get absolution quickly.

What a way to live! As I grew to be a teen and more independent, I pulled away from the Catholic Church out of sheer emotional survival. Because of the guilt trips induced—and Catholics are not the only imposing religious organization—one progressive priest started recovering Catholic groups to help reduce guilt and fears caused by the previous "wrath of God" philosophy. My story illustrates how emotional blocks can cause resistance to not only organized religion but to belief or interest in God at all or any openness to spiritual growth. How could there be God when there was so much suffering in the world? The answer—almost a revelation—came to me one day.

Revelation

Curly locked, beautiful baby,
angelic faced—perfect.
Screaming, wailing, pitiful,
Mother turned demon.
Smothering, maiming,
Tearing her limbs off.
Petite sparks of electrical activity
Blip through baby's bitty brain.
Tiny intelligence cannot grasp
The meaning of this experience,
Her personal hell, her horror.
Unable to perceive possibility, future—
The burn of the rug on her chubby knees,
The cutting of the freezing wind,
Whipping and chapping her tiny body
Into a premature popsicle.
Mother floundering against
The able resistance of baby's kicks.
Mother exhausted from a day's work at 7:00 a.m.,
Trying to push perfect pink arms and legs through sleeves
Crumpled to the size of pinholes in the tussle.
Trying to slip the little cocking round head through the neckhole
Of Grandma's newly bought, perhaps a-tad-too-tight,
Hot pink infant jumpsuit.
A little too tight, yes, yet warm, soft, pretty, protective—
Against the upcoming day's trials
And winter's bitter chill.
7:05 a.m., mother emerging victorious from battle,
Tired but not beaten,
Only her pride wounded.
Revelation
Bullied into awareness.
They say, "No pain, no gain."
She had asked, "Why?
Why do good people suffer? Where is God?"
Revelation,

A flash of insight through intellectualization,
Her downfall and her freedom.
Major waves of electrical activity
Blip through mother's adult bitty brain.
Mother—young, pain reactive, feeling enraged—
Wondering, "Are we merely tiny ants
Thoughtlessly crushed or gassed
If caught scrambling across the kitchen counter
when the Master decides to fix breakfast?"
Revelation,
An awakening through angel fairy dust
Graciously shimmered over her willing heart.
If baby is too young to comprehend,
Perhaps so has mother been. How dare she claims
Exclusive Higher Intelligence?
To moan fate, karma, while gaping holes
In the pieces of life's puzzle
Lay hidden from her view.
To judge God—to judge eternity
On the basis of split-second hardship.
Revelation.
Mother—once too immature, vain, egotistical,
Unwilling to admit possibility,
A bigger picture, a grander scheme of things
Beyond her own daily planner and finite intelligence—
Grasps now the joke, "Want to make God laugh?
Tell him your plan."
Are not human years but minuscule moments
In timelessness?
And human pain petty
In the vastness of eternal bliss?
Revelation.
For truly is there suffering in the split-second
Appearance of pain?
Pain, intended simply to warm, protect, guide
The intervening by an
All-loving, providing parent aware of the grand plan.
All occurrence for the good right now.
This moment.

Like a trillisecond ago
When baby's razor-sharp nails dug paper cuts
Into her mother's soul, searing a wound which healed
Into the understanding of pain
And life
And love.
"Hush, baby. No need to cry. For you sway
Gently, firmly in the protective arms
Of your mother-father.
Unsquelch your tight, prune face.
Unsquint your angry eyes.
And when the tears pass,
You will see Paradise."

—A. Filosa, PsyD

When I was trying to dress my five-month-old daughter, she was screaming bloody murder, acting as if I was trying to maim or kill her as I attempted to put her arms into one of Grandma's cute little pink outfits. All I was doing was clothing her to keep her warm and protected on this cold winter day, yet you would have thought by her cries that I was suffocating her as I scrunched the sweater hole over her beet-red, enraged little head. I realized that we all are limited by incredible ignorance! How dare I expect to understand the mind of God and divine plan as anything except the appearance of tragedy—comforting blessings much like the fleece cloth was to be to my child.

Some people reject the concept of God as too unscientific, too unintellectual and invisible, and unable to be perceived with their five senses. However, spirituality is a genuine experience, a feeling, a knowing. Who has ever seen love and yet does not believe in love? What is God—the ultimate creative love power?

Other people have abandoned their spiritual search because when they beseeched God for help, their prayers appeared unanswered and they felt abandoned. Prayer is not begging some grand old man in the sky to bend down and make life better. Spiritual searching is more like exploring one's own sexuality. It is a unique personal journey that involves doing and exploring what feels right for you. Prayer is not an external force but a connection with your own divine birthright, your own inner sacred place of your higher power. Remember we are children of God made in the image of God and that God is in everything—which logically must include us. Therefore, where should we look for God but in us and around us?

The spirituality I am referring to is not the same as institutionalized religions with doctrines and rules spelled out for you. Meeting your spiritual needs may include belonging to some church or group of your choice that gets you to focus in on your inner serenity and harmony. Your spiritual self means that special part of yourself—of peace and goodness, of God and love. It is when you transcend everyday life situations and experiences and connect to the larger than life—the divine—if you will. It is a state of perceiving purpose, goodness, life, and trust that things are progressing as they should despite outward appearance of difficulty, even in the face of tragic life events. Like my little girl who did not understand as a baby that her parent was clothing her to protect her, likewise, our adult brains are infantile compared to the divine and cannot understand that the appearance of suffering is actually protection and good coming to us from on high from the divine. Being in touch with your spiritual self helps you stay in touch with this realization that you are always provided for, protected, safe, strong, powerful, well, good, and full of purpose and hope.

Evaluate your religion—your spiritual nourishment or addiction?

Your religion is necessary to your growth. It is meant to nourish you spiritually. If, however, it causes you to hate or oppose others—anyone—then it is distracting you from its purpose, which is to help you grow in love. It is then an addiction—not spiritual nourishment.

God is the ultimate source of love. Exclusive religious clubs are about its opposite—fear. The key to igniting your power is your relationship with the universe, with God—with your higher power. Your religion is simply your vehicle or transportation to the *higher ground* or higher consciousness beyond the primitive consciousness of material struggling to meet basic security and safety needs, such as for food, shelter, and so on. Religion is the clothing or the dwelling that protects and shelters you so you can go about your business of growing spiritually.

Religion is to be guarded against as an escape from life's problems, a way of filling the void, an addiction. Your spiritual self is the core or foundation upon which you draw strength and receive guidance to live a happy, fulfilling life.

If your spirituality is not helping you feel good and take care of yourself, your religion may be more of an addiction rather than a true spirituality. When you think about your religion's teachings and your organization's rules, do you feel consistently good, loved, positive minded, or sometimes guilty and fearful about yourself? Do you feel loving toward everyone regardless of the differences they may have from you, or do you look down on some individuals or groups?

To become a fulfilled person, you must discover your spiritual self. You have to believe you are good, one with the ultimate good, and always provided for and worthy of a good life. You must believe that life is good and life is unfolding as it should, even though outward appearances suggest suffering. If your religion makes you feel unworthy and guilty, how can you acknowledge and stand up for yourself? If you see the world as accidental or cruel in nature, why bother to try to change your personal situations? Your religion needs to support your emotional growth and well-being.

Daily spiritual or religious practice

To change your life, you must seek God or your higher power, as you perceive it, and pursue the development of your spiritual source of abundance, peace, and harmony. Each person's journey is individual. One must begin by realizing the necessity of this journey. Daily spiritual practices are of many types but are a necessary part of your spiritual development, much like the physical exercising of muscles is necessary to bodily health. You start willing yourself to exercise, and you begin to see the rewards. Likewise, regular spiritual practice of positive thinking leads to positive attitudes, self-confidence, and hope and changes your life circumstances through the self-fulfilling prophecy nature of our lives.

Religions that outright teach you the techniques to train your thoughts to empower you are the New Thought type: Religious Science—which has nothing to do with Scientology—and Unity denominations. In fact, surprising as it may seem, cognitive (thought) psychotherapy—the most effective therapy—is very much the same as these scientifically based New Thought organizations. New Thought, sometimes known as New Age Christian Thought (not to be confused with Scientology), is a religious philosophy that is progressive and open-minded that accepts that all religions provide pieces to the puzzle of God. It emphasizes that the basic tenets that most religions hold—namely, that God is the universal source, everywhere and in everything, the loving creative force that provides for all. Given that, God provides us free will by which we can express—thus, our thoughts, our words, our beliefs, and our consciousness creates our reality in a self-fulfilling prophecy manner. As cognitive therapy research has demonstrated the effectiveness, New Thought provides the theoretical metaphysical underpinnings for its effectiveness.

For those already attending a church and are affiliated with a religion, daily practice might involve reading spiritual scriptures daily or practicing spiritual guidelines. It involves daily prayer or meditation in which one connects with the divine. For those at the beginning of their spiritual journey, look for a spiritual or religious association or church that suits you. Perhaps return originally, as I did, to the church of your childhood if that is where you felt comfort and love or, as in my case, to work through or heal some of the traumas that came from being part of a religious organization as it evolved from a wrathful God image to a proper God of love and understanding.

If your concept of God is nature, take walks—commune with nature. For others who have an Eastern religion perspective, who see God as a divine within, learn and practice meditation regularly. In other words, focus inward on peace and love to transcend intrusive life worries. Practice connecting to the source of goodness daily. To keep yourself accountable, join and attend a religious or spiritually oriented center or group that fits your beliefs and feels truly right for you.

The daily practice of positive affirmations is beneficial to everyone. Affirmations are positive statements we say to ourselves at regular times during the day, such as "I am good," "I deserve good things," "I have good things," and "I see joy in my life." These are uplifting and energizing, not a religion forced on you or condemning you to behave certain ways to avoid future pain of hell. They give you power.

Homework: Regular daily spiritual practice maximizes your chances for happiness. So make the time to clarify your beliefs about God, the universe, and your life purpose. Find that special place inside yourself of peace and goodness where you receive a state of goodness in life and trust that things are progressing perfectly and that you are safe and well.

Start out at least five minutes a day and work up to half an hour.

God is the universal source of love—not the chairman of an exclusive religious club

> *Human beings are part of the universe but they experience themselves as separate…that is an optical illusion of our consciousness.*
>
> —Albert Einstein

> *We are each of us angels with only one wing. And we can only fly embracing each other.*
>
> —Luciano De Crescenzo

God is the universal source, the higher power as you conceive it. All religions are related by a few basic concepts about God. People in different religions have been caught up in the dissimilarities between different religions' belief systems and have adhered to different religious organizational rules. This is fine if it helps you grow in love and peace. The difficulty comes in when others' religions or organizations are rejected. Then conflict and even wars occur. Religious wars make no sense. How does killing people in hatred relate to God, the unconditional source of love for all?

More wars and deaths have occurred over religion than any other cause. Is this kind of religion related to God? Spirituality is being connected to or recognizing oneness with God—the one source of universal power. Your spirit transcends a particular religion that you believe in. Your spirit is the eternal and divine part of yourself that stems from God and that lives forever. You can come to understand that in many different ways, as many religions show.

Religions basically hold the same core concepts, and religious war does not relate to the concept of God. All religions have a common thread. At the center is God, that universal all-knowing, all-powerful source. Two points that are important are that all religions hold that God is love and all of us believe in love. The second part is that God is in everything. Therefore, if God is in everything, then God must be in you. God must be in all. There must be good (God) in everything. Logical analysis—and latest quantum physics research—supports this.

If we could stay with the basics, we probably would not have any problems on the earth at all. There could be no enemy because God is in your enemy. There could be no concept of evil, except as it is needed for our good. There is no devil, except as we create it. God is in everyone and everything. God is love and God is good; that means we are good and we are love. We are spirits. A spark of divinity. All religions see God as being in everything, which means in us as well as in people of other religions.

Moreover, if we logically carry out our belief that God is a loving creator and provider of all that exists, how it is that one person can condemn another person as being rejected by God? That is taking the whole meaning of God away. Because if God has unconditional love, he would never do that. Think about yourself. Would you condemn your worst enemy to eternal hell? No, and nor would God. If these concepts of devil and hell are our desire, we will generate them. They are man-made, born of man's thoughts and God's willingness to let us create or imagine whatever we wish to experience or feel in order to express and grow. Nevertheless, this is not of God. This is simply man's thoughts—man's creative expression.

A wonderful story illustrates how ridiculous separatism among religions is. The story goes that a Middle Eastern group of tribes got their water from a variety of wells. Each tribe had its own watering hole, and each secretly believed that its water was the best and the purest. Until one day, a diver explored beneath the wells. Surprisingly, he found that all the wells drew from the same body of water, thereby dispelling the supremacist arrogance each tribe held.

We perceive God or our higher power through our personal filters of perception—what we have learned from our organized religion, our culture, our family, and our personal experiences. That explains why we have so many religions and why our perception of God may differ from others. God is God, however—not our differing perception of God based on our own perceptual filters. Thus, our religions are good as long as they move us along on our spiritual journey and we learn to create our lives from our spiritual core. Acting like our religion is better or that we are better than others, and especially fighting over, this is the opposite of what God is all about—and it is just our personal egos and not about God.

We need our egos as a catalyst for our own growth. Our religions are vital to our growth. Again, however, if we focus on external power or control, we are not doing the spiritual emotional work that can actually transform our lives—because it is the creative power of our thoughts, not external stuff that empowers us truly. In other words, focusing on the external does not permanently or deeply change your life. When you grow internally in God, in a core positive belief, there is a good reason for everything. When you apply the metaphysical laws, when you focus on the good to seeing it manifesting in your life, this creates a happy fulfilling life for you and everyone else.

My poem(s) are based on true experiences. However, if I start to sound like a concert opening act that a friend of mine attended, during which a cat lady sang a song she claimed was dictated by her dying cat, please feel free to dismiss them as fanciful. If you think they are too outlandish, just learn from the rest of the text.

Oneness

I'm on a shopping trek.
A strange urge overcomes me— To experience a car wreck And feel its intensity.

"No, don't go there!
Watch your word.
Each thought's a prayer— I may be heard."

I wrench the foul thought away,
Yet I, a therapist by trade,
Receive a call later that day,
Answering the request I made.

A client had an accident.
Her car's damaged, yet she's fine. She needs a listening
ear, to vent, To release the emotional time.

She shares each scary moment.
As I absorb the details
Of the traumatic event,
Shocked how my earlier urge prevails,

Especially when she intuits,
"It was as if someone had a bad thought, Then quickly stops and changes it.
Then the car crash ends, and I'm overwrought."
For hit hard from behind,
Her car then stopped out of the blue. When changed,
the other's mind To restore all to anew.

We meet together to ease her stress
And decide to try some hypnosis. And as if she knew our weird
connection, Which she chose politely not to mention,

As if she knew my secret wish

While in her hypnotic trance,
Her half-shut eyes on me eerily fix
And stealthily hold my glance As if to prevent me any future tricks.

I've heard we are all angels and all one,
Come to earth as God's way to express—
Except we're one-winged, so each flies as none, Unless embracing all the rest.

Was this lust a backward demonstration Of our gift of free will and intent?
Did my morbid inner conversation Help miscreate her tragic event?

Or is it that we know,
In the depths of our hearts, Everything about friends
and foe— For they're simply our other parts.

—A. Filosa, PsyD

One Source

That God is the ultimate source,
all good, all loving, all-powerful, all knowing,
everywhere and everything,
creating and providing for all.
From whom we are molded in his image.
He created the world, people, the entire universe
through his thought, his desire, his word.
And has given us free will to create our lives
with his power through our thought and words.
We are, in essence, divine sparks expressing God.
All we need to do is become the hollow bone
through which God can express.
Put simply, thoughts create.
Thoughts create because there is an underlying
orderly spiritual or metaphysical law,
just like any physical law,
such as gravity and electricity.
Like with electricity, we can fry a man (electrocution)
or feed a man (the cooking stove).
Our thoughts can create good or havoc
in our lives or the world.
This is why cognitive therapy works,
in my opinion.
Proven through research, we know it works.
And that's my opinion why it works.

—A. Filosa, PsyD

The pillar of words in world religions

Our thoughts are prayers and we are always praying.

—Unity song

All the religions share another common characteristic. All believe that words have power which spring from a spiritual fountain. Let us look at different religions and what they believe about words to understand that the power of words comes from the spiritual law and level. To define, "thoughts" and "words" are terms that mean essentially the same—a word may be a thought silently, written, or spoken aloud. No words exist without thought behind them—even though we sometimes comment that somebody is talking without thinking.

In the Christian Bible, John 1:1–3 states: "In the beginning was the Word, and the Word was God. Nothing was made without the Word, and without the Word was nothing at all made." When we speak the Word, knowing we are God, that is the power, God speaking the Word. God had the power to speak the Word unto himself as God. Jesus states many times in many ways, "Ask anything in my name without doubt and it will manifest." Thus, to paraphrase, "Ask the mountain to rise up and move, and it will be done."

Fundamentalist Christians might say that the Word is Jesus, but why then is the Word discussed in Genesis in the Old Testament when God was creating the world before Jesus was born? Logically, the Word must refer to something else. The Word is the spiritual law—the ways and means of our power to create through thought—the power of the source God.

Because the Word is power, the Word is the power more than Jesus Christ is. Christ was not even his proper name but referred to his ability to have the sort of spiritual positive consciousness that we have been talking about. Jesus Christ told us about the use of the Word to create our lives. Jesus was not the Word, although he was the Word when he demonstrated all his miracles and he simply stated the Word, his oneness to God, and what he said manifested in physical reality. He said, "Rise up," to the dead, and they were alive. He told the blind to see. And affirming his oneness with God, speaking God the Word, he made the blind to have perfect vision.

Christians, in general, believe in their power of words in the form of prayer. New Age Thought Christians—people who believe in Religious Science and Unity teachings, its sister religion—expand on this. They believe that "healing of every condition is possible. No condition is incurable where there is faith in God's power." In order to receive and utilize the prayer energy, you must be in a receptive mode. "We ask you to daily affirm and hold in mind the affirmative that best suits your need."

If you are placing another person's name on the healing list, please share the affirmation with him or her.

> I believe in the healing power of God;
> I am renewed and restored in mind and body.
> Divine love enriches me. My life is teeming with abundance.
> Divine life flows through me as radiant health.
> Divine light shines through me; I make wise choices.
> Divine peace permeates my life; I live in serenity.
> I breathe the breath of life and my body is vibrant with health and vitality. Praise God!
> I am a channel for the inflow of light and wisdom. I know what to do and I do it. Praise God!
> The presence of God within strengthens and nurtures me.

> The spirit of God permeates my life, richly prospering me.
> The peace of God fills me with serenity.
>
> —Unity prayer

Now we have crossed over the part of the book that you can buy or not buy, take or leave as it suits you at this time, but it is very important that you have read it. Words are the basis for creating your life. I, and many, believe that words have more power than you may realize. Most people who have any kind of religious openness will accept this part of the book, but I am going to explain some things about it regardless of your religious orientation.

If our thoughts are in tune with God, that higher power that is love which fulfills our needs, then we have faith. And faith gives us a hopeful attitude about life. Medical research has shown that people who have faith do better medically. The medical profession is becoming more aware that certain thoughts and feelings relate to our physical condition. For example, research that shows that frequently cancer is preceded by significant depression—or underlying resentment turned inward—occurring about a year and half before the diagnosis and is a good reason to seek help for depression for more information. Essentially, the type of thoughts we have leads to how we feel, which combines to lead to how we behave, which leads to our physical outcome manifesting in our life situations, events, relationships, and more. Ultimately, thought creates everything that exists in the physical world. There is Louise Hay's book, *You Can Heal Your Life and Heal Your Body*, which provides insight into the thoughts that underlie diseases and conditions and how to change your thoughts and heal yourself. She cured herself of cancer through changing her consciousness as well as some natural healing methods. Her story is in her book.

A well-known author of our time, Gary Zukav, calls this the power of intention. Many decades ago, Norman Vincent Peale wrote numerous books about the power of positive thinking. The most effective psychotherapy, per psychological research, is cognitive therapy or cognitive behavioral therapy—psychology of thought. Cognitive therapy has been found to be as effective for depression as psychopharmacological drugs, like antidepressants. This form of psychotherapy involves the therapist helping clients become aware of their thoughts, particularly self-statements, and to change these self-statements from negative to positive ones, thereby relieving their depression and changing mood from unhappiness to positive feelings.

Some thoughts, beliefs, or attitudes are unconscious or subconscious. This means that we are not aware of them, but they are still affecting us. Usually, the thoughts we say to ourselves, if we would tune in and listen to our inner voice, check our inner voice mail, are fairly easy to notice. What we might not know is the underlying belief of what these thoughts add up to. With some analysis, we can figure this out. If you notice yourself saying negative things a lot while you were going about your business in the exercises, you can believe you have a negative self-image.

Exercise: Once again, notice what kinds of comments you make to yourself and use this to give you a clue as to your underlying self-esteem, self-worth, or self-image. This leads you to your negative core issues—awaiting positive transformation.

The problem is not the problem. The problem is my *perception of the problem.*

There is a wonderful book called *Your Word Is Your Wand.* The book is a series of affirmations to help a reader find the right words to say to change negative thoughts into positive thoughts about a variety of categories, including relationship, money, work, and self-worth. Your magical, mystical, metaphysical wand, words are the key to empowerment. Turn to the next chapter for the scientific proof.

(Di)Vision

I love a rocking chair.
So when I was a teen,
I would often sit there,
Radio on—rocking
Like a music fiend.

I would relax, close my eyes,
Let my imagination soar.
Music flies us somewhere nice.
Mine could race to the face of a lion's roar.

What were these visions for?
Once I fell almost asleep,
When in my drowsy mind's eye,
I envisioned a white jeep
From an aerial view on high—
On which, I began to spy.

I watched the white jeep make its way
Up neighborhood streets nearby,
Then stopping in my own driveway.
As my vision bid goodbye,
Then I too dropped from up high.

The doorbell rang, and I could hear
My mother called out to me,
"Honey, come down. John is here.
Would you please hurry?"
He'd arrived unexpectedly.

Peeking out my bedroom window,
Assuming I would see
His flashy red Camero,
When astonishingly
A white jeep winked at me.

Since 'cross town is far,
With his car low on gasoline,
He drove his parents' car,
One I'd never seen,
Except in my recent daydream.

Now had I become insane?
Teens hormonally deranged can be,
So as not to sound inane,
I kept this secret locked inside me
And no more indulged in crazy revelry.

Until later years,
I took an ESP class,
Which banished my fears,
Explaining at last,
This odd experience of the past.

"There are three ways to be psychic,"
My clairvoyant teacher said.
I thought, "How wild! What a kick!"
Still in confusion, scratched my head—
As to the class, she spoon-fed,
"ESP is not scary.
Nor is its use wrong.
No reason to be wary.
This skill we, each of us, can hone.
It's like talking on the phone."

Though not superathletes, like Magic J,
We are each able to throw a ball.
Psychic talent is the same way,
An ability shared by all,
Requires practice—and a little gall,

And knowing your own channel,
Personal awareness
Of how this gift to all,
You, as an individual,
Best process your private sixth sense.

The first way is "knowing,"
Popularly called intuition.
Also related, the second, is "feeling."
The third still sparks suspicion,
The art of seeing a psychic vision.

Are knowing and feeling things acceptable?
Because all can intuit—all can do it?
Since seeing things not all are capable,
Exclusionary religions "throw a fit,"
Denying anyone who can do it.

Ages ago, I regularly did client psych evaluation
For a Christian counseling group.
And once I made a mistake to mention,
Throwing the boss "for a loop,"

Could psychic vision explain
One boy's hallucination?
Though fine for his counselors
To "feel" another's prayer,
Psychic seeing must be the work of the devil
And visions an invite into Satan's lair.

So pounding his fundamentalist gavel,
He fired me then and there,
With no time to discuss
Great Saint Joan of Arc,
Her heard voices (clairaudience).
Her special psychic mark.
Nor my astral travel like a lark.

—A. Filosa, PsyD

CHAPTER 5

Words—Your Magical, Mystical Wand

Your word is like a mystical magical wand—a spiritual law like gravity is in physics.

Biology and physics as well as philosophy, psychology, theology, and spirituality all support that thoughts and intention are powerful

*N*umerous great thinkers have addressed and proven through experience, theory, and research how thought empowers us to create our lives, our world, and ourselves. Oprah Winfrey, the very popular TV talk show host, introduced to the public *The Secret*, a video documentary and book by doctors, ministers, physicists, and other great minds which includes research in quantum physics and biology and proves the power of thoughts. *The Secret* describes the law of attraction—like attracts like and what we think about and what we visualize manifests in and create our everyday life in reality in general. Oprah has been committed to help people understand their spirituality. Previously on her show was Gary Zukav, who wrote the best seller *Seat of the Soul* about the "power of intention," which brought this concept to the public. Many decades ago, Norman Vincent Peale wrote numerous books about the "power of positive thinking." Neal Donald Walsch, in *Conversations with God*, wrote about "sponsoring thoughts" to describe how our underlying thought patterns create our lives. He envisioned making a million dollars—and, within the year, had almost achieved his goal as he was inspired to write his best seller series.

As was stated, Louise Hay, in her best sellers, *You Can Heal Your Life* and *Heal Your Body*, wrote about the idea of "probable cause"—the negative thinking patterns which cause our negative life conditions, including physical conditions and diseases. She developed her own list of negative probable causes and corresponding positive affirmations to counter them in life areas, such as health, work, relationships, prosperity, and more. She healed herself of cancer through the power of intention—only used natural alternative health treatment. As was stated earlier, a less well-known but a wonderful book called *Your Word Is Your Wand* is a series of positive, poetically phrased affirmations that help the reader find the right words to change negative thoughts into positive ones about similar life categories.

As was described earlier, in psychology, the most effective psychotherapy, according to research, is cognitive therapy. "Cognitive" refers to cognition, which is the psychological term for "thought." In the science of changing human behavior and enhancing emotional well-being, the most successful treatment focuses on changing unhealthy mental or thought patterns. Most good, experienced therapists, even if they do not call themselves "cognitive therapists," help their clients become aware of their cognitions (their thoughts), particularly their self-statements (what they say about themselves to themselves when thinking), and change these self-statements from negative to positive ones. Cognitive therapy has been found to be as effective as drugs for depression, like antidepressants. Cognitive therapy relieves the depression by changing the discouraging thinking that fosters their bad mood or unhappiness to enhance more positive, uplifting, encouraging feelings. Cognitive therapy can ameliorate the gamut of mental disorders—even psychoses if the ill person can be convinced to recognize their hallucinations as something to dismiss and ignore.

Robert Lipton, PhD, a neurobiologist, has done extensive research probing and proving that belief affects biology. Medical research has shown that people who have "faith," which involves positive thinking, do better medically, such as in heart surgery. When cardiac patients are prayed for, their surgery outcome improves. Interestingly, when alcoholics entering rehabilitation centers are prayed for, their outcome is not as improved because of the mixed message significant others send. The attempt at positive thinking tinged with resentment toward the alcoholic's presumed weakness and character issues interferes with the positive thinking.

The medical profession is becoming more aware also that certain specific physical conditions are often preceded by certain attitudes or thought patterns. As was stated, Louise Hay's contributions have connected many more specific thoughts to specific health conditions and have provided much insight into the underlying thinking patterns and emotions of disease and illness.

Scientific research proves the power of intention

Frontier scientists at the cutting edge of quantum physics discovered that we humans and all the universe are made up of tiny microtubules, hollow light tubes of pulsating, mutable light energy, a light field which can be influenced, altered, and transformed through the power of intention—the observer effect or "focused attention," as it is called in experimentation. Lynne McTaggart presents the tremendous body of empirical evidence research proof in quantum physics and neurobiological and human behavioral sciences in her very readable book, *The Field*. The quantum physicists observed that subatomic particles occur in a zero-point field—a space in which there is random activity of photons that could explode into infinite possibilities—that crystallize or freeze into a set reality as a function of being observed. The power of intention creates reality through our thoughts, our consciousness, our intention, our words. We can influence and create physical reality.

Lynne McTaggart's *The Field* is a readable book that summarizes the research evidence—which provides compelling proof for what the great spiritual masters have been trying to teach us. As a friend of mine put it when he or I have an intuition, "We're a little physic"—meaning the person was a "little psychic." Judging from the current scientific research on intentionality, physics and psychic phenomena are the same. Here is why.

Frontier scientists in quantum physics experimented with the observer effect, the power of focused attention and intentionality by living beings—human and animal—on physical reality. They found that even baby chicks through their intentionality to imprint—to bond with the first object they see and assume is the mother figure—could cause machines to move toward them. Some experiments ran over two and a half million trials with statistically significant positive results—proving the power of intent. Human intention was found to be able to influence and alter everything from bacteria and yeast to ants, mice, cats, and dogs, etc., to animate objects.

The observer effect or power of intention was proven at a statistically significant level to be able to change the cells of human beings as well as people's brain waves and other human physiological reactions. For example, when subjects were being measured for their physical indices of anxiety and were stared at by experimenters through a one-way mirror, they reacted with increased physiological reactivity indicative of feeling anxious about being watched. When they were not being watched, their bodies were calmer. Interestingly, when subjects were previously required to stare lovingly at another's eyes and then participated in the experiment, their physical reactions to the being watched unbeknownst actually increased their calmness rather than diminished it.

Moreover, researchers found that when more than one person thinks the same thing or sends the same vibes, the power of the observer effect increases—particularly couples who were involved with each other affected reality more powerfully than an individual did.

The movie *What the Bleep Do We Know!?*—the documentary on the law of attraction, which is known as the observer effect in scientific experimentation, includes pictures of water, photographed after being influenced. A monk blessed water, and the water molecules lined up in a beautiful pattern. Likewise, he sent the vibes of love to the water, and the photographs revealed another aesthetic design. However, when he sent the feeling of hate to the water, the water molecules combined in a dark and ugly configuration. Since humans are 90 percent water, the authors of the documentary point out and question, "What effect does love or hate have toward another person?"

Medical advancement now involves exploration of the use of light energy with the goal of utilizing this knowledge to diagnose and treat people based on their spectrum of light energy. White light is the combination of all colors of the spectrum. I believe that this will also serve not only to advance medicine but also to raise and dispel the human race's consciousness regarding stereotypes, like gender and race. All people are one light energy field. Then too people can grasp also that spirituality is simply psychic plus science equals cutting-edge physics.

My personal awakening to the power of thoughts

I was taking a class at a church, where we were studying Louise Hay's *You Can Heal Your Life*. The assignment was to choose a personal ailment to heal. I frequently had colds and infections to remedy. I had become involved in holistic health treatments and improved considerably. However, I would still, at times, succumb to sickness. In Louise Hay's book, she describes the underlying cause, or mental pattern, of colds as "mental confusion and small hurts"—in general, being stressed out. The affirmation to alleviate this experience is "I allow my mind to relax and be at peace. Clarity and harmony fill and surround me" (page 161).

At first, I resisted and even resented the idea that I could in any way be influencing myself to develop colds. Ironically, a proclaimed believer in the power of thought, I called myself a cognitive, although eclectic, psychologist! However, I certainly did not consciously desire to get sick, although I was aware that I appreciated the rest I would take when I had "caught a cold." This was when I "caught up" on reading, which I enjoyed.

Being a willing student, I decided to state the affirmation whenever I felt confused, stressed, hurt, or disappointed. I noticed myself thinking and making self-statements, like "I have to rush here," "I'm stressed," "I'm overwhelmed," "I don't know what to do," etc.—which were all contributing to this underlying mental pattern of confusion and feeling discombobulated or harried. I also knew that belief in germs and catching cold play into becoming ill. I became aware when I would claim such ideas, such as "Oh no, so-and-so's cold is contagious. I've been exposed. I'm going to get sick."

Whenever I made an unhealthy self-statement—I told myself I was stressed and/or I was going to get sick—I would thought stop these ideas and state Louise Hay's affirmation. I found myself becoming healthier to the point that I took on so much responsibility without getting the slightest down in the weather that I feared I would blow a mental socket! Whereupon, I stopped saying my affirmations and, of course, became sick. Then I reinstituted the negative thought stopping and reactivated my positive thinking plan. It worked!

The true challenge came to me one day when a coughing, sneezing, contagious client rushed into my office, saying she had just come from the doctor's and picked up her antibiotic from the pharmacy! Silently to myself throughout the therapy session, I affirmed the affirmation. Usually before an interaction with a sick person ended, I would already be experiencing "sympathy pains," a slight headache, maybe a scratchy throat. In this case, I never became ill at all! Mind you, I religiously said the affirmation to myself every single instance I had a potentially negative sickness-inducing thought—at least fifty times during the therapy session, probably every time she coughed, for example. All in all, I probably repeated what became almost a mantra three hundred times the first day, between fifty and one hundred times the second day, and so on, gradually weaning off the rest of the week, until I truly believed that germs had no power over me and that I was perfectly healthy. At times, admittedly this was tedious, but well worth it, to me because I experienced complete control over my physical health for the first time!

This is based on a true event:

Words

    I'm sure you have heard
      And don't doubt this,
    "Better watch your word.
    You may get what you wish."

    A ministerial student
From a center of New Thought
Said, "I am not going to madly vent
But practice what I've been taught."

    By trade, he drove a truck,
And each day when the sun rose up, Before rigging his
    haul to work, He needed to stop and gas up.

    . And each and every time,
    Forever he seemed to wait, in a long, long gas line, Which left him almost irate.

    So as a simple test,
He spoke his word to Grand Mind,
      Stating his very best About what he hoped to find.

"When I reach the station today, No one will be there.

I will have it my way.
The place will be bare!"

While trucking along, he chanted,
"When I arrive, I'll see
An open pump space I've landed Which I'll use freely."

Wow! The gas station was empty— No line, no trucks, no cars.
He fueled his vehicle quickly, Thanking his lucky stars.
A magical demonstration Of the power of Positive Thought.
He'd created this sensation, Which in church class he could flaunt.

When it was time to pay, Can you imagine?
On this miracle day, What's going to happen?

Yes, inside, he waited and waited, But no cashier ever came.
The words he spoke had fated, And no other was there to blame.

The wish he had chosen to say— That no other would be there today,
Forgot that he'd need someone to pay, And he waited forever anyway.

To create your vision, This student had learned:
Be precise when you envision
Or you may well get burned.

For what you see
Is what you get. Choose words carefully, So they do not limit.

—A. Filosa, PsyD

All of us have had an experience of thinking about something or commenting negatively about something, like "I hope the washing machine doesn't break down," and shortly thereafter, it does break down. This is being ignorant about your power. You put forth your word, your desire, and God is simply saying yes to your free will to *create*—only you are using the spiritual law backward. This could also be an intuition.

Exercise: Ask yourself, "When have I predicted something negative happening and then it happened?" From now on, replace a negative thought with a positive one. Practice thought stopping.

Man's world religions and worldviews

Our worldview is our own personal metaphysics or cosmology. Although recently "metaphysical" is used interchangeably with "New Age Thought," Aristotle coined the term "metaphysics" to describe the complement to "physics" (the laws that govern physical reality), the invisible laws that govern our invisible realities, the spiritual laws that govern our deeper spiritual lives. A complement is something that completes, makes up a whole, or brings to perfection.

Throughout time, in all cultures and countries, man has sought to understand himself beyond pure physical reality. He has recognized that there is some higher power, creator, or force that he is a part of and with which he seeks to find harmony. The majority of people have some form of religion. In the United States, only about 7 percent of people don't claim a particular religious preference. At some level, we realize that we are not here accidentally and that the world is not just haphazard but rather that there are some natural laws, some forces to be understood at a deeper spiritual level. Even if we have not spent much time thinking about it or have not been consciously on a spiritual journey, we can analyze our beliefs to come up with some semblance of a worldview that we personally believe in.

Your personal metaphysical theory or worldview is crucial. A positive, planned worldview to your ultimate life course is as essential as having a specific destination in mind and directions or a map to get somewhere in your car. Not knowing your worldview is like getting into a car not planning to go anywhere but rather to just sit there and finally drive aimlessly. Not having a plan is like getting into a boat without having any navigation guidelines. A little steering off course and you could wind up in China when you were intending to go to Bermuda. We need to plan our journey and get maps to guide us. We want to be fulfilled and happy, and we want to know clearly how to get there.

Religions and philosophy try to provide us with methods and direction. The purpose of spiritual philosophy and religion is to give us beliefs, understandings, and insights about our purpose and ourselves in the world. Through this, we connect with the higher power of good underlying our physical reality, our deeper, more everlasting spiritual reality. Our worldview stems from our basic beliefs about our self-worthiness, which determines our lives. Our sense of self-worthiness (composed of our self-statements about ourselves and how we fit into the world) leads to how we feel. Consequently, this leads to how we react to events and how we behave. These choices affect how life is going to treat or react to us.

Likewise, our self-worth is bound up with our life philosophy, which relates to our religious and spiritual beliefs.

My son and his best buddy were in the back seat of my car on the way home from shopping while I was thinking about writing this chapter, when they noticed a Glad wrap box sitting in a grocery bag. They began cracking themselves up with jokes based on the old commercial in which a person's food dropped out of some form of plastic wrap because she or he had not used Glad wrap, the best brand per the TV commercial. The Glad man would say, "Don't get mad. Get Glad." Synchronically, my son and his friend were helping me understand that this viewpoint of positive thinking at the superficial level could seem sappy. They made up various scenarios: "My friend just fell off a cliff. Oh, don't get mad. Get Glad." "I just took a bullet to my head. Don't get mad. Get Glad." They laughed uproariously. Their play was especially interesting and synchronistic because they had no idea about the topic I was addressing in my mind about my book.

If our thoughts are in tune with a belief in a higher power of love, which provides for our needs, and if we have some faith, our lives feel hopeful. It is hard to believe, yet tragedies or cruel life events are only so temporary in appearance—with a deeper spiritual understanding explaining them differently and positively. Tragedies or cruel, harsh experiences are as such in appearance when taken in light of the broader spiritual picture. For example, some of the greatest misery that has faced humankind—such as the Holocaust, the September 11 attacks, Columbine High School massacre, and the Virginia Tech shooting—served to elevate our consciousness to a vastly more unified worldwide desire for love and peace. How do we not know that the souls or spirits of these people didn't contract with God to go through these painful human experiences to aid others and elevate the human race to a higher state of lovingness and that they too, through polishing their diamond with friction so to speak, elevated their spirits to be one with God's unconditional love? Have you heard only the good die young? They have graduated early.

Thus, our lives can demonstrate to us what our beliefs are—because we are "driving our car" in a certain direction without taking charge to head there. That is the point of this book: to encourage you to take heed of your destination so you create happy outcomes for yourself or, if you will, so that you fulfill your purpose harmoniously in tune with the spiritual universe, our deeper reality of life.

The point of this discourse is to encourage the reader to take charge of his or her destination and to learn to create a happy, harmonious life in tune with the deeper spiritual reality. Our lives are but a demonstration of our direction whether or not we are consciously aware of where we are heading. If our thoughts are coordinated with the higher power of love and an understanding that our needs are always being provided for, we are renewed in faith and hope and can take conscious charge of our life course and manifest outcomes positive in appearance as well as essence.

Learn from the common threads tying together the world religions

And what place is there in me in which God can come, even He who made Heaven and Earth? Is there anything in me, Oh, Lord, my God, that can contain Thee? Or, should I rather say that I should not exist unless I was in Thee, from whom are all things, by whom are all things, in whom are all things?

—Saint Augustine

This part of the book *may be controversial* to some and hopefully will not offend anyone. This is what has given me a greater understanding of God and source and represents my attempt to see the good and value in all religions—to rather bring us all closer together in harmony and brotherhood.

In this melting pot of cultures and belief systems, Americans practice most of the great world religions from Protestant and Catholic to Hindu, Buddhist, Islamic, and Judaism. We can approach religion as exclusionary clubs, such as claiming that our religion is the only true source of truth. Or we can accept that there is a common thread among the religions and that each religion asks different questions about our spiritual nature and thus comes up with different answers, but each provides us with pieces to the puzzle of the mystery of life.

Let us get back to basics, folks! God is love. Love is the essence of God, and anyone who believes in God of any religion must accept this. Aggression and war are not expressions of love and therefore manifest only man's willful mistake, not God's nature!

The underlying concept of all religions is that God, or the higher power, is the source of ultimate good. The exclusionist view, which has led to more deaths and wars than any other cause, is hardly consistent with the basic premise of God at all. More wars and deaths have occurred over religion than from any other cause. Is this kind of religion related to God—a spiritual or religious belief recognizing one's source, one's closeness with the universal reservoir of power and good? How can we wage war in the name of religion when all religions' core belief is that God wants to provide all good for all of us? The exclusionary club mentality of religious organizations makes no sense, a contradiction in terms because it actually violates the one core concept underlying all religions—that God is the abundant provider of all good for *all of us*! Billy Graham, the great evangelist and a fundamentalist Christian, supports this belief that God loves everyone.

When we address the commonalties among the religious views, we find the common thread and truth that resolve the differences between religious organizations as well as show why our words and thoughts are spiritual power. All the religions have a common thread of truth. They hold the same core concept of God, even though at the organizational level the practice of claiming that one's own religion is *the* only right religion, which guarantees exclusive admission to heaven, contradicts this essential belief.

At the center of each religion is God, as we call him in Catholic and Christian religions, or the Buddha or Enlightened One in the Buddhist religion or Yahweh in the Judaic religion or Allah in Islam, etc., the universal source of all creation and good, the higher power by any name.

Most religions agree that God is present everywhere, which means, taken to its logical conclusion, that God must be in everything or that everything is in God. For example, as young children, Catholics learn in their little catechism books the principle that God is invisible and everywhere. This is what "omnipresent" means. Even the religions, like the Islamic and most of the Christian Protestant religions—that place God in heaven in a separate place from humankind—smatter the word "omnipresent" or "omnipresence" in their ministerial sermons, hymns, or scriptures, showing their underlying belief that God is everywhere. Again, Christian organizational dogma contradicts the hidden core principles of all religions. Man-made specific organizational assertions sometimes allow for exclusivity of God favoring certain people over others. For example, in the Koran, the Islamic Bible, God is described as closer to man than his own jugular vein, which sounds like God is in us, yet in practice, this crucial statement of God's word is ignored and man continues to be demoted to a mere earthly creature and possible worthless sinner who could be banished forever from God if he misbehaves under the watchful, potentially wrathful eye of the Father in the kingdom above.

The development of exclusive religious clubs

The idea that God favors certain groups over others originated more than two thousand years BC with a struggle over territory that stemmed from mere politics—nothing to do with God or religious beliefs at all! When Abraham, a Jew, couldn't bear a son with his wife, Sarah, he was allowed by tribal law to procreate with someone else, an Arab woman, with whom he had Ishmael, who became the father of the Muslim lineage. Because supposedly in her old age, Abraham's wife Sarah did bear him a son, Isaac, who became the father of the Jewish line. This son became the true heir to the land. Envy raged between the two brothers, as the one was deposed. Hence, the two camps of the Jews and the Arabs emerged. Over time, their cultures produced Judaism and the Islamic religions. The conflicts from a political struggle resulted in God being interpreted through differing cultural filters rather than one religion representing the true nature of God.

In fact, Mohammed, the spiritual leader of the Islamic religion of the Muslims, was not born until thousands of years later when he was deeply entrenched in Arab culture and competitive with the Jews politically. Moreover, when Mohammed did what is called channeling a spirit guide—he went into trance and the angel Gabriel spoke to him—another individual had to interpret and write what he heard because Mohammed was illiterate. So the Koran actually was secondhand information. Furthermore, although taken superficially, the Koran endorses violence. The true meaning of passages related to aggression actually refers to fighting or challenging one's own negative consciousness or thinking!

Let's look at some specific examples from specific sects within religions. For example, take born—again Christians of the fundamental Christian religion. They believe that they are saved from eternal hell or damnation by the personal presence of Jesus Christ in their hearts and their lives. They are saying basically that Christ is within. They experience the feeling of Christ inside themselves. That is the born-again experience. Even though they also see themselves as sinners and still place God outside themselves, their actual experience is one of personal connectiveness with God.

Likewise, the born-again Christians who value their personal relationship with Jesus as fundamental to their being saved or born-again—often who describe a sense of being filled to overflowing with him in their hearts and soul—turn around and contradict themselves in accord with the other Protestant denominations and express agreement with the concept of Judgment Day or Resurrection Day—the God of the sky deciding who's been bad or good and thereby bestowing his gifts accordingly. Does this sound strangely similar—although meaner—to the myth of Santa Claus? What is most important is that this idea denies the true feeling of closeness born-again Christians know they have been saved—that they are connected to and feel within themselves Jesus (name for God). The Holy Trinity being the Father, the Son being Jesus, and the Holy Ghost.

Moreover, truly religious or spiritual folk feel and know they have God in their hearts, a part of themselves. God, like love and being love, is only experienced this way, as a feeling of the heart. The core belief all religions share is that God is love. Therefore, where does God exist or reside? Love, which can also be recognized as intense positive feeling, is the limitless spirit of God and resides within us.

For another example, in the Buddhist religion, they do not use the word "God." They refer to the higher power as the Buddha or the Enlightened One. Buddha was a young prince sheltered in the palace, until one day he inadvertently witnessed a sick, dying man. He fled the palace and gave up his riches to try to understand why there was suffering in the world—and he became a spiritual leader. He found that external sources of potential happiness, such as money or material possessions, did not necessarily equate with happiness. People who had a lot of money might still be suffering. He concluded that connection to the oneness—the universal source—supplied happiness. An inner experience, the Buddhist practice was to meditate and connect with the one source to experience the oneness of what now for the Buddhist is known as Buddha or the Enlightened One. In Christian terms, this would be thought of as God. This is to experience transcendental communion with the almighty presence. That this removes suffering is because one realizes ultimately that we are one with God. We are one with divine, the ultimate white light energy, the source, all good, all power, all knowledge, and all eternity—the source of happiness. Understanding experiencing this truth, the Buddhists exemplify the Eastern religions, which each, of course, have different practices, different terms, etc., but come from a similar state of "tuning in" to experience the connection with the one.

The born-again Christians talk about their salvation as having come from an experience of Jesus Christ coming into their hearts. They intellectually believe in a separation between man and God. In actuality, their happiness comes from the experience of their oneness with God through Jesus Christ, who is the spiritual leader in the Christian religion as the Buddha is in the Buddhist religion.

All religions assert that God has the qualities of omniscience (all knowing) and omnipotence (only power). There is nothing God cannot know or understand because God is not only everywhere present but is the intelligence of everything that is! God is omnipotent. That means he is all-powerful; there is nothing greater than his power. Exclusionary clubs and their defensive religious fortresses and gala finale Judgment Day contradict the core concept of omniscience. If God knows everything, has all power, and is good, why would God commit anyone to eternal damnation? Do you know anyone who is good, loving, and caring who would commit someone to eternal damnation if they could prevent it?

The practice of religions—even within sects of the same religion—differs greatly. This shows how man-made the actual specifics of the organizational practices are. For example, even in the Buddhist religion, there are numerous sects divided according to how these concepts are applied and practiced. In Christianity, there are many Protestant denominations.

Even though practice differs within religions as well as between them, there is no reason for actual division or conflict about one religion being the true religion and the others being wrong once we agree to observe and uphold the crux of the core beliefs that are essentially the same. Moreover, the core beliefs about God oppose exclusion of anyone or rejecting anyone else's religion. We need to own our oneness with love and love one another, however our neighbor chooses to understand his God and express his own spirituality.

Healthy participation in religious organizations

Let us review: We define God by all its names as the universal source, the only higher power, as we perceive it. We know all religions share some basic concepts, although some hide them well and we have seen religious organizations are caught up in dissimilarities between their exclusive practice of religion and their underlying knowledge or core beliefs.

To participate in a religious organization can be a good thing because it gives us a sense of community and belonging as well as accountability for growing spiritually and emotionally. The difficulty lies in one religion refuting another religion, and conflict erupts. However, all religions hold that God is love, and all of us do believe in love even though we cannot see it. Second, most religions hold that God is in everything and is everywhere. So philosophically and logically, let's look at this: If God is everywhere, then God must be in you. God must be in all, in everyone. If God is love and good, there must be good in everything and everyone, including those from other religious beliefs beside one's own. For example, when Jesus—the master of one of the great world religions, Christianity—was asked what commandment was the most important, he replied, "Love—love God and love your neighbor as yourself."

If we could stay with this basic idea, conflict on earth would be gone. There could be no enemy because God is in your enemy. There could not even be a concept of evil, except as we believe to perceive it because everything is good. There is no devil, except as we create and perceive it as a product of the free will God has given us. If God is in everything and is all-powerful, how could there be another powerful force for God to compete and reckon with—unless, of course, we want this.

The crux of all the great world religions is God is love and God is good. That means we are good and we are love. We are spirits—sparks of divinity. Furthermore, everything that happens to us is good because God is everywhere and all good. The higher power or source has also, according to most religious beliefs, given us free will to make our own choices and create our lives. Hence, even the idea of the devil, if a man chose to believe in such, is in accordance with free will. In other words, when we make mistakes in our choices—choose to think negative thoughts, like the existence of an alternate evil power or force—we experience suffering. This, of course, is in appearance only, not at the deeper level of spiritual reality.

There cannot be two infinities opposed to each other! There must be one infinite power, which we can use constructively or destructively; but from the universal, all are in harmony with as one principle, which is always in unity!

There is suffering on the appearance level. However, should we choose to see all things as good and think positively, should we choose to acknowledge the truth of our beings as sparks of God of divinity with eternal spirit, and should we choose to acknowledge God's omnipotence, omniscience, and omnipresence, then we also know that all is progressing toward good and love. Ultimately given, God is good and love and is in charge despite appearances to the contrary due to allowing us our momentary free will to express in detours.

Another commonality, in concept, among most great religions, although Judaism may question this at times, is that humankind is made in the image and likeness of God with an eternal spirit. Eastern hemisphere religions of the Orient see our spirits as becoming one with the higher power through meditation, whereas

Christian and Catholic religions talk about the soul as the eternal spirit part of humans. Thus, what is earth age suffering when measured in the timeliness of eternity? The misery some experience stems from our precious gift to express that is our birthright and even reflects backward use of the spiritual law or a brief phase of "no pain, no gain."

For another example of the misuse of the law from my own life—that I recognized and then turned lemons into lemonade—as the end of the holiday season drew near, I grew sad wishing there was more time for family togetherness. The next day, when the children were to return to school, it snowed. In my city, a little snow causes a shutdown. I got my wish. By then, I had adjusted to the idea that the holiday was over and had made personal plans I was looking forward to. When my expectations, although not my heart's desire, were dashed, I began bemoaning and cursing my fate. Want to make God laugh? Tell him your plan. Then I realized the desire I put out and that I had received an answer to my "prayer," so I enjoyed the extra time (two weeks) with my children to the fullest. Sometimes, we forget what we wanted and don't see the good in our experience because we hold certain expectations about how the outcome should look. We need to replace "should" with "could"—knowing in the ocean of God that all is well and recognizing how we are creating our lives through the thoughts we put out.

Acceptance is the key. Spiritual masters, such as Jesus or Buddha, acquired the approach of holding no expectations and rather substituting preferences with acceptance. For example, the Buddha, while giving a lecture, is reported to have been confronted by a heckler who threw a tirade of insults at him. The Buddha said not a word until the man insulting him exclaimed, "Why aren't you reacting to what I'm saying?" To which the Buddha replied, "If a person brings a gift to someone and that person doesn't accept the gift, whom does the gift belong to?"

Moreover, once we accept these concepts as the basic truth, or common threads, as the hidden principles underlying all world religions and we logically and rationally take the basic concepts to their logical conclusion and go beyond traditional religious organizational doctrine, dogma, and rituals, we shift to the divine level of expression God originally intended for us. That is, we manifest in our life experience through our thoughts, our beliefs, our consciousness the state of mind of heaven on earth on an ongoing basis through expressing into the infinite universal intelligence or mind only positive words and only positive thoughts consistent with the truth of us—that we are the divine sparks of the eternal, all-good, all-powerful, all-knowing, all-creative, and abundant provider, one source, and that we can and are creating heaven on earth.

We need to come to grips with the good in all religions as each has important pieces to the puzzle of the meaning of life, and each answers its unique questions regarding metaphysics—our life or spiritual philosophy—such that when combined, they may complete the puzzle of the mystery of life and provide the deep, broad picture of the mysteries of life that we seek. The specific differences of the religions occur because understanding of God is expressed and interpreted through different men's perpetual filters or perspectives, not because one is right over the other.

The actual beliefs and sayings of Jesus and Buddha are remarkably similar (see *Jesus and Buddha, The Parallel Sayings*). Evidence, in a monk's book discovered recently, indicates that the mystery years of Jesus's life—the years between puberty when he studied in the temple and the beginning of his ministry at age thirty that are missing in the biblical accounts of his life—were years he spent in India studying the teachings of the Buddha! This explains the similarities to his and Buddhist teachings. Of course, Jesus understood or related the Buddhist wisdom in terms of his culture and era so his people would understand his teachings.

The common thread in religions of the concept of free will explains the appearance of suffering in the world. It is known that the higher power, or source, has given man free will to create our own lives or make our own choices. When we make mistakes in choices, we experience what appears to be suffering. Although conceptually we know that because of God being all-powerful, in everything, always present, always there, we will ultimately come to good. Finally, because God is in, around, through everything—including us—we are eternal. This means that this energy, our spirits within us that is the image and likeness of God, is eternal. Our journey is to progress more toward the obvious appearance of expressing God and experiencing our true nature of God through a consciousness of the heavenly state of divinity—achievable in our everyday life!

How can we do this and experience the joy and fulfillment intended for us? First of all, by relinquishing our exclusive favoritism religious snobbery. Accept and respect each human being's right to understand and relate to their higher power individually—appreciate the spirituality of all persons. The shocking events of September 11, 2001, have made most vitally aware of the need for worldwide unity in love and oneness—harmonious peace—rather than waging war under the guise of defending God! The Holocaust certainly raised our consciousness against bigotry. The September 11 attacks raised our consciousness against religious snobbery.

Second, we need to understand that the source of our personal power to fulfill ourselves comes from learning how our words, thoughts, beliefs, and attitudes create our lives. Prayer, contrary to popular belief, is not somehow cajoling the big guy in the sky to pay attention and swoop down to meet our needs. The power of prayer stems from our aligning ourselves with God in our hearts and praying from within and from remembering that God created the physical world to express itself physically and that God works through us and allows us free will so it can express myriad experience. This combines meditation to attain oneness and peace of mind that the Eastern religions teach us—with the Western religion concept of prayer—our desires manifesting in reality. This is also a good example of how the world religions combined form pieces to the puzzle of God.

You can accept the power of our thoughts and words as a spiritual law much like acceptance of the law of gravity in physics, or you can accept this purely based on psychological research, which proves the power of positive thinking. Helping people change their thoughts is the most effective form of psychotherapy known today to treat unhappiness (anxiety, depression, and other painful emotions) and create a sense of positive emotional well-being.

Why entertain the possibility of the spiritual law underlying the power of positive thinking? Because this enables you to use the power more clearly and effectively. Bear with me on a little more philosophical discourse that could completely transform your awareness to realize how we can live life on the divine realm.

Words, the powerful wand of religions

Our thoughts are prayers and we are always praying.

—Unity song

Most religions share the common belief that words have power, which springs from a spiritual fountain. They assert that prayer and/or meditation are the source of our power. This power is truly at the level of our thoughts' creative ability since we have free will and our words are the way and means of our birthright to express. As the great philosopher Plato postulated, there are corresponding images in God's mind's eye that actually correspond to our ideas or thoughts. As we think, the image is actually representing the perfect correspondence in the plane of God. In the language of quantum physics—zero-point field—at the moment of subatomic random activity and infinite possibility, through the power of intention, reality is manifested.

For this discussion or explanation, "thoughts" and "words" are terms that mean essentially the same thing; words may be thought silently, written, or spoken aloud. No words exist without thought behind them. Even though we may have heard that somebody is talking without thinking, this is not actually the case. Our words in this light are powerful, as we intuitively remind ourselves with "Better watch your words" or "Watch what you wish for." It will happen!

Let's look at different religions and beliefs about words to understand that the power of them comes from the spiritual level. Charles Fillmore, one of the founders of the Unity religion, defined "word" as "the vehicle through which ideas make transcendence manifest" and "the opening by which God reveals Himself…God's creative power…" (I think of the "word" as "expressing the thought" or as "giving voice to the thought.")

In the Christian Bible, John 1:1–3 states, "In the beginning was the Word, and the Word was with was God and the Word was God." In the beginning was God; nothing was made without the Word, and without the Word was nothing at all made. What is the Word we are referring to? It is not limited to a person, like Jesus, because the Word is universal, which cannot be limited to one physical expression. When we speak the Word, knowing that we are expressing God, we are expressing the power of God. God created us from a desire for us to have the power to speak it's Word unto himself as God such that it could express infinitesimally—through our individual sparks of divinity—but, of course, only to ultimate good as it is good. Logically, we accept gratefully that God has the power to speak through people. In essence, we speak as God and create as God. We acknowledge our oneness and the spiritual nature of our own personal word—our thoughts. Jesus stated this many times and in many ways, "Ask anything in my name without doubt and it will manifest." To paraphrase Jesus, "Truly I tell you, if you have faith the size of a mustard seed, you will say to this mountain, 'Move from here to there,' and it will move; and nothing will be impossible for you" (Matthew 17:20).

Fundamentalist Christians might say that the Word is Jesus, but why then is the Word discussed in Genesis in the Old Testament when God created the world, which was prior to Jesus's birth? Because the Word means the power of God expressing it, which creates stuff of our reality. "Word is the power" does not refer only to Jesus. Jesus Christ told us about the use of the Word so we too could use this power to create our lives and even demonstrate miracles. As he said in the Bible, "This and more you can do" (The Holy Bible).

Jesus was not the only Word, although he was the Word when he demonstrated all his miracles and he simply stated the Word, his oneness with God, and whatever he said manifested in physical reality. He said, "Rise up," to the dead, and they were alive. He told the blind to see, and affirming his oneness with God, speaking God the Word, the blind had perfect vision.

Jesus Christ was not even his proper name. Jesus was. Christ was added later to indicate "Christ consciousness"—his consciousness or awareness of his oneness with God.

Christians, in general, believe in the power of words in the form of prayer. In Judaism, children are taught about the power of words, a whole category of ethical sins that involve *lishonha'rah* (evil talk). Orthodox Jews are taught to refrain from speaking badly about others or to repeat anything confidential if it would bring harm to another. In other words, they recognize the power of the word. Their practice indicates the underlying belief in the power of words.

In the Eastern religion, chanting is used because words have power. They repeat chants sometimes all day long, hours and hours of the same sound to be in tune with the oneness of the higher power. They recognize that certain sounds, or words, bring them to the level of communing with God—raising their transcendental experience of oneness with God where they know the truth of themselves of their perfect, whole, pure, divine spirit selves connected with the oneness of the universal power and presence. They use their words to recognize this about themselves in order to bring their lives into balance.

The Native American Indian's belief in the power of words is manifested in practice by medicine men or high-level priests whom the rest of the tribe rely on in times of need—they only know the special way to heal with sounds. The Tewoh are a tribe who devote themselves to the practice of chanting in the Native American way, knowing that positive words create physical objects. The different Native American tribes have different medicine wheels or different practices—which way they dance, clockwise or counterclockwise, or which direction they face, etc.—yet the underlying belief is that they are putting out their word, and it is manifesting in the universe. This is how the medicine men and the people of power within the tribe actually get their power. One of the five pillars—required practices—of Islam is the designation of five special times per day to connect with God and pray. This reflects a healthy enlightened awareness of the need for daily regular practice of connecting in oneness with Allah (God) and using their words to create positive reality.

All the great religions of the world—even sects within religions with differing doctrines and rituals—rely on some form of prayer (words, thoughts, chants) to *generate* spiritual power.

This is based on true events:

To See the Sea

A young woman,
Cross-legged on a blanket of sand,
Meditates—
Face to the horizon at sunrise.

Beautiful blindness—
The sunlight shatters and scatters
Infinite crystals
Of shimmering yellow-white light
Which dance across
The azure ocean.

Her young beau,
Lame from illness,
Seduced by his love of the ocean,
Possessed by his masculine extremes,
Crawls across the hot shore
Toward the cool water
And hurls his contorted body into the vast sea.

The cresting waves free and carry him
Beyond the surf toward the tranquil ocean depths.

Her breath quickening anxiously,
Prayerfully, she envisions
The yellow-white light of the endless sea
Conspire to greet and love him,
Uplifting him protectively in its wisdom.
A flash of doubt

As dark gray fins are sighted soaring toward him.
"I can swim away," his mind says
As the fins thrust themselves upon him!

Stunned—in awareness—he experiences
A school of dolphins gracefully slide
And swivel around him,
Inspiring him to breathe in their magnificence
And the magnificence of the universe.

This same young woman,
A mother,
Some years later,
Cross-legged on a cozy vacation beach,
Watches her young son wade happily in the surf.

Desirous to protect him
From her own awful imaginings—deep sea devils,
malevolent creatures
lurking in the depths nearby—

Prayerfully, she sees the sea as all loving.
She speaks her desire,
"Even the sharks are friendly."

A flash of dark gray fins respond—
Déjà vu?
Stunned again—in awareness—
To her horror, five feet from her little boy,
A school of sharks swim by,
Revealing the innocence and the cooperation
Of the universe.

—A. Filosa, PsyD

New thought

Let us make this plain. If one is not attracting good into his life, *there is something wrong with his unconscious thinking. The subjective state of his thought is wrong. The subjective state of his thought constitutes the sum total of his belief, it is his habitual attitude toward life and living. This inner thought is the sole medium between the Absolute and the relative, between causes and conditions. When this inner thought is clarified, that is when it knows the truth; it will reinstate the outer man in peace, poise, health, and happiness. This inner thought becomes clarified as we unify with good; this is the inner quickening. Following this is the outer quickening—the outward sign of the inner belief.*

—*The Science of Mind* 475:4–5, Ernest Holmes

All religions and/or spiritual philosophies contribute valuable pieces to the puzzle of spirituality. New Thought is a spiritual philosophy, which provides what the name implies—the newest information about thought (word) and our power. Although New Thought is often considered a Christian religion because followers emphasize Jesus as their main way shower or spiritual master, New Thought actually embraces all faiths as many paths to the one source and views all the religions as sharing threads of the truth of our spirituality—hence, the motto "Where all paths meet as one." Congregations or spiritual organizations of New Thought, such as Religious Science (which is different from Christian Science or Scientology) and its sister religion, Unity, have members who are Buddhist, Jewish, and other faiths and who are open to learn about their spirituality through the teachings of Jesus Christ as well as other spiritual masters.

New Thought reminds us that there is truly no power in the physical because the physical is the end result of a spiritual idea manifested. Any condition of life, including problems in living, such as illness—misery of any kind—is just so by appearance. Suffering is created in the same way abundance and happiness is, through our thinking. In the case of problems, our thinking has been negative or backward. And consequently, what manifests or is demonstrated in our lives is negativity.

The spiritual law that "thought creates experience" works like gravity or electricity in the physical world. It doesn't matter whether we are plugging in a toaster to fix breakfast or putting our own finger inadvertently in the socket—electrocuting ourselves. Put something into an electrical socket, and electricity occurs. Furthermore, we may not see or understand electricity, yet we see its manifestations of power in our lives. Likewise, when we think and put out our words, we create our worlds. This is the spiritual law of thought creates.

When people are ignorant of the law, much like toddlers who don't know better than to stick their toys or fingers into electrical sockets, disaster can be created—certainly not what we consciously intend. The law goes awry when ignorantly people speak and think negatively—consequently creating negative experiences for themselves and others because our physical experiences are simply manifestations of our word and thoughts.

We know that the invisible spiritual law exists because of the outward demonstration of the power of thoughts and words in the tangible world. Electricity's outward demonstration occurs when we plug something in, and power in some form, like a lamp, is turned on. Therefore, we know that this thing called electricity exists. Likewise, we know that the spiritual law of the power of the word exists because we can see the physical manifestations of our thinking and beliefs in our own living—in the observer effect, in psychology, in the self-fulfilling prophecy. We can trace back our life experiences to our underlying core beliefs about ourselves and our worlds as well as to specific thoughts or words we have emitted. We can also access our core beliefs and choose enhancing positive thoughts and positive words to create happiness for ourselves.

Science of Mind is the religious philosophy devoted to making a science out of how the ultimate intelligence and power of God works. It was at a Religious Science class that I had my emotional breakthrough—rather than a mere intellectual grasp based on my education as a psychologist—about the incredible creative power of our thinking. I was taught that I, not an outside factor like germs, was stressing my immune system out—my sickness orientation and confusing thoughts. These New Thought religions clarify scientifically the way we can use positive thinking to create better lives with clear step-by-step guidelines. Thought, directed with belief and intent, produces a physical effect, result, or condition. A new thought will produce a new effect, thought, or condition.

To reiterate a good example of a bad example, my mother used to "catch" herself and wish she had not spoken, even though she was not trained in this idea—that thoughts create. She would comment that it had been a long time since any of the appliances had broken down. Immediately, she would try to retract the statement, saying that she did not want "the big guy up there" (God) to hear her. Sure enough, something would soon break down. What had she done? She had put out her belief in her words backwardly or ignorantly or innocently, that if she said something could break, it would—and it did. God only says yes to what we believe. This is giving us our free will. Thus, innocently, we do crimes to ourselves, which is the true meaning of sin. It could also have been intuition. They feed into each other. Either way, the negative thought is best changed to a positive one—to create a positive experience.

When we are conscious of our connection with God, through the power of our word, we can experience our heart's desires. This is the spiritual principle that thought creates experience. This is different from praying to, begging, and beseeching God, apart from us in heaven, to meet our needs. The ultimate spiritual or religious truth—the piece of the puzzle that New Thought brings—is we are spirit, sparks of divinity, and we need only to recognize and affirm this for such to manifest. The more we acknowledge that we are ultimately the image and likeness of God—perfect, whole, complete, healthy, and abundant in all ways—the more our lives reflect our heavenly and magnificent state of consciousness through outward demonstrations of loving, peaceful, abundant, prosperous, fulfilling lives!

Whether you adhere to the Big Bang theory, evolution, or Genesis in the Bible, you can understand that the higher power or only creative source was exploding or putting itself out into infinitesimal sparks of its divinity as a way of experiencing itself in the physical form. God cannot experience without free will; thus, God says yes to whatever we say. So we need to be careful what we say and mean it. The intense realization that we are good and deserve only goodness must be ever present in our heart of words for us to manifest the glory of God in our daily lives.

Myrtle Fillmore, who with her husband Charles originated the Unity teachings, had suffered for numerous years with serious physical conditions. Medicine hadn't helped. In fact, the doctors had given up on her case. She began to talk and send love to all parts and organs of her body and see them as whole and healed. She believed this was true because her spirit had a fundamental connection with God and since God is pure and perfect, hence her basic core was too. She was completely cured through changing her thought pattern even though doctors were no longer involved. She used and discovered the spiritual law properly and programmed into the universal mind the positive self-enhancing healthy statements to counter all the negativity that she and others had been vocalizing based on her appearance. She had been, after all, an invalid for many years. So it was easy to fall into the trap of negative appearances leading and entering into a vicious cycle of negative thinking and miserable experiences.

Prayer treatment

Religious Science, a sister church of Unity—which is almost the same as cognitive or thought therapy—spells out the procedure for effective prayer (called prayer treatment):

1. Recognition. Acknowledge the mightiness and benevolence of God in whatever name(s) you recognize your higher power (divine spirit creating and fulfilling my heart's desires, the Almighty God, Lord, universal source, etc.).
2. Unification. Feel yourself uniting with God. Experience the sense of oneness with God, the personal relationship, and presence. "I am one with my higher power."
3. Declaration. Claim in the *now* that you have your desire—prosperity, abundance, love, health, whatever your need. "I am now prosperous, loved, healthy…" Visualize specifically how this would look and be.
4. Thanksgiving. Give thanks for this and all blessings. "I am grateful for…"
5. Release. Affirm that you know that you're provided for, that your desires are met without any doubt. "I release this to God, knowing it is true. So it is."

Exercise: Write up a prayer treatment following the five steps. Carry it out and observe the manifestations and demonstrations in your life. Remember the form your answer takes may not be the exact form you anticipated; however, your need will be met.

Gratitude

The latest cutting-edge information we have received for our spiritual growth is this New Thought that challenges us to remember who we truly and deeply are and to realize that as we recognize and savor our goodness and the goodness in all, so will the good grow and manifest in the wonderful lives we have and deserve.

Open up to guidance synchronicity

Synchronicity refers to meaningful events that occur simultaneously, events that many people would just call coincidences or accidents. Perceptive people with higher abstract reasoning or metaphysical awareness would comprehend and learn from these events as the world working in an orderly manner to bring more order, harmony, and flow to life. This is a skill most people can cultivate and use for the betterment once they understand. For example, some things are meant to be or not, and life pulls you in a direction or signals you. For example, numerous people tell you the same thing or events pull you off your course of action because it was meant to work out that way. For example, a person misses his flight and the plane crashes.

Intuition

Intuition is reading between the lines—perceiving what to others is invisible. It is picking up on vibes or light energy fields that others might miss. Sometimes, some people are able to lower the frequency of their brain waves—when awake—to a level that most people would be at when almost asleep and, in that dreamy state, are able to perceive life more deeply or penetratingly.

For the purpose of this discussion, the first and fastest level of brain wave frequency is beta—when a person is active or alert and doing things. The next level down is alpha—when one is not physically doing things—and rather is thinking, learning, realizing. For most people, when their brains go down to the next level of theta waves, they are falling asleep—going unconscious, lying down, out of it.

What research has shown through measurement of the brain waves of people engaging in intuition is that these people—they are hooked up to an EEG (electroencephalography) equipment having their brain waves measured—are actually standing up, awake, and talking, yet their brains are at low-level theta. They are able to commune with the higher intelligence and be aware—perceive in a penetrating way—unlike most persons who are going to sleep and don't notice this information about events and happenings that they could if they tuned into their intuitive level of brain functioning.

Of course, most people have had the experience of being intuitive at least once. They have inadvertently or accidentally changed their brain functioning to this dreamy level and reaped the benefit while awake. You are referred to the Silva UltraMind ESP program, which teaches you through relaxation and visualization how to be intuitive.

This is based on a true story:

Guidance

A while back, I planned
To visit Disneyland.
And as the trip grew near,
I began to fret and fear

That my condition
Would spoil the fun.
For heavy stuff I'd carry
Did make my back too weary.

So I "prayer treated"
For help which I needed
And later found myself
Standing next to a store shelf

With my daughter at Rack N Sack.
I'd stopped by the backpack rack—
Not a place I shop for me.
I waited patiently.

When holding up a backpack—
Which resembled to me an old sack—
A customer said twice,
"This, this will work out nice."

Her daughter agreed, "Yes!"
And what next, can you guess?
They depart hurriedly—
Leaving the sack by me.

Another mom and teen come by.
"How perfect," they both cry.
At that same pack they spy,
Then they too sped on by.

I get the picture!
This is a message for sure
When two more, as if in line,
Pick up the pack and say, "How fine!"

And again, drop it abruptly.
So I turn grudgingly
To check it out and see
And find it very light to carry.

My daughter comes. "Let's pay. Hurry."
But I say, "These straps look hard to me."
"It'll be fine," she protests. "You'll see."
And I buy it—reluctantly.

I decided to heed.
It was meant to meet my need,
And my trip was great.
The backpack was fate.

I use it daily since.
Still, its purchase made no sense!
Often happens, coincidences
Are not mere accidents.

Like mission control
To the astronauts,
We've got a spirit patrol
To kink out our earthly knots.

We have guidance.
If we tune in,
Are willing to listen
To our intuition.

Attention one needs to pay
As messages fly by one's way.
The questions one asks today,
Something will answer in some way.

Want to make God laugh?
Tell him your plan.
We can't know our path
Unless led by his hand,
For the form our journey hath
Meets our need, not our demand.

—A. Filosa, PsyD

AP FILOSA, PSY. D.

Dream interpretation

Since age thirteen or fourteen, when I began studying Freud's dream interpretation analysis and Carl Jung's symbology and archetypes, I familiarized myself and used all kinds of dream interpretation and methods. The following is my integrated approach to dream interpretation—a way of interpretating dreams—to help people understand themselves and resolve life problems.

First of all, dreams, no matter how scary or frustrating, are good and positive. They are existential meaningful messages from your unconscious—your deeper intuitive self—meant to enlighten and assist you about your life.

During the day, we think and analyze in words, whereas, at night while we sleep, we think and problem-solve in picture form—like in movies. For example, dreams may give you clues about unconscious memory. A woman in her midthirties had some creepy recurring dreams about multiple males coming on to her sexually. This helped her recover real-life sexual abuse memories by multiple offenders. For another example, dreams may help you realize fears and insecurities that you have been keeping on the back burner and encourage you to face and resolve them in your life.

In order to interpret dreams, they cannot be looked at concretely and superficially. For example, you cannot assume that your dream of zombies materialized simply because you watched a zombie movie that week. Remember that the content of dreams is symbolic and the issues dealt within dreams are about your own inner conflicts and troublesome life situations. You have to be a detective to figure out what those symbols mean because, after all, a picture is worth a thousand words.

There are four main types of dreams—although one dream can serve multiple functions.

1. Wish fulfillment: Expresses and fulfills a wish—a need not met adequately in your life right now. For example, you dream of having sex. That indicates that you want more emotional and/or physical intimacy in your life right now.

    How to benefit from the dream: First, enjoy it and do not feel guilty. Second, use this understanding of yourself to increase intimacy in your life.

2. Releasing or catharsis of fear and insecurity: Releases suppressed emotion—anxieties—that have been nagging at you in the back of your mind which you have not been facing.

    How to benefit from the dream: Recognize and face your fear. Realize that the nightmare served a purpose of releasing some tensions. Use the focusing process to figure out the problem and take action on a solution. For example, a woman dreamed that she was wandering in her neighborhood at dusk. Other people were walking around at a distance. She felt comfortable—until she heard a strange animal howl. Turning around, she saw a wolf coming toward her. She knocked on the door of the nearest neighbor and asked him to allow her to come in because the wolf was chasing her. Safely inside, she watched in amazement while the other neighbors played with the wolf—acting as if it were a neighborhood pet. When she opened the french doors slightly to look out, a pit bull tried to get in, and she pushed it away nonchalantly. Then she woke up.

    In real life, the woman lived two houses down from neighbors who owned a pit bull. They had no fence, which allowed the puppy free reign of the neighborhood. Children often played with it. It was a sweet, loving animal although at times acted aggressively. For example, the pit bull jumped on a three-year-old, and someone had to take a stick and beat it off. The woman's own ten-year-old son had told her that while he was riding his skateboard, the pit bull had actually jumped on the skateboard and pushed him off, and the dog began to ride the skateboard! The woman who had this dream owned two little dogs—whom she would let out to play in the front yard contained by an invisible fence that others, including the pit bull, could cross. One of her dogs would snarl at the pit bull—not necessarily a smart move to an animal that has been bred to grab a bull tenaciously and not let go until it is slain.

In the back of this woman's mind, she had been worried about her children and her dogs—that the pit bull might become aggressive toward them. The nightmare came to help her face this fear. She took it upon herself to talk to the neighbors and give them her invisible fence company's phone number. As a result, they followed through and got the pit bull an invisible fence.

The nightmare, which appeared scary, was actually a positive message to herself, encouraging her to take care of herself and loved ones. Interestingly, when the woman did not get the symbology of the wolf representing the real-life pit bull puppy, a pit bull came up to the french doors in her dream—as if to say, "Come on, lady, I'm a pit bull—not a wolf." The wolf symbolized the real-life pit bull.

3. Problem solving: Presents actual solutions to real-life problems you are having and has guidance or information that you have not previously thought of.

    How to benefit from the dream: Before bed, think about a problem you are having and ask to have a dream that will give you information about how to solve it. For example, I had misplaced an item and asked for a dream to help find it. My dream that night suggested a certain chest associated with a person from my past. The symbol was not an actual chest that existed in reality, but it had some qualities of a piece of furniture that I own. Sure enough, when I looked inside this piece, I found the item. You have to realize that dream content is symbolic and use your associations to figure out what it is being symbolized.

4. Intuitive or precognitive: Picks up on vibes and gives you information that you may not be able to make sense of until later on when you are awake and in the real-life situation that it was referring to. For example, a woman had a dream about a friend whom she only saw occasionally. However, in the dream, she kept telling her friend, "You're my best friend. You're my best friend." Within the week, she saw her friend at a holiday gathering. They chatted, and she told her friend that she was so financially strapped she could not buy a futon for her child to sleep on. As she left the party, the friend stopped her and offered her $10,000, her savings account—if the woman needed it! What do you think the recipient of this generosity said? It was, of course, "You're my best friend!"

    How to benefit from the dream: Be on the lookout for situations that resemble the contents of your dream and utilize its guidance.

How to interpret your dreams:

1. Before going to bed, put out your intention—your desire—to remember your dreams. Visualize yourself remembering your dreams. When I was a teenager and studying dreams, I was able to remember four to five dreams a night because of my desire.
2. Keep a dream journal or diary so you can record accurately your dreams. Keep a pad and pencil by your bed so that as you awake you can write them down quickly before you forget them. Prior to falling asleep, put forth your intention to remember dreams to increase memory.
3. You can also program yourself to receive guidance or problem-solving solutions. You are referred to the Silva UltraMind System. To summarize it, you relax your body fully. And then you imagine the numbers 3, then 2, and then 1 to bring yourself down to the theta level of brain activity. Then you visualize your problem in front of you. Then you look to your left and visualize what action you are taking in your life right now to overcome the problem. Look even further to the left and visualize your life as it would be without the problem—perfect, whole, and complete. You will receive guidance in your dream—or everyday life—that will bring you a solution.

4. Ask yourself, "What are the main qualities of the dream? What emotions did I feel? When did I feel similarly in my past life? How does this relate to my life and parts of my life situation or myself? What associations come up?"
5. What are the symbols in the dream representing? For example, the wolf equals the pit bull.
6. Does the dream represent a wish fulfillment, a venting of fear, a problem-solving or possibly intuitive content—or a combination of them?
7. What action do you need to take to benefit from the message your unconscious is sharing?

Tip: The closer to your morning awakening time the dream occursdf, the more likely the dream functions to provide problem-solving solutions. Your mind has pondered it longer.

Chapter 6

Speak Your Truth

This above all: to thine own self be true, and it must follow, as the night the day, thou canst not then be false to any man.

—*Hamlet*, act I, scene III, William Shakespeare

Up to this point, we have talked mostly about our inner words, our self-talk, and our internal dialogue. This chapter is about communicating with other people and how to do so in a constructive manner. First, we need to follow the exercises in the previous chapters to get clear about who we are and come from a place of love and positive values about ourselves and others before we express healthily to anyone.

Using anger as a guide to clarify yourself

Before we express our anger to anybody, we need to *tune into the true source of anger* and clarify where we stand to ourselves. Anger is an indication we need to strengthen the I (not as in "I don't need you," however). It is a guide to clearer self (Harriet Lerner, PhD):

Ask yourself:

* What about this situation that makes me angry?
* What is the real issue or problem?
* What do I want to change or accomplish?
* Who is responsible for what?
* Do I need to express to someone to achieve my goals?

After we have answered these questions and made a life decision about what we want that is consistent with our values and beliefs, then we can *approach the other person*. Venting anger is no solution. Fighting usually keeps the relationship or problem the same. Our job is to make clear our thoughts, feelings, and needs in a nonblaming way. We can request others to change, but we must remember *we can only change ourselves*. We control our lives by making decisions about how and in what we choose to participate. Harriet Lerner, PhD, in her fabulous book, *The Dance of Anger*, elaborates on this.

Healthy assertive communication

We therapists find it much easier to help people enhance their self-esteem and become assertive than we do to help people who have antisocial tendencies to control themselves and stop hurting others.

Psychotherapy is a process of echoing a person's voice until it becomes stronger. Thus, the voice becomes stronger and the person begins to express more. As when learning any new skill, we don't do it as gracefully at the beginning. The people in therapy begin to speak up for themselves, often saying no too many times and stating their needs in demanding ways. This pitfall comes from (1) being a new skill and thus grossly executed and (2) misconception about what assertiveness is.

Communication generally falls in four categories: passive, assertive, aggressive, and passive-aggressive

Let's take the three unhealthy ones first. Passivity means being overly concerned with other people's feelings. In other words, you say nothing and do not speak up for your own feelings, needs, or likes. The passive person acts as if other people have all the rights, allowing others to take advantage and hurt their feelings. The passive person is quiet, overly polite, holds in thoughts and feelings, and does not express.

Verbal aggression is how we usually speak and were taught—in "you messages." Aggressiveness is being concerned primarily with one's own feelings, thoughts, and needs and violating the rights and needs of others by expressing in ways that put down, blame, or aggress against the other person. This is the use of "you messages," as in "You did this to me" or "You did this wrong" or "You're selfish" or "You're rude," something to that effect. Lashing out falls in the category of aggressiveness. This can be very damaging to other people and to relationships. Unfortunately, most people do not know how to speak, except in you message—blurting out in an aggressive manner. The other person becomes defensive, and since they are not listening to you, there is no benefit.

Passive-aggression is a combination of passive and aggressive. One doesn't outright lash out at the other person aggressively. The passive-aggressive person doesn't actually express needs at all; rather, he gets anger across passively (and gets a similar negative response from the person it's directed toward) by indirect ways, like rolling eyes in disgust, forgetting others' requests, or otherwise getting back at the person. This is like cutting one's nose off to spite one's face and leads to depression. He deprives himself of something to get back at somebody. For example, the person refuses to go to a movie that he's actually been looking forward to just because he's mad at his partner and wants to deprive her. The other person doesn't know why he is acting this way or what is bothering him, so you can't meet his needs. Still, the other registers the covert attack and reacts negatively.

I messages versus you messages

What is assertiveness? Assertiveness is when you express yourself, speak your truth, and talk politely with the other person about your feelings and needs in an I message form.

You begin your sentences with I. Fill in the blanks: "I feel…" "I need…" "I like…" "I've experienced…" "I was raised…" "This works for me…" "This is my style…" You talk about your needs, feelings, thoughts, style, and experiences—all about I. You do not ever use the word "you" in the sentences. You let the other person know where you are coming from. You also do not use the word "angry" because anger often provokes the other person to take a defensive stance. The word "anger" reduces the other person's listening ability and provokes the person to prepare for battle. Even when you are talking specifically about a behavior of the other person, you do not have to say the word "you." You can simply say, "When other people do this" or "When this kind of situation happens to me, then I feel…"

When making I messages, you talk about self, feelings, needs, style, what works for you, how you were raised, and what your life experiences taught you. In other words, you share about self. Do not mention the other person or even say "you." Objective: let the other person understand you. If they care about you, after they think about it, you will see change in their behavior without pointing out their faults.

Versus

In contrast to what we have been taught, even in past assertiveness training courses, it is best not to make you messages. Don't use the word "you" ever in a sentence. Don't say, "You did this wrong" or "You should do it this way"—often how we speak. This puts the listener on the defensive and makes him want to counterattack, which defeats the objective—getting the person to listen and understand.

Example situation: Children mess up the house which the mother uses as a home office. House looks messy when clients walk through to use the bathroom.

Mother's possible ways of giving feedback to children:

Passive—says nothing, just runs between clients to clean up the house
Aggressive—says, "You slobs! Clean up this mess!"
Passive-aggressive—says nothing and, when finished with seeing a client instead of fixing dinner, cleans up the house and starves them temporarily
Healthy assertive choice—says, "I use this house as a professional office, and I like it kept neat during my working hours, especially [specify room or rooms] that clients may need to walk through to the bathroom. I am working and I cannot do both—keep the rooms neat and clean while I am doing therapy. I'd like these areas to be project-free, shoe-free, etc., and all things in bathroom drawers and cabinets so it looks like a respectful restroom for clients."

Notice that there was not any kind of nagging or blaming of the children for being "little, spoiled brats" who "do not do anything" and "expect me to do everything," which would have been a negative you message to deliver to them and probably would not have been as well received.

Of course, the woman's consciousness in this situation would also need to change to include the belief that she deserves time, respect, cooperation, and energy to carry out whatever she needs to do and that others will take appropriate responsibility.

Exercise: Identify your styles of communication. Which of the negative types do you use?

Create boundaries to support your efforts to communicate

Assertive communication is best delivered when you're calm, not intense. Intense or angry expressions often lead to similar reactions from others. Wait until you are calm and suggest that the person sit down and have a discussion or have a businesslike meeting with you. Ask when it would be a good time for you to share something with them and then have a special spot where you actually sit down in a businesslike, peaceful manner to share your I messages. This is assertiveness.

As you probably noticed when reading about the process of focusing inward, some self-expression is usually involved. However, don't express until you're clear about how much is actually related to the current situation versus past situations—and until you're sure what is really bothering you and why and what would really make you feel good.

Empathy and active listening skills

Empathy—the ability to "put yourself in the other person's shoes" to understand another person's thoughts or feelings or viewpoint.

Active listening—the process of communicating to another person your empathy or understanding of his or her viewpoint and feelings.

Possible ways of listening actively

Listen: Look at the person. Don't talk or move. Think about and concentrate on what the other person is saying. Say back to the person what he or she said.

A. Parrot—just copy what the person said.
B. Paraphrase—say what the person said, only in your own words.
C. Check out your understanding. Ask, "Do you mean…?"
D. Describe how the person feels: "You must feel angry, sad, etc."

When to use active listening or empathic statements:

1. Regularly in conversation.
2. When you believe an argument is beginning and want to disarm anger or prevent conflict.
3. To resolve conflicts. Each person gets a turn to deliver I messages while the other person does the active listening. The person should deliver a fairly brief I message and then allow the listener to repeat it. This listener's feedback should not include any questions or personal views. The sender keeps giving I messages until he feels complete. Then they reverse roles, and the process repeats with the other person saying the I messages while the other person parrots back his or her I messages.

    Example, sender's I message: "I like to be talked to in a calm voice. I like to feel comfortable. I get rattled when people are angry."

    Receiver's active listening: "You don't like loud voices or yelling."

    The sender continues in little bits until complete. Then roles reverse. The sender becomes the listener and vice versa until both viewpoints are expressed and heard.

    Don't be passive or bottle up your feelings or needs. Don't be aggressive by making "you messages." Don't tell people by telling them what they are doing wrong and act like you have all the rights and know everything. Don't be passive-aggressive which is a combination of passive and aggressive. Passive-aggressive is when you indirectly show them you are angry but don't actually tell them what your feelings and needs are. You just give them the cold shoulder, roll your eyes, and act mad, and they don't know why or what is bothering you.

    Usually, people become defensive when they hear or feel put-downs. Being verbally aggressive or passive-aggressive does not have good results because the person stops listening. To be healthily assertive, make "I messages": "When [describe the incident], then I feel [describe emotions] because [describe the impact on you]. The final step is when you make a specific small behavioral request. For example, they run late to meet you at a restaurant. When they arrive, you say, "When someone runs late and I don't know what's going on and I am at the restaurant alone, I feel disappointed, anxious, and alone because I don't know what is going on, if the person is going to show up or even if the person is okay. Step 4: "Would you please call and text me and make sure that I know when you will be here?"

The listener does not share his own ideas at this time. He acknowledges or paraphrases what the other person said and then state that it wasn't his intention to distress the person and apologize. When the sender feels complete, then the listener becomes the sender who is acknowledged by the listener. At the end do win-win negotiation about what they have heard each other say. Remember to have tactful polite communication—one person is the sender, one is the listener.

Send out the vibe of love and desire to receive love back

Set the stage for your message to be responded to well. The procedure for this is to visualize at the top of your head (what is known in Eastern medicine as your crown chakra) opening up and white light coming through your head and filling you up with divine love. Visualize your heart center. Imagine your heart opening up and send love from your heart, a positive vibe to the person. Actually, compliment the person internally (telepathically). Then request that person to meet your specific needs, which you need to state very clearly.

Results can be amazing. For example, a repairman was trying to fix something at my home. After about two hours, when he still had not located the source of the problem, I did this procedure with a prayer that the problem would be fixed, immediately at no cost since the hassle had taken such a long time. Within two minutes, the repair person repaired the problem and offered the service free because the service call would have cost so much and the simple repair should have only taken a few minutes.

Visualization

Visuals can be used in many ways. For example, do dogs understand human language? No, except for a few words if they have been to obedience school. Hence, when you want to send them a vibe, think in picture form. To illustrate with a funny story, I was teaching this to my adult children and closed my eyes, encouraging one of the puppies to nibble on my son-in-law's ear. When I opened my eyes, my son-in-law had been biting the dog's ears. I freaked them out because they misunderstood my closing my eyes (just an easier way to visualize) as indicating my belief that I could use my mind to control the dog, rather than this just being the natural telepathy that we all have with each other.

Think about times when other people have read your mind or finished your sentences.

Exercise: Send out the vibe of love and desire to receive love back. Observe what you manifest.

Win-win negotiations

Once both sides have shared—all the pieces of the puzzle are out on the table—you can proceed to win-win negotiations. Knowing fully now each person's viewpoint, needs, and concerns, solutions that can make both people happy can be negotiated. Possible ways include taking turns, giving in to the person who needs the most now with the understanding the favor will be returned, finding middle ground that makes both parties happy, or whatever solution leaves both people feeling that they have won and feel satisfied.

Tip: Make your suggestions in I message form—suggesting what *you* plan to do to change, not what the other person should do to change.

Exercise: Allow an hour or less to practice the communication process with your partner. One person is the sender, and the other is the receiver. Then switch roles. Stay on the same topic until both feel completed. Carry out the win-win negotiation. Remember to start to send out the vibe of love, and desire to receive love back.

Coping with feelings of anger and anxiety that can block our appropriate expression

A supervisor of mine, Jan Morris, PhD, developed an excellent anger control training program to help institutionalized juvenile delinquents to learn to control their tempers. Following are excerpts from her manual that we can all benefit from.

There is a big difference between feelings and actions. We *have a right* to have *feelings*, including anger. We *do not have a right* to express our feelings in *actions that hurt people*, such as verbal and physical aggression and destruction of property.

Feelings are good when *we control them* and use them in a positive way. Feelings are bad *when they control us* and when we act out our feelings in a way that hurts ourselves or others.

Anger is good *when we control it*. Anger is a sign that tells us something we need to do to help ourselves. Anger makes us strong, gives us energy, and makes us feel in charge and able to take care of ourselves. It can give you strength to do things and take care of yourself, if you know how to use it. It is good if you express it in a verbally controlled or assertive way to make people aware of what you are feeling. This causes them to behave differently toward you. You get stuff off your chest and relieve tension.

My example: A friend of yours is late a lot, which bothers you. You calmly tell your friend, "When I wait around for somebody, wondering if they are going to show, I feel anxious and disappointed. I'm not going to do this anymore, unless I'm sure about the timing." Result: Your friend starts being on time or you stop scheduling time to get together with them.

Anger is *destructive* when it controls us. It makes it hard to think, and we act too quickly, hurting ourselves and others. We express it in actions that get us into trouble. We use our anger to try to show we're tough and to hide other feelings.

Anger can become *troublesome*. When you feel angry about too many little things too many times. When your anger is too strong and overwhelming.

Exercise: Think of some examples in your life when anger was a good thing.

Exercise: Think of some examples in your life when anger has been a bad thing. Now that you realize that lashing out in temper is not inevitable and that anger is just a feeling, not a behavior, how would you do things differently now?

Ways to cool down or chill

Ways not to overreact when your husband, wife, mom, dad, brother, sister, teacher, friend, or whoever drives you crazy

1. Time-outs. This means put yourself in a time-out. When you get so angry that you might do something you regret, like getting in trouble or major conflict, take a time out. For example, go away and do something to calm yourself down, like reading, writing, computer, crafts, sports, gardening, TV, anything to get your mind off your problems and anger until you are calm enough to think straight and talk assertively about your feelings and needs and are ready to "negotiate" (consider the other person's feelings or needs too and present solutions that show you care not only about yourself but the other person too).

    Homework: Use time-outs a lot today and this week.

2. Positive self-talk. What we think and say to ourselves affects how strongly we feel. We can say certain things to ourselves that make us angrier, or we can say certain things that calm us down. Examples of things we might say to calm ourselves are "I can get my needs met," "I can relax and take a deep breath!" (breathe), "I can count to ten and walk away when I'm getting too excited,"

and "I can keep my cool [temper]." We can also say things to reward ourselves when we've done something good, like control our temper. Things like "I'm proud of myself," "I didn't yell, demand, tease, hit [or whatever]," "I'm learning to keep my cool," "It's hard but I'm getting good at this," etc.

* Take out a piece of paper and make a list of things you believe will help you stay calm (things you'd say to yourself).
* Take out a piece of paper and make a list of compliments you say to yourself when you do stay calm and in control of your anger:

Do not say things to yourself that are mean, put you down, or might cause you to get more upset. Tell yourself, "Stop!" when you say, "Things should be different. I'm being treated unfairly!" (shouldism—don't should on yourself), "Nothing will ever work out. Everything is ruined" (catastrophizing), or "He hates me" (putting self down). Do this for homework.

3. Reframing. When someone does something that bothers you, see the good in what the person did, not the bad. Reframe it in another way. In other words, from a spiritual perspective, see all is for the good, despite appearances otherwise. For example, when your mom takes a pan you wanted to use, instead of getting mad, think, "Gee, Mom is trying to help me cook the dinner so I won't have to do everything. Look, she is making the vegetables. I bet she didn't even know I wanted to use that pan. Mom is nice. She'll get me another pan if I ask." How mad can you be at your mom now? Another example is when your little brother or child throws water on your friend. "Hey, he likes us and wants to play. He is trying to get our attention." In other words, it comes from the spiritual perspective that all is for the good, despite appearances otherwise.

* Today, try to see the good in what others are doing. This will help you be less angry and less likely to want to lash out at them.

Exercise: Keep a list of things that happen to you today and how you chose to look at people's irritating behavior in a nice way, as if they were being nice. Take out a piece of paper and list ways you see good in others.

4. Refocusing. Sometimes when we get irritable or angry, it is not because of what's happening but because something else is bothering us. Instead of immediately blaming the other person, go away and think about what you really need that might have nothing to do with the other person. For example, you might be tired and need a rest. What's below the anger? You might be sad, not angry, or scared and need reassurance.

When you start to get too angry, stop! Think! Use the focusing-inward process. "What's really bothering me the *very worst right now*?" Imagine the problems are boxes on the floor. Each box has a label: "I'm tired," "I'm worried about getting to practice on time," or "I don't have the right friends." Which one is really the worst problem (feels the yuckiest)? Take care of that problem first.

Exercise: Try to do this focusing process daily until it becomes a reflexive, second nature.

5. Love letters (adapted from *What Your Mother Didn't Tell You and Your Father Didn't Know* by John Gray, PhD). Sometimes it is best not to discuss what's bothering us with a parent, spouse, friend, sibling, etc., and rather better to sort out our feelings first. We can do this by writing a love letter when we believe someone criticized, hurt, or angered us—before talking to them.

This is the form of the letter. Write and fill in the blanks:

Dear [the person you are upset with],

I am angry because… [Fill in your words.]
I am hurt or sad because…

I am disappointed…
I am scared because…
I am embarrassed because…
I am upset because…
I feel rejected…
I love you (or care for you) because…

Read over your letter and figure out which feeling most bothers you. This helps you clarify your feelings and needs.

Then write a reply love letter. Write the person's words that you'd like them to say. In other words, write their apology letter to you. Make sure to include everything you wanted to hear. This really helps you feel better and return to good feelings about your relationship with the person.

The form for the other person's letter is:

Dear [your name],

I am sorry… [Fill in their words.)
I regret…
I understand…
You deserve…
I love you because…

When you write yourself an apology love letter from whoever hurt or angered you, you help make yourself feel better, more loved, and calmer. This returns you to feeling loved and supported before you approach the person. This is for your healing. Read both letters to the person only if you want to and believe this would be beneficial.

Exercise: Write a love letter and reply this week when you feel in conflict before you express yourself and your discomfort to head off an angry confrontation.

6. Assertive communication. Standing up for your rights and needs in a way that considers the other person's feelings and needs too.

   A. I messages
   B. empathy and active listening
   C. win-win negotiation

   Exercise: Role-play with someone the I message or active listening or win-win negotiation.

7. Affirmation. This is like positive self-talk. It is a sentence or phrase you say to yourself a lot to keep your mind focused on what you are aspiring to. Example of affirmation to control your temper: "I set boundaries in a firm, caring way," "I can be patient and keep my temper!" and "I can get my needs met in a nice talking way after I cool off."

   Exercise: Your affirmation can be "I can be patient and keep my temper! I can get my needs met in a nice talking way after I cool off." Write your own affirmations.

   Homework: Use it and say it this week.

8. Triangular breathing. Imagine a triangle. As your eyes go up the first (left) side, inhale and say a mantra (such as "with God" or "peace"). Exhale as you visualize down the triangle (mantra "be

still"). Just gently hold your breath as you visualize the bottom half of the triangle and say, "Relax," to yourself.

Exercise: Following is the breathing cycle. Don't control your breathing; just observe or follow it. Imagine a triangle in your mind. As you visualize traveling up the left side, simultaneously inhale. As you imagine going down its right side, exhale. At the bottom side, pause, rest, or hold your breath, and internally say, "Relax." Do this at least three minutes.

Rest, hold, and say, "Relax"

From the Cat Masters Series, story #1

Lacy Speaks Her Truth (by A. Filosa, PsyD)

Once there was a cat named Lacy. She was a slim, pretty, gray cat with several large beauty-mark-like spots. Lacy was an unusually clean, well-behaved, and independent kitty who, being talented artistically, had a vivid imagination. She was so creative that the sandpiles in her litter box were breathtaking (that's a pun).

Lacy, however, like many of us, had a major weakness. Given her supreme imagination, Lacy's weakness was the love of gossip. Gossip! Gossip! Gossip! She spent most of her waking hours in this delicious endeavor. How does a cat gossip? you say. Why, "meow, meow, meow," of course, in cat language.

One lovely, crisp-aired, blue-skied morning, Lacy set out for a little fun. She crept through the cat door to go spy. Lacy liked to kill two birds with one stone, collecting delicious gossip about her kitty neighbors while catching a tasty animal or two in the process to keep her energy up!

On this fine morning, Lacy was feeling good, fat, and full as she scurried past one of her favorite "mouse stalking" holes to visit her friends and peek into their business.

What luck! As Lacy peered through the window grate of the Johnsons' basement, she spied Tabby. Tabby was a tabby cat, as you might have guessed. Her owners didn't feel particularly creative the day she wandered onto their doorstep, so they named her Tabby. The plain name fit, however, because Tabby was plain looking and loved the simple solitude of a good, dark basement, especially one full of mice for "dinner guests." Tabby distinguished herself though as the orangiest color a cat could be. The Johnsons could have christened her with fancy, fun names, like Sunrise, Fire, or even Pumpkin.

Lacy peeked with difficulty through the dark basement's thickly encased grate. The window was very dusty, but soon Lacy perceived with crystal clarity that Tabby was pregnant!

Lacy rushed to spread the news, her nails clicking with a frantic, staccato beat across the sidewalk. *This news flash is major and awesome*, Lacy's mind raced. Her little brain fantasized all kinds of petty, kitty-gossip thoughts. *Why? Tabby rarely comes out of the basement. Who knows if she has been out at all? And who knew she had a boyfriend? The size of that orange stomach is enormous! No doubt, the newborn kittens will arrive any second.* Lacy hoped the kittens would reveal the father by the color of their fur.

Click! Click! Click! Lacy's long nails scratched the cold but uncomplaining spavement as she journeyed to Garbage Alley. This was where many of her close friends congregate on sunny autumn mornings. Today's menu promised to be sweet. It was November 1, the day after Halloween.

"Girlfriends!" Lacy meow shrieked as she arrived at the local dining spot. "Girlfriends! You won't believe it! Tabby! Who knew? That mousy little cat in the Johnsons' basement is about to deliver!"

The first to react was Tom, a tomcat, the lone but never lonely male member of the bevy. Tom, whose name was another product of lazy-minded yet intuitive owners, was ever ready to pay visits on solitary female cats. In a slow, charming, Southern drawl, he meowed, "Who needs de-live-r-y? Ah shall make a house call and pick up the mouse from this kind lady."

"No, you tomcat! Not deliver a mouse, deliver some kittens," Lacy informed him.

"Ah see. Perhaps Ah will stay here," Tom drawl meowed.

An angelic voice coo meowed, "Kittens! Oh, I love kittens." This was Miss Lovely, a beautiful black cat with luminous, dark eyes. Her unsuspecting owners named her Miss Lovely as she seemed so sweet and demure when she graced their doorstep. With large, pitiful teardrops, she beseeched adoption. Little did her new owners know that Miss Lovely had been abandoned numerous times by previous owners. Soon, she scratched and hissed, jealously scaring and chasing away other pets to maintain her newly adopted status!

Then as everyone planned the kitty-shower party, they speculated as to who the father of these soon-to-be little lives was. Like fireworks, excited loose tongues sparked. "Meow, meow." "Oh, meow, meow, meow." "Oh no! Meow, meow." And on and on.

"We must go and tend to her," Miss Lovely cooed as a raindrop-glistened teardrop fell from one of her bejeweled eyes.

"Yes, we must. This is a once in one of our nine lifetimes!" cried the sister cats and Tom together.

Off they hurried toward the Johnsons' basement, stopping only to gossip meowed to other cats along the way. "Tabby's pregnant and about to give birth."

By the time they reached the Great Johnson Grate, as it is now called, the group of cats probably numbered forty! When they all pushed in to glare at once, no one could see anything. Poor Tabby, frightened by the invasion, bolted up the steps into Mrs. Johnson's kitchen.

Mrs. Johnson, busy with housework, was not used to having shy Tabby under her feet. She distractedly picked Tabby up and set her outside on the porch. A multitude of cat ears simultaneously perked up as they heard the porch door snap shut. The group ran so swiftly to the porch that they resembled the blur and whir of the blades of an electric fan speeding by. Their wind chilled the air one would have thought a ghost had passed through.

"Aaah!" all shouted with cat-whiskered mouths wide open in surprise. That is, except Tom who drooled, "Ooh," appreciatively. There was Tabby with terrified deer-in-headlight eyes, sleek and slim as ever!

"Where are they?" demanded Lacy.

"Yes," territory-hungry Miss Lovely hypocritically sympathized, "where are the little darlings? Left alone? I pray tell."

Tabby swallowed nervously and whispered, "The mice…they are okay."

"Mice? What mice?" Lacy interrogated. "Where are your new kittens?"

Shaking her little head bashfully, Tabby whispered, "No kitties."

Then a cat of high visual intelligence named Spy bellowed, "Let's go look again. Single file, one cat at a time!" She led the way. The stilted procession looked weird to the onlooker, yet this scientific approach worked.

Upon reaching the Great Johnson Grate, each cat took its turn, using its nocturnal senses to full advantage as they stared at Tabby's "litter." And what did they see? Right where earlier Lacy perceived young Tabby resting ripely was—her twin. No, not twins plural, just her twin. No, not even truly her twin, for she was too roundish to be her twin. No legs. No paws. No eyes. Just a big orange stomach. Why, a round orange stomach!

Wait. This was the human-eye version. The cats with their supersonic night vision knew right away that Tabby had simply been reclining on a discarded backside of an old jack-o'-lantern, a pumpkin!

From this day forward, Lacy no longer claimed her decorative christened name. She was known now as Loosy, L-O-O-S-Y, not to be confused with the usual spelling of the name Lucy, L-U-C-Y. Loosy signified the loose tongue that drew forty cats away from a fine, fall morning feast to slurp, burp, and smack vulgarly on a shy, retiring, little tabby who had done nothing to warrant such a tongue-lashing. She just chose to rest and recline on an old pumpkin.

Loosy, of course, did not like the nickname the group gave her. "Yo, Loosy! Whassup, Loosy?" was the greeting she faced daily from her fellow cats.

As the legend had it, the nickname stuck like bubble gum in a cat hair, until Loosy, no longer a fan of gossip, instead spoke only of truth and of love. To accomplish this, she attended therapy sessions with a cat psychologist who helped her learn to meow from her true, authentic self.

Although a challenge requiring self-discipline, one can stop one's focus on others' business and not nose into others' problems, judge, or blame them. Loosy learned in her therapy to make I statements. She began her sentences with "I meow" to express her own personal thoughts, feelings, needs, and style. Considerate of others' feelings, she communicated her ideas politely and respectfully so the other cat was not put on the defensive. The cat was open to hear what she said.

Miraculously, once she spoke her meow, meow in the direction of truth and love at all times, she immediately became her original decorative self for good—Lacy. She did not talk negatively about anything, herself, or anyone again—let alone gossiped. Nor did she draw to her self-insults or gossips from other cats—no more Loosy name-calling. She mastered her life lessons of speaking with integrity and said only what she knew to be true and good.

At age twelve, she fell ever so gently from a tree where she snoozed, the innocent sleep of a baby, and henceforth began her second lifetime and her quest toward her second life lesson—to not make assumptions or take what others say personally.

Summary of healthy communication principles

1. First, use your anger as a guide to clarify yourself. Ask, "What's below the anger? Sadness or fear?"
2. Heal past emotional wounds.
3. Use the focusing-inward process to figure out what will make you feel better—whether talking to someone about your feeling is necessary—before expressing yourself to anyone.
4. Do whatever you need to put yourself into a positive thinking mode (refer to "ways to cool down or chill" in this chapter and "how to be a whole, fulfilled person" in chapter 8).
5. Send out the vibes of love and the desire to receive love prior to approaching and making a request of the person.
6. Structure the discussion in terms of I messages and active listening.
7. Negotiate to achieve a win-win solution.
8. Remember that you can always take your power back by not participating in negativity.
9. Boundary setting healthy communication—Say "I want to have a caring healthy loving functional relationship with you but I can't do this if there is nastiness coming at me. I need niceness, not accusations and criticisms, complaints, threats, demands." And "if we start to argue, we need to call a truce or timeout where we go our separate ways until we can talk nicely and calmly to each other. Thank you."

Chapter 7

Create Healthy Relationships

I release all fear and accept only the joy of the moment and the harmony of my relationships. Every man is a golden link in my chain of good. My apparent enemy becomes my friend and is a golden link in my chain of good.

—paraphrased from *Your Word Is Your Wand*

Relationships that are vital, healthy, harmonious, loving, and peaceful are essential to a healthy, harmonious, peaceful self. Think about it. If you are upset with someone, how happy can you be? Or do you find yourself feeling disturbed or perturbed? In addition, if something is awry in your basic thought atmosphere or thinking pattern, if you have mistrust or negative beliefs about relationships, this will manifest in your life in disturbed interpersonal relationships. For example, a client sought marital counseling, wanting her husband to work on his trust issues. His previous wife betrayed him—she had an affair. He kept repeating incidents of abandonment. When he was a teenager, his car broke down, and he was stranded. And when he called his alcoholic father to pick him up, his father refused and told him to hitchhike home. This man kept reenacting the rejection he experienced as a child. In other words, if you hold the belief that you are rejected or that you will be abandoned, you will create this in your current life situation.

Learn from relationships

Relationships are the window to your soul—your psyche.

Do you remember the discussion on defense mechanisms—children's adaptive survival mechanisms to cope with dysfunctional family situations—which become blind spots as we grow up? Do you remember the difference between being a projector or a camera—projecting your own past stuff on to others and misperceiving reality? Projection is the defense mechanism where you blame others for your own problems or misperceive others' behaviors as problematic because you have been hurt in the past. Everybody projects to some degree, which is why we need to strive to not take anything personally.

Couples come together at an unconscious level to work through some underlying issues that both share, although each partner may take the opposite stance. For example, in the case of issues of trust, one partner might be very controlling and clingy, the other one independent and distant—having chosen the opposite means of protecting themselves from abandonment. Your partner will often assume your shadow self. Your "shadow self" refers to the repressed dark side of yourself. For example, the controlling person, the one who has deep-seated needs for control, may often project this out and perceives the spouse as extremely controlling. They may even misinterpret their partner's selfless behavior as selfish—not recognizing and owning the projection of their own shadow.

Relationships are essential to healing, to growth, and to understand where our thought processes and beliefs have gone amuck. When anyone bothers us, particularly if we feel intensely or chronically bothered, this signals that a button has been pushed in us and we need to do some healing work. We can ask ourselves or the higher power, "How can I see this differently? How can I release the fear or agony that I am experiencing and learn something from this experience in a loving, gentle way?"

No one can hurt you without your permission. No one can make you feel inferior without your consent. You ultimately want to recognize that whatever anyone else is feeling is his or her own stuff—not to be taken personally.

For example, a man had issues of feeling dominated or overcontrolled as a child and had issues of feeling rejected or left out of things as a child. When he moved in a cohabitation situation, his partner made some comment about an area of his office that is well lighted and might not need a lamp. His response was "What are you trying to do, control my life? Don't you think I know whether or not I need a lamp?" She felt hurt. Clearly, he overreacted to a little comment about how bright the room was. However, they were scratching each other's scabs. He reacted from a place of feeling overcontrolled. She had rejection buttons to be healed, or she probably would have found his comment humorous and could have been supportive to help him look at his own buttons—reassure him that her comment was not intended to control but was rather offered to be cheery about how great his office was.

When an interaction with someone triggers an angry feeling, before conflict sparks, it is best not to immediately express your irritation. The anger signals a time to go within, to go internal, to focus—to see what is really bothering you, why it bothers you, and what will make it feel better—rather than engage in a conflict that makes you feel worse afterward. You may discover that your intense feeling is out of proportion to the comment or situation, such as in the above example.

This is an opportunity to discover what unresolved feelings of hurt and fear have been provoked. Then to heal, you need to talk about and release feelings from the past wounds or traumas to heal. The example of the client who was feeling rejected by his wife because she was going to bed early is a good one. Their relationship healed and helped him realize how much pain he still had about his relationship with his father, which he needed to deal with. Had he argued and divorced her because he felt that she did not give him enough attention, he would not have healed. Pushing each other's buttons helped them both heal and be able to trust and have an intimate relationship.

Feel Your Feelings

THE FEELINGS CHART

Love (Happiness)

Happy
Contented
Amused
Pleased
Confident
Excited
Fulfilled
Comfortable
Satisfied
Joyful
Loving
Appreciated
Wonderful
On Top of the World
Thrilled
Blissful
Fun
Interested
Playful

The Iceberg Model
FEAR =
False
Evidence
Appears
Real

Fear (Sadness)

*The surface
Or tip emotion,
Anger:*

Annoyed
Furious
"Ticked Off"
Irritated
Disgusted
Resentful
Hate
Dissatisfied
Irate
Frustrated
Aggravated

**What's Below?
Afraid**

Fearful
Frightened
Nervous
Anxious
Scared
Insecure
Terrified
Shy
Apprehensive
Ill at Ease
Shocked
Inadequate
Jealous

**What's Below?
Sad (is Loss
Fear)**

Down
Low
Depressed
Disappointed
Hurt
Rejected
Despondent
Sorrowful
Unappreciated
Grieving
Lonesome
Discouraged
Guilty
Embarrassed
Miserable
Hopeless
Bored

What is the shadow?

A concept introduced by the psychologist Jung, the shadow is your unconscious wounds—your deeply buried, fear-based negative energy. You take your shadow everywhere, like a black cloud. Then one day, out of the blue, it rains on you parade. Even metaphysicians and positive thinkers who regularly visualize and create positive life experiences—money, love, success—are haunted by ghosts from their past. When they least expect it, some trauma—their shadow—disrupts their life's peace and success.

Why does this happen? Because life is your mirror. Outside events reflect your inner life, even your unconscious beliefs and unresolved issues and wounds. Until you heal and release them, these shadows keep appearing, unbidden.

So how is your shadow created? From generation to generation, pain, not love, is too often the legacy. To heal yourself, you must heal the wounds inflicted by your mother or both parents.

An adult who grew up with an alcoholic parent may unconsciously and compulsively demand perfection from his own children. For example, a man may compel his introverted son to sing in the choir, even though the boy would rather not. The experience is unnerving for the child, but instead of receiving compassionate understanding from his father, he's forced to deal alone with his fear of standing in front of the church. He must adapt at all costs.

Consequently, the son learns to push himself to overachieve to please his dad. This pattern eventually causes him to become a successful overachiever, but he develops chronic fatigue syndrome. The child carries the shadow of his father's perfectionism until he learns to release it. Only then can he find balance and create a life that really works for him.

To free yourself from your mother's pain and to move from fear to joy, you must tap into and release your shadow. Accepting your parents' pain is part of the work. Once you become aware and accept your shadow, you can release unconscious negative energy and limiting fears based on your beliefs and attitudes. That frees you to use the law of attraction. Healing from the pain of your parents' love frees you to become a hollow bone through which spirit can pass. You can then function completely in the law of attraction, loving yourself and your life. You're no longer imprisoned by your unconscious needs and wounds and no longer projecting negative energy and creating mishap. You're able to live in the moment and at peace. You can set boundaries to please and satisfy yourself, rather than living with resentment or terror because you're operating from your true spiritual purpose and joys. Shattering your shadow is a model to help you dispel the fears you absorbed from your parents' unresolved emotional wounds and become pure love.

When embarking on this journey of self-discovery, you can picture yourself as a broken window about to be transformed into a prism of a gorgeous array of colors. Rather than just patching the damaged panes, you're replacing the whole window with your truth, passions, and joy. Shattering your old self makes room for new authenticity, beauty, and perfection—a beautiful stained-glass mosaic that is uniquely you.

Advanced inner child work—the shadow

To accomplish the task of healing and wholeness, shadow work is necessary. This is the ultimate shattering of self to completely clear any inner negativity and connect you to a sense of oneness, security, and, yes, even bliss.

Current negative relationship experiences are actually your key to complete healing because they provide the clues to identify your shadow—your deep, dark, repressed, secret part of yourself, your blind spot that holds your worst wounds and pain. This may be unconscious or subconscious to you now, and you need to identify these negative core beliefs because they impair and limit your freedom to be truly fulfilled and joyous. Your deep insecurity needs to be fully healed so you can accept and approve of yourself as complete, perfect, and whole and to manifest a wonderful life.

Shadow work is an advanced inner child work technique that was purposefully not included in the chapter "Heal Emotional Wounds of the Past" because, without preparation, this healing role play could be too intense and emotionally difficult.

Healing the self therapeutically is like peeling an onion, whereupon each layer is lifted gently, not nuked. This is not to discourage anyone from attempting this because if you are to feel complete and secure, this procedure is eventually necessary—one must face one's inner demons and convert them to pure love. Prior to this work, the painful effects of life trauma should have been addressed and released—preliminary discussing and working through abuse, neglect experiences, major losses, etc. Your inner child should have been soothed and comforted many times. The inner child work (see chapter 3) was a role play whereby you move from seat to seat, taking turns, as your natural adult caretaking side soothed, comforted, and loved your wounded, innocent child part to provide insight, problem-solving, guidance, and, most importantly, love to restore your inner child to a happy, innocent, secure state of being.

The shadow work—shatter analysis

After preparation, it is safe to do the deepest level of personal healing, the shadow work. However, it is a little like what the disclaimer on TV states when a professional stuntman is about to pull some outlandish maneuver, "Don't try this at home. You must be a trained professional to do this." Shadow work is *best supervised by a trained psychotherapist*, although the client, once instructed properly, may choose to do some of the process at home for homework.

Step 1: Identify your shadow by thinking about some person in your life who really bothers you or with whom you are angry intensely and/or frequently.
Step 2: Feel free to rage or vent about this person's horrible qualities. Do this with the knowledge that your intent is not to put the person down or spew negativity; you are simply getting in touch with the intensity of your dislike. Be sure to put out your power of intent to the universe that you are not truly desiring to inflict damage on this person but rather getting in touch with your own feelings. To yourself internally, name-call this person in terms of his flaws. For example, to yourself, call the person "rude, disrespectful, selfish," etc.
Step 3: Ask yourself, "In what way are you like this?" This is your shadow self, the deeply buried, repressed, dark side of yourself, that nasty part that you do not wish to acknowledge—which is actually your most deeply wounded child self that needs your total love to heal.
Step 4: Ask yourself, "How do I accept and work with this part of myself already?" In other words, first of all, "How do I cope with this part of me already in my life?" For example, a woman in the example below tended to be rather compulsive and was task oriented to the point of sometimes not being empathetic to others' feelings. She tried to cope with it by overcompensating, being compulsively pleasing to others, catering to them. This is how she worked with it. She now needed to truly understand, embrace, and love it.
Step 5: Set your intention to actually learn to accept this aspect of yourself. Recognize that only a higher power can heal this part. Only your higher self or higher power within could dispel your deep terror, rage, and unforgivability. Only love can conquer fear.
Step 6: Begin a role play with your higher self, reaching out to your shadow self—that wounded inner child that is the ugly, crazed, inner self that feels out of control with pain. Your nurturing adult self must

connect in oneness with your higher power, as you perceive it. If you will have the power and unconditional love necessary for your wounded child to open up, trust, and be reachable to heal, he or she *can*.

How to heal your shadow—the role-play technique

First, decide on a quiet place, where you will not be interrupted for at least an hour. It may not take this long, but plan on it anyway. It may take multiple sessions, however.

Create a visual image of your shadow. One client had a dream as a teenager of someone who seemed to be a crazed Bipolar woman, unkempt hair sticking out, who was trapped in an attic, scratching with long red fingernails to escape from the tiny space she was locked in. This represented her dark side—the rage she feared would escape and destroy herself and others. She used this image, recognizing it as her shadow self.

Connect with your higher self, your higher power, feeling complete unconditional love. As you sit on the couch or love seat where you can move back and forth fairly easily, begin by sending the vibes of love and desire to receive love back. When you are doing this deep level of inner child work with your seriously wounded shadow part, you may experience this pain as so intense you will realize this is the only way to reach your wounded self.

Keep going back and forth between your higher self and shadow self. Let the shadow self express the source of the wounding. This will probably bring you back to some buried grief or traumatic experiences. Your higher self needs to supply unconditional love and a big-picture perspective to the little wounded self. For example, this woman, who had a lot of preparatory therapy before she took on this exercise, realized during the shadow work that she had regressed to her birth trauma experience when her mother had been in labor for two full days and she had been squeezed breathlessly in a limbo, frantically trying to survive and not understanding her torment and wishing she could fall asleep and be dead and escape the pain—thus, her dream of the lady with the red fingernails trying to scratch her way out of the attic, which was a visual image of her painful birth experience. The nurturing parent part was able to help the wounded child understand the situation and help her feel not so alone and to realize everything was okay and that she was about to embark on her life adventure! In the past, she just coped with her shadow by hiding her desperate survival instinct or compulsive task orientation with pleasing behaviors. This woman would tend to reenact physical discomfort experiences in her life or be attracted to people with physical problems which would be reminiscent of the confining birth trauma, but she had no insight into it until this shadow work.

Build healthy support system

Long-lasting couples' relationships

Some of the following ideas come from Michael Broder, PhD, and Phil McGraw, PhD, a prominent psychologist with a popular television show who also serves as a life coach by helping people identify their problems and begin their process of getting help. Qualities of most long-lasting couples include:

    A. They have a "we" attitude. They are team players. They know that if something is affecting one person, it will affect both of them.
    B. They are friends at the basis of their relationship. They like, trust, and respect each other. They share power. They are able to have fun together, not just sexually but in life in general as companions.
    C. They give each other attention and show appreciation.
    D. They have time for their relationship, and they give undivided attention to each other.

E. They are concerned about each other's well-being at the present and in the future.
F. They live in the same thought atmosphere or thought world. They have a similar life or spiritual philosophy. For example, one is not extremely cynical and the other positive minded. For another example, one is not agnostic, and the other is a devout Catholic.
G. They communicate well with each other, particularly because they are in the same thought world. They are on the same general wavelength, so communication can be deep and rewarding.
H. They take time to have a regular powwow or peaceful discussion, almost like a business meeting, where they can politely share their needs with each other through I messages. They recognize venting is harmful, and they do not do it. Therefore, one sign that a marriage could break up is constant arguments or one spouse or partner constantly criticizing, complaining, or ridiculing the other partner.

Couples with good communication skills disagree, but each partner listens attentively and empathically to the other side, versus partners with poor communication patterns, in which the men tend to "cut off"—withdraw from conflict and refuse to talk at all. This has been termed "stonewalling," which is almost as awful as actual physical or emotional violence for women because women need to feel validated and responded to. Therefore, this is violating a basic need.

Many people expect way too much from their significant others, spouses, family, etc. Some people even believe that their partner should be their primary source of happiness. Individuals need to be able to fulfill themselves and let a loving or romantic relationship be simply one part of fulfillment—icing on the cake. We are responsible for fulfilling ourselves and making ourselves happy emotionally, spiritually, mentally, physically, intellectually, and socially. These are our own responsibilities. We need to make time to take care of ourselves.

Sometimes we may wear too many hats—leaving little time for really wearing any of them with style. For example, one survey showed that the average couple only spoke to each other about thirty minutes a week. Externally oriented and trying to live up to the American dream with the big house, children, successful dual careers, and all the other status items involved, there is little room for a relationship. Make the time.

The principle of divinely guided harmony—win-win negotiations

Abusive and neglectful communication needs to be stopped. Now is the time to raise consciousness so women are revered as whole, perfect, wonderful, and lovable! Both partners need to affirm that they have healthy, loving, peaceful, harmonious, and mutual relationships. These affirmations will lead to positive, mutual relationships. The opposite underlying negative thought patterns manifest in intimidation by men. Women need to claim their own thoughts and beliefs about their importance and believe the process of conflict resolution will reflect a balance of power.

When there is a disagreement, "divine harmony" (in other words, what is higher power's plan for the highest good) is pray treated for, and both partners need to be open to what they are intuitively guided to. What works for one couple does not necessarily work for another couple. Couples need to be open to finding any solution that comes to them that feels right to each of them. There needs to be a bubble around the couple unit; they make the decision because it works for them. The solution may seem highly untraditional to other people. Whatever works for them is good and right.

Couples' therapy

A good marital therapist can be helpful in assisting partners to learn better communication skills. They can help individuals look at their own negative thought pattern and heal old inner wounds brought to light in the relationship because buttons are being pushed. If there is chronic dissatisfaction in the marriage for either party, it is useful to seek professional help. If you get to the stage where there are chronic arguments, damage is being done by things being said or done to each other. The problems become harder to fix.

Choose the right people to be in your life

The three love connections: Soul Connection, Love of Life, or Firework-Type Love Relationship

There are three primary connections that need to go both ways between partners to make for a very satisfying, long-lasting relationship—the soul connection. The three connections are:

1. The romantic chemistry or physical attraction connection—that you are having a satisfying sex life and affection with this person.
2. The parenting connection—you are best friends and nurturing "parents" to each other, devoted and concerned, as you would be to your child.
3. The spiritual or life philosophy connection, compatibility where you see things in the same thought world, which allows you to communicate at a deep level and grow personally, emotionally, and spiritually.

To have a satisfying long-term relationship or partnership, the couple must share at least two connections both ways—for example, be mutually attracted to each other and caretaking of each other. Another example is that, although they are not romantic, they are best friends and share similar life philosophy, so they grow in the relationship and feel supported. Having only one-and-a-half connections—for example, a mutual physical attraction but only one partner feels parental or devoted to the other's well-being can be satisfying only in the short-term, such as for a year or two boyfriend-girlfriend-type relationship, and aren't enough connections to make for a happy marriage. The love of life connection—all three connections, romantic, parenting, and life philosophy—make for a most satisfying long-term commitment with fireworks, like in a romantic movie.

Don't marry someone unless you're positive you have at least two connections going both ways. You can be happily married to someone that you do not have all these connections both ways with. It is more compelling and overall more satisfying to stay together if you do have these connections. I know, for example, a female therapist friend of mine whose husband, with whom she has a good long-term relationship raising three children, lives in a different thought world or spiritual philosophy from her. He is scared of her spiritual metaphysical inclinations. Still, they get along well. She fulfills herself by having intimate friends that she can communicate with on this spiritual level.

Exercise: Ask yourself, "Which of these connections do I and my significant other share? Are they mutual? Do the connections go both ways or just one way?" For example, your partner desires you sexually but you don't him. Remember, go back to the beginning of your relationship for this connection. Anger, conflict, and children can reduce this drive. You are trying to determine if there is some basic connection. How much compatibility do you have in these three areas? You need at least two connections both ways to have a long-term satisfying relationship. One and a half will work for a while in your chain of boyfriend-girlfriend-type relationships but will not last for marriage.

Marital myths

Healthy couples are not limited or affected by marital myths or human race consciousness about the institution of marriage.

Partners in healthy marriages know that they are not clones. Being on the same wavelength does not mean that they are going to see things exactly the same. They are two individuals. They are going to have differences with need for discussions or powwows. And with healthy couples, they do not get to the point of abusiveness or impoliteness.

They will not necessarily share the same passion or hobbies together. They certainly will share some interests, but their specific hobby does not have to be shared. For example, a partner who has multiple sclerosis is not going to be a dance partner, yet that does not stop the other one from dancing independently if this is his or her passion. Separate vacations can be rewarding from time to time.

Human race consciousness regarding male-female relationships and partnerships

Issues that affect relationships that go beyond the specific partners stem from human race consciousness. In his book *Men Are from Mars, Women Are from Venus*, John Gray explains that men's brains develop in a goal-directed, fixed manner. Out in the wilderness, faced with hunting potentially dangerous animals originally, males would have been unsafe or impractical to discuss a lot among one another when a problem arose—it was time to kill the prey or protect themselves. In contrast, women—communicating, cooking, and caring for children—talked among one another and worked together, such that they can talk, do, and feel simultaneously. In contrast, men do not do, think, and feel simultaneously. They may need more time and space to process their feelings. According to Gray, men go into their "caves" and, when intruded upon, breathe "dragon breath" to shoo people away to get their processing time.

Couples' research supports that women have more relationship communication skills. Comfortable with sharing their feelings, being psychologically intimate (which is a critical ingredient in a successful relationship), they are quick to sense trouble and steer around confrontation. They focus the discussion before it escalates. They are less likely to tune out or withdraw from conflict than men. On the other hand, men, the hunters, will force a solution before they have heard their partners out, yet women care deeply about being heard and understood. According to John Gray, what men want most is to be respected and trusted. Gray gave the example that if a man takes a woman on a date and she does not like the movie, he feels terrible. In contrast, if she says that she does like the movie, he is beaming as if he ultimately produced, directed, acted in, and executed the entire show for her!

Polarized masculine and feminine energy

I refer to "masculine and feminine energy" rather than "male and female" because all people have masculine and feminine energy. What do these differences signify? In our collective thought pattern, or collective unconsciousness, feminine power (the creative, nurturing, calming energy) versus the masculine (driven, controlling, and goal oriented) is not well accepted yet. Research and surveys have shown that women today work out of the home and still assume the bulk of the responsibility for housework and childcare. Why is there not equality over mutual responsibilities? Equality between the sexes cannot occur until men are as competent and willing as women to raise children. Until then, the childbearing burden will fall on mothers—and marital conflict related to childcare will continue. Research shows that marital satisfaction takes a nosedive once children enter the picture. Women cannot actualize themselves as fulfilled people and relate intimately if they are overburdened by responsibility. This relates to a consciousness of a lower value and lower respect for women. Men hold this, and women hold this—or women would not allow themselves to be abused or allow themselves to be overworked or ignored.

This thought pattern needs to be changed on a mass consciousness level. This can be done individually and can begin with you. Realize the important power and force that feminine energy has to exert—to create, to calm, and to nurture. Once woman power is valued, then there will be peace on earth.

The inequality between husbands and wives today is at the root of the societal, second-class citizenship of women that is in our mass consciousness. Women struggle to achieve equal status with men. Women got the right to vote less than one hundred years ago. Women entered the workforce and began to be allowed to use their minds and creativity in the world a little over fifty years ago. Today, women continue to fight for equal rights in the workplace, such as equal pay.

Women have been treated in a conspicuous and authoritarian way by men. This necessitated the women's movement to balance the power and to increase the respect between the sexes. Although often disguised or unconscious, this inequality persists. Socialized and societally conditioned to be homemakers, women have developed superior skills in the caretaking of others (family, spouse, and children). Women have been encouraged to be sensitive to feelings and to care about maintaining harmonious relationships. Men were socialized to go into the world and achieve dominance over their environment from the original hunting of cavemen up to present day when men work careers to provide financially for their families.

When a stereotypically feminine person conditioned to sensitivity meets and partners with a stereotypically masculine person conditioned to dominate and control, the foundation for authoritarian, unequal, and disrespectful relationship is laid. As we move away from traditional gender roles, these roots of the male-female relationships need to be addressed. A good therapist noted, "A relationship is like a boat journey. If the boat gets a little off course, it could wind up in China—or somewhere else you didn't intend."

Race—human race—consciousness or collective unconsciousness sets the sail and needs to be readjusted. It shackles women to most of the household and childcare responsibilities—to work 24-7—if a husband talks in a verbally abusive or neglectful manner toward his wife and keeps the wife feeling intimidated. The men are usually stronger and bigger and so, at a primitive level, are intimidating anyway. They may assume postures that threaten with outright glaring, menacing looks (towering over posture or actual aggressive threats or behaviors). Stonewalling (cutting off) is a good example. Per research, when conflicts arise, many men tend to project blame or responsibility for problems to external causes, including their partner. Many women, on the other hand, tend to introject or assume the guilt or responsibility for what is going wrong.

Why do women tolerate these negative behaviors or comments toward them? The fear of being physically hurt—although this may be unconscious. Particularly, women who have experienced emotional, verbal, and/or physical aggression growing up in the family of origin have a core belief thought pattern that they are not lovable or that they are not worth much. In a vicious cycle, this allows them to tolerate being treated like this. Women who come from any type of dysfunctional family of origin (and how many do not?) may have low self-esteem. They may believe their husbands when they say that they are overemotional, crazy, etc. Yet they fear that if they do not keep things in an organized manner, chaos may break out. Women, often good at managing highly demanding situations, may try to carry out overwhelming responsibilities. We can only do two things well at a time. Women today are attempting to tame an octopus with many limbs—home, marriage, children, and work. Paradoxically, when women overfunction and do it all, they neglect the deeper relationships. The woman's nurturing, intimacy-building, creative power is going to waste.

Open, honest communication and setting boundaries

People can be toxic to us. The next couple of sections are guides to help you evaluate the supportiveness of the people whom you are in a relationship with. For your well-being, choose to distance yourself or set boundaries when certain individuals are being toxic to you. There is no point in allowing yourself to be verbally, emotionally, or physically aggressed against. Walk away from that situation. Say, "Excuse me," when you see it coming and go to the bathroom, if necessary, if you live with this person. Do not allow yourself to be abused. There are no victims. You allow yourself to participate in that scenario and can withdraw from it when you make the choice to do so. In chronic arguments, if at all possible, calling a truce is called for.

Any time interactions become toxic, it is best to withdraw, journal, think, and get professional help, etc., in order to see what is really going on. Be objective and look inward to the buttons that are being pushed and what you personally need to heal to make the situation better. Recognize that there is something calling from an underlying belief about yourself if you are having interpersonal problems. Do something to heal your buttons. Then when you interact, no matter what the person's response, you will not be able to be hurt as you were in the past.

Know that it is always okay to make an I message—to let the other person know your feelings, needs, and experiences. The only exception to this rule is if your sharing might provoke someone to become physically aggressive to you. Then it is best to avoid. Do not speak. Judge based on *past behavior predicts future behavior*—if the person reacted aggressively in the past in a similar circumstance, it could happen again. People involved with those who have temper problems need to make their own safety a priority.

Choose supportive people to be in your life

We need to surround ourselves with supportive people of like-mindedness, in terms of our life or spiritual philosophies—people who are accepting and validating of us. A psychotherapist, like a licensed clinical psychologist, can be a good person to start with if you do not have friends or family members whom you feel truly validate you. Ultimately, you would like to have several close friends too.

Toxic people, caretaking providers, and empathetic listeners

Toxic people are people who say or do things that disrupt or hurt you in some way. No matter how many times you try to let them know they are hurting or upsetting you, they persist in the same damaging behaviors.

Good people to be in relationships with fall into two types:

The *caretaking provider* is the person who will offer you a hand when you need it. He or she will do something to reduce or lighten your load, and in the process, he or she won't also burden you or cause you trouble, making his or her help not worth as much in the balance because you have a personal mess to clean up afterward. A good example of a bad example is someone who appears to be a caretaking provider yet is acting toxically, like the grandma takes care of your child so you can go to the grocery store peacefully and you return to find out she just fed your child what she is allergic to despite that you brought her a snack to give your child. So you go home to unload your groceries with a sick child.

The *empathetic or empathetic listener* is the person who will listen to your woes, provide support, and validate and advise when appropriate. This person doesn't make you feel worse afterward about yourself and what you shared. On the contrary, you feel better and have a better handle on your situation. For example, you talk to your spouse, cry on his shoulder, and get support and he is okay with this.

People usually will not be good at both; they'll either be hands-on types or lip-service types. And when pushed out of their comfort zone, they may not respond as effectively to your needs. So don't expect the same level of support in both areas from the same person.

Zero expectations

Any negative interaction is an opportunity for us to be able to grow and learn—once we accept zero expectations about what others will provide for us. For example, a woman had a conflict with her mother-in-law (go figure with our race consciousness about in-laws, especially mothers-in-law). In actuality, she was probably one of the best guiding forces in her life. She had helped her from mundane everyday matters, such as finding her most flattering clothing colors to wear and starting her on her own spiritual journey. Yet for an example of how toxic the mother-in-law can be, when the daughter-in-law called her to tell her that her three-year-old was going to have her tonsils out, her mother-in-law's immediate response was "Oh, I just heard of a boy dying from a tonsillectomy"—a very toxic response. She had an ADD problem and would blurt out anything that came to her mind.

To deal with this on an everyday basis was not healthy for the daughter-in-law. With overinvolved grandparents, she did not have much of a life beyond work and family. It was, in a strange way, a blessing that her mother-in-law did toxic kinds of unreliable or almost cruel things, which helped the young woman to distance herself from the in-laws and actually have time for herself—turning a lemon into lemonade. Expectations for her—given her limitations with the untreated, unrecognized ADD problem—were too high. Handled with proper boundaries and zero expectations of her, this fun-loving grandmother could be a wonderful guide—as she was energetic and shared lots of information.

People can have numerous problems that are not any reflection on you, although they will affect you—such as the person having an ADD disorder. For that reason, they are not reliable. They blurt out things inappropriately, or they act impulsively. This is disturbing but is not to be taken as personal rejection. The person you are involved with could be depressed or have a chemical-dependency problem with other kinds of toxic tendencies. There are things about people's basic natures that cause them to be the way they are, and you cannot expect them to change. Even though they may not fit with your expectation, they are the way they are.

Mental disorders

Why give power to the negative and discuss mental disorders? People can have mental problems that interfere with their power of intention. It is also important to understand one's limitations because these limitations do need to be faced and released for one to be able to utilize the principles in this book. You can have love connections with others who have significant mental problems that interfere with healthy relating. Remember the analogy of the car trip? You have to be aware of where you are right now and accept reality to take action to start moving in the direction of your destination. If you know who you are and accept your strengths and weaknesses, you can change your life.

Intelligence is the ability to process information and learn from it. Being defensive and denying problems keeps you stuck with the problems and unable to learn and grow. If you work on yourself, you are more able to have satisfying relationships. If you understand what other peoples' weaknesses or problems are, you are able to adjust your own expectations and behavior to take care of yourself and not participate in negativity. How do we stay aware and accepting of problems without giving them power? In an earlier example of the car analogy, we need to know our starting point in order to make our way to our destination. We need to understand where we are originally—our limitations—and accept them so that we can progress toward our goal. This does not preclude or prevent your power of intention. Visualize yourself and others as whole, complete, perfect. And then set proper boundaries to prevent negativity from affecting you, based on the current appearance.

The following is a list of many of the major mental disorders to help you better understand people and their challenges. Consider the possibility that when you decide to express in the physical—when up in God's buffet, you saw something that looked interesting—you or others may have chosen certain challenges to develop yourself, like a diamond needs friction to be polished and to shine.

First-year medical students often begin to diagnose themselves with whatever diseases they come across in their textbook. This is not a guide for you to diagnose others or yourself, although you may recognize some symptoms and may desire to seek professional help to get a proper diagnosis. When people are struggling with their lives—with their schooling, their career, their relationship, and so on—there is a good reason. They have challenges interfering with their ability to keep their focus and accomplish their goals. In addition, understanding and accepting that people may have mental conditions will help you see people as they are and to have realistic expectations about their behavior. You can protect yourself from negativity through setting appropriate boundaries. You can have a peaceful life by not participating in negativity—even with someone with a mental disorder. If you are frustrated with a significant person in your life, that may be a clue that this person has a serious problem that would respond to professional help and be way beyond your capabilities to rescue or do anything about. Caretaking them would hinder—not help the problem. Everyday insanity is doing the same thing over and over again but expecting a different result.

Here are some mental disorders that could affect you and others:

Addictions or dependencies, such as substance abuse and compulsive eating
　　Definitions and symptoms: Addictions have been dealt with throughout this book. The next chapter—about the whole, fulfilled person—is devoted to the topic of addiction and recovery.

Chemical dependency
　　Definitions and symptoms: See glossary for Adult Children of Alcoholics and Alcoholism. A person can be an alcoholic and never drink or drink only on weekends or drink to relax a couple of times a week. It is a progressive disease. Don't confuse the out-of-control, nonstop drinking late phase with alcoholism and miss early or middle phases.
　　Treatment: See twelve-step programs in the glossary and chapter 4, "Open Up to Help" and chapter 8, "Be a Whole, Fulfilled Person" for information on recovery from addictions. What you need to know is only 2 percent of people can recover without an intensive ongoing support or treatment group, like Alcoholics Anonymous or Narcotics Anonymous. And those people are usually facing doctors who tell them they will die from a life-threatening illness if they don't quit.
　　Famous people: The headlines are replete with substance abusers, including celebrities.

Compulsive eating
　　Definition and symptoms: People are generally overweight because they take in too many calories and burn too few and because they eat to reduce stress, comfort themselves, fill a void, or are addicted to unhealthy food. There is much support for a toxic food environment.
　　Cause or etiology: Food was frequently an issue of control in the families of origin and may have been used to pacify children, or the compulsive eater may have used food to comfort himself because he wasn't getting his needs met in the family situation. People with any kind of eating disorder often experience their sense of control over their lives by controlling their food intake, even if it means to overeat unhealthy foods when they feel like it.

Treatment: Psychotherapy is useful to get insight to the origins of their compulsive eating. Dieting only results in a yo-yo effect of losing and putting on weight. People temporarily loses weight on a diet because they have not allowed themselves to eat food they normally eat. When they return to eating off the diet, they still have not learned how to eat in a healthy manner or to eat foods they enjoy in proper portions. They have lost muscle mass, and their metabolism has slowed down because the body normally reduces the metabolism when less food is coming in. Hence, when they return to their typical eating patterns, they put on weight even faster. Weight Watchers is the only dietary program that I would recommend because you don't have to just eat their foods. You get a consciousness about your foods and how to eat in a way that you don't put on weight.

Famous people: Almost everyone who is overweight. People are stress eating in our fast-paced, toxic food society.

Attention deficit and other processing disorders

Definition and symptoms: Attention deficit hyperactivity disorder (ADHD) is the term used to describe a variety of attention deficit disorders—symptoms of chronic inattentiveness since childhood, careless mistakes, missing details, lack of follow-through on instructions, poor listening, difficulty with organizing activities, loss of everyday essential items, forgetfulness, and avoidance of sustained mental work, like homework.

Behavior Modification Chart

Set 3 goals for your child and monitor daily: at the end of the day give them a check, happy face, or sticker for each of the goals they achieve that day. If they get two to three, then they get to have a small prize and if they get three or four good days at the end of the week they get a big prize. Example of awards or prizes is a treasure chest like at a pediatrician's or teacher's office, a small amount of money, a treat, whatever rewards your child. If they a good week like three or four days at the end the week they can get a special outing or shopping trip to reward your child for a good week. This reward system increases the dopamine of the child so they are focused on their goals and are more cooperative.

	Mon	Tue	Wed	Thu	Fri	Sat	Sun

Goals

1. Keep hands and fee to self, no hitting, no throwing
2. Speak in a friendly voice, no yelling or name calling
3. Your prosocial choice for your child such as good hygiene, completing chores, being organized, or keeping reminder lists

Some types include:

Inattentive type without hyperactivity: Usually referred to as ADD. All the above symptoms. Tends to be passive, bonds with others who are present although does not take initiative without the presence of structure, and has difficulty keeping life focus.
Hyperactive type: All the above symptoms, plus overtalkativeness, fidgeting, on-the-go behavior, climbing and running as a child, restlessness as an adult, blurting out whatever comes to mind, or interrupting conversations.
Obsessive-compulsive, moody, overfocused type: All the above symptoms, only the person gets overfocused and has difficulty with transitions, and also has negative mood problems—depression or anxiety—compared to the often happy-go-lucky ADD inattentive type.
Bad-tempered ADHD type: Has the ADD symptoms only, often looks like Bipolarish (see description of Bipolar later in this section).

Cause or etiology: Neurological—genetics, brain infection, etc. Parts of the brains of individuals with ADHD are either overactive or underactive, depending on the type. The electrical activity is either sluggish or overstimulated or both, such as in the overfocused type. For example, in ADD inattentive type and most of the others, the prefrontal lobe of the brain—the sites of executive function, organization, thinking before acting—are sluggish. The moody type shows a sluggish or overstimulated emotional center of the brain (such as in the temporal lobe).

Associated features: defensiveness, denial, minimization, and projection. They have been screamed at, yelled at, and punished, which cause defensive ways of relating to protect their self-esteem.

Other related disorders: ADHD has been considered to be on the mild end of the spectrum or continuum of autism, with ADD or ADHD being the very mildest type of problem. Learning disabilities, such as dyslexia, and other processing disorders, like auditory and visual, being next in line. Then pervasive developmental delay. Next, Asperger's disorder, individuals with mild autism who can function. Finally, autism, the most severe type on the autistic spectrum.

Treatment: Readers are referred to the following authors who have done a lot of ADHD work—Daniel Amen, MD; Thom Hartmann; Ned Hallowell, MD; and Dr. Frank Lawlis—for specifics regarding treatment, such as supplements and diet and medication if truly needed, behavioral organizational strategies, behavior modification and school accommodations for children and teens, best school situations, life organizational coaching for teens and adults, neurobiofeedback, and psychotherapy to increase self-esteem and reduce self-defensiveness and develop coping strategies.

The physical bodies of people with ADHD are theorized to not detox chemicals, preservatives, and processed foods as well as other people do. Therefore, the processing speed of their brains—the speed that the brain chemicals neurotransmitters flow—is only about 90 percent of normal people's brain processing speed. Cutting back or cutting out processed, chemically laden foods have been found to be very helpful. Increasing nutritious food increases the oxygenation of the brain and enhances life-focusing functioning. The omega-3s 5000 mg daily (good for improved prognosis for Bipolar too)—fatty acids, like fish oil and flaxseed oil—have been found through research to be as effective as psychostimulant medication, such as Ritalin, and they get to the root cause of the condition rather than artificially speeding up the processing speed with amphetamines that are addictive.

Per Internet, famous people with ADD or ADHD or learning disorder: Beethoven, Alexander Graham Bell, the Wright brothers, Winston Churchill, Leonardo da Vinci, Walt Disney, Thomas Edison, Albert Einstein, Benjamin Franklin, Galileo, Abraham Lincoln, Napoleon, Isaac Newton, Picasso, Edgar Allan Poe, Eleanor Roosevelt, Thoreau, Van Gogh, Robin Williams, and numerous other celebrities.

Ed Hallowell, MD (*Driven to Distraction*), a psychiatrist who himself has as well as specializes in ADD or ADHD, says he would not trade it for the world because it's like being a Lamborghini—unique blend of spiritedness and creativity. You just need a special mechanic and a special oil."

Anxiety disorders

Definition and symptoms: Anxiety disorders include:

Generalized anxiety disorder: chronic, excessive, uncontrollable worry, irritability, difficulty concentrating, tension.
Social phobia: fear of humiliation in social situations, sometimes confused with agoraphobia.
Agoraphobia: fear of and avoidance of places and situations where something bad or embarrassing could happen—including fear of a panic attack.
Panic disorder: an anxiety attack with symptoms including sweating, heart pounding, shortness of breath, chest pain or tightness, and fear of going crazy or dying.
Obsessive-compulsive disorder (OCD): obsession—persistent reoccurring, intrusive, distasteful thoughts; compulsion—repetitive behaviors or mental act, like excessive handwashing and counting, to ward off dreaded events to reduce stress.
Posttraumatic stress disorder (PTSD): Experiencing or witnessing a life-threatening event results in anxiety symptoms, such as flashbacks, nightmares, sleep problems, intense distress, withdrawal, hypervigilance (little bit like paranoia), concentration difficulties, and exaggerated startle response (jumping in response to a loud noise).

Treatment: Although fear and love are the root emotions, anxiety symptoms indicate unresolved grief, in my opinion. Anxiety symptoms are like the lid on a boiling pot that shakes. Anxiety is the clue that intense emotions rage below—sadness, grief—which needs to be released. Medications, like Clonipin, Valium, and Xanax, are addictive substances that mask problems and should be reserved for acute symptom relief. Focusing—using the focusing process to figure out what's really bothering you—to guide you to make life changes to reduce your stress level provides a more permanent healing approach. Psychotherapy includes support, desensitization, hypnosis, eye movement desensitization reprocessing, emotional freedom therapy, and stress management or relaxation techniques.
Per Internet, famous people with OCD: Howard Hughes and numerous other celebrities

Bipolar disorders

Definition and symptoms: People are familiar with Bipolar I disorder—the biochemically based mental illness. People affected by Bipolar cycle from severe manic episodes symptoms, such as being on the go, not sleeping for days, not having boundaries, impulsiveness, overspending, oversexing, overdoing, overtalking, generally being over-the-top, either being grandiose or paranoid and irritable until their biochemistry depletes and then they crash into depression—not moving, talking much, withdrawing from everyone in life and feeling hopeless, guilty, and suicidal.
Bipolar II disorder may go unnoticed yet is still a serious medical condition that is biochemically based and needs treatment. It does not follow clear cycles, nor are the highs and lows as extreme as in Bipolar I, so the problem is not as obvious. People with this disorder are still on an emotional roller coaster. Their thoughts race. They act like someone with ADHD although they may be better organized. Their moods are

very changeable. They can become irritable and mean over trivia. They may function fairly well, like holding a job and meeting family responsibilities. Likewise, overworked mothers may get what I call "Bipolarish III."

Cause or etiology: Genetic predisposition (runs in families). However, there is a difference between genotype (your genetic predisposition) and phenotype (what you develop in real life). By keeping your stress down and keeping healthy routines in sleeping, eating, and exercising, you can prevent underlying conditions or disorders from manifesting and affecting you. This goes for all disorders.

Treatment: Regular healthy routines, especially regular sleep times, are necessary to control bipolar disorder.

Psychotherapy helps to help the client maintain a stable lifestyle, as well as focuses on helping them learn to express and solve problems maturely rather than "act out" to stop bottling up feelings and needs and then go "chase something shiny" by "putting one's running shoes on," which is the typical way people with bipolar disorder use to release their inner cocktail of positive mood, enhancing neurotransmitters (where in an acceptable fashion was) because they can do this themselves without having to go to a bar. In therapy, they learn to slow down and think before acting to express appropriate needs so they can work out interpersonal issues maturely. Bipolar is a form of depression; unipolar forms of depression are described next. Bipolar is a chemical imbalance, which shouldn't be treated with an SSRI (Selective Serotonin Reuptake Inhibitor), like for Unipolar depression, because the bipolar person knows how to increase their serotonin, and too much can have adverse side effects, mania, and increased depression "because what goes up must come down" so SSRIs like Paxil, Zoloft, Cymbalta, Prozac, Lexapro, etc. are appropriate only for those with unipolar depression. The problem is people rarely do come in to visit their PEPs and complain about being very happy "manic"; they only complain about depression, giving the doctor the misimpression that they have a unipolar instead of a bipolar depression.

Medications, which I have observed clients to receive, include Lamictal or lamatrisine for the irritable outbursts or some form of atypical antidepressant like Wellbutrin with a mood stabilizer, like Lithium or Abilify usually combined with Cogentin to control Abilify potential side effects. An antidepressant by itself is too stimulating to control "me-mania," so combination of atypical antidepressant (not SSRI) with a mood stabilizer of a medication with born like Latuda, which relieves depression while controlling mania, is used.

Per Internet, famous people with Bipolar disorder: Abraham Lincoln, Ernest Hemingway, Patty Duke, Linda Hamilton, Vivien Leigh, Robin Williams, Jimi Hendrix (also substance abuse), Edgar Allen Poe, Virginia Woolf, Vincent Van Gogh, and numerous other celebrities

Depression

Definition and symptoms: A depressed mood (feeling low, down, blue, hopeless), lack of interest or ability to take pleasure in life events, over- or undersleeping (early morning awakening and not being able to get back to sleep), under- or overeating with weight loss or gain, low energy, feelings of worthlessness, low self-esteem, impaired concentration, social withdrawal, and impaired life functioning.

Types include:

Major depression: All the above symptoms, including intense guilt, suicidal thoughts, plans and possibly attempts, and inability to function.

Dysthymia: Chronic mild depression for about two years or more. Both of these types are a body chemistry problem. The next two are more situational unless they have what we call the vegetative symptoms that indicate the body chemistry is out of whack, like eating and sleeping problems.

Postpartum depression: Depression following childbirth.

Grief: Reaction to loss.

Situational depression: Sad reaction to life stress.

Cause or etiology: Genetic predisposition for depression—significant losses, disappointments, negative thinking or interpretation of events, and low self-esteem that can lead to a biochemical imbalance.

Treatment: Under age twenty-five, antidepressant medication is associated with increased suicidal risks. Otherwise, SSRI medication is usually helpful. There are natural alternatives to medication: St. John's Wort, a herbal SSRI, and the omega-3s and omega-6s—flaxseed and fish oil (fatty acids). Normal people who do not get a good night's sleep are found to be depressed, so the first line of attack would be to help people get a good night's sleep. Natural remedies include hops, melatonin, Quietude, chamomile, Sleepytime tea. It is also important to reduce caffeine and sugar—not drink coffee or iced tea, for example, after eleven o'clock in the morning, believe it or not. Aerobic-style exercise, including walking for at least thirty minutes, three times a week or more raises your serotonin, the biochemical responsible for positive mood. Cognitive behavior therapy—positive thinking—is the most effective treatment to eradicate the negative core beliefs that the person is not good and has no power over their life. Taking one's power back and setting boundaries so that one can take care of oneself is essential. Grief needs to be released.

Depression can be a vicious cycle. Depressed people withdraw from life. Research shows that if a depressed person engages in pleasurable daily activities, it will help the depression lift. Variety is the spice of life. For depression, schedule in personal satisfying or well-rounded activities every day for at least one to two hours (see chapter 8, "Be A Whole, Fulfilled Person). For example, include physical activity at least three times a week, uplifting spiritual or religious practices, mentally stimulating or creative hobbies, like reading, crafts, etc., and social interactions which are vital—even if you need to start by chatting with neighbors or talking on the phone with friends and then eventually join a recreational group of your choice.

Per Internet, famous people with depression: Brooke Shields, Princess Diana, Hans Christian Andersen, Michelangelo, Charles Dickens, Peter Tchaikovsky, Robert Louis Stevenson, Ralph Waldo Emerson, Irving Berlin, F. Scott Fitzgerald, Ernest Hemingway, and numerous other celebrities.

Dissociative identity disorder (DID)

Definition and symptoms: This is a much more common disorder than previously realized—even by psychotherapists. Believe it or not, you know people that have this—people close to you that you interact with regularly. We need a celebrity to come forth with this diagnosis to raise our awareness about its prevalence—like Karen Carpenter's death from anorexia nervosa raised our awareness about eating disorders. DID is currently misdiagnosed or co-occurring with Bipolar disorder and borderline personality disorder.

A person with DID has two or more distinct identity or personality states, which are often perceived by others as just being moody. These identities or states have distinct patterns of thinking, perceiving, and relating to the world. The different identities—also known as alters—are experienced by the person like switching eyes or sunglasses with different tints. For example, if you came into a room with no glasses on, the room would seem normal. If you wore rose-colored glasses, the room would seem pink. The person with DID switches from one alter to another, so the perspective switches.

Only one alter can be out at a time, although the rest are suspected to be listening in. The host personality often does the integrating or interacting with the everyday life functioning to manage the person's life. Other common parts or alters include student or worker, part that holds emotions like depression and anxiety and may have panic attacks, a tough guy or controller or intimidator protector part whose "terminator" job is triggered by stress or conflict to protect the host from the enemy, the person with whom he or she is experiencing current stress, a therapist or internal self-helper or guide, etc.

The original personality may tend to be insecure, depressive, or introverted. This type of person may be withdrawn to keep stress and conflict down. Too much going on causes the switching to occur. People who have this disorder do not realize they have it because this is all they have ever known.

They look ADD-ish or very moody to others because they lose time to some degree, depending on the degree of what's called coconsciousness—which depends on how thick the amnesia walls are between the parts. The person's experience is like what you might experience if you were reading a book while someone is watching television. You may pick up the name of the show or some significant action, but you would not own responsibility that you were watching the show or know the details because you are reading a book. People who have this disorder are often accused of lying, but they have actually just switched and one of their parts did something, and when that "part goes away," the other part comes out and has difficulty recalling personal information, including important events. Another indicator of DID is that a person may be able to see themselves—for example, see themselves pouring orange juice or walking down the steps.

The defense mechanism they use is dissociation. Normal dissociation means escaping into a TV show, movie, or book temporarily to get a break from reality. In the case of dissociative identity disorder, which is a major mental illness, the dissociation is pathological. As a child, the person may have been in a chronically abusive or neglectful situation from which they could not, for example, get in a car and run to a therapist's office to get some help. So the child created a way to escape the situation by creating identities to handle these bad situations so the original self could go away and not experience them.

Associated features: In my opinion, pedophiles or child molesters often have undiagnosed and untreated DID. They were sexually abused as children, and they have been sexually acting out parts that came or originated to handle the abuse. These parts later in life get triggered by situations that resemble the abuse experiences that happened to them. For example, a child was sexually abused at age eight and, as an adult, is sexually attracted to eight-year-olds. That is how the cycle of abuse occurs. The part or alter does not have the big picture, like access to the painful feelings that the person had as a child when he or she was being sexually abused. The sexually acting out part has only the limited viewpoint of what the sexual experience was like. It's not that he or she doesn't remember the feelings; he or she never had the feelings. Another alter has the feelings and the ability to be empathic. The sexual part or alter has the ability to be sexual. People with DID commonly have other disorders; different alters have different disorders, including somatoform disorder (excessive worry and preoccupation with physical complaints because of repressed negative emotions), borderline personality disorder, depression, eating disorders, etc.

Cause or etiology: Developmentally, babies have four distinct states of being—the sleeping baby, the fussy baby, the crying baby, and the quiet or awake baby (after their needs have been taken care of). Infants do not actually realize that they are one distinct baby. In other words, the crying baby does not realize that it is the sleeping baby.

When the baby is between the ages of two and three years old, he or she develops a state of being called the authorial-self—the author of the self or observer of self. This part helps the baby begin to understand that it is one flowing unit. Just as we understand that we go to sleep, we may wake up feeling kind of groggy, yet we are still the same person. When a young child, from the age of two to eight years old, experiences chronic traumatic incidents, physiological arousal is heightened. They are not able to comprehend what is happening and thus do not integrate the different parts of the self into one self properly.

This is the beginning of dissociative identity disorder. The person, who may have an intelligent creative artistic type of temperament, employs dissociation to escape situations. They create a part of their brain to handle the incident. When the trauma passes, the host personality comes back out. Just like wearing your four-year-old shoes would be too tight for an adult, once the adult has left the abusive family of origin—dissociation—which has become a habitual way of being becomes troublesome. For example, a woman who was raped near an elevator may have amnesia about this, but the part that holds the memory will be triggered by the sight of the elevator. The person will experience a panic attack without knowing why and will be passively influenced. They often have parts that act out sexually if they have been abused this way. The host personality will not feel responsible for the sexual acting out. People with DID hear voices in their head kind of arguing with each other or talking with each other, but they think it is their own inner voice. Significant others of people with DID often feel jerked around because of the changeability of the person, which they attribute to moodiness. They wonder sometimes, "Who am I talking to?" or "Didn't we just agree?" In other words, the person with DID is inconsistent and does not make sense.

Treatment: This is a psychological, not a biochemical, disorder. It is treatable and curable by long-term psychotherapy. This has five phases, which are ongoing diagnosis to help the person realize they have the disorder. First, diagnosis is by dissociative evaluations scale and by the therapist, asking alters to "come out" once the client feels safe with the therapist. Second, the client begins to identify the part of his inner system—the different identities or alters or mood states. Third, the client's parts begin to communicate with one another—to make decisions as a group harmoniously—so that the body can handle life in a consistent manner. In other words, they work together. Eventually at the grief and trauma resolution stage, the parts share sensitive secrets about the trauma and do the healing work. Finally, they integrate to one self or develop a working harmony so the person can have a decent life.

Per Internet, famous people with dissociative identity disorder: Herschel Walker, a famous football player and Heisman Trophy winner, in his book *Breaking Free*, has recently admitted that he is being treated for DID. I am so proud of him for coming forth to try to help people be aware that this disorder is much more common than we thought and that people can be successful with it. DID, formerly known as multiple personality disorder, can allow the person to multitask and avoid periods of stress or pain through losing time (amnesia). There can be dire consequences because each part may not realize he is part of the greater whole and may do things that are dangerous. Psychotherapy is essential.

According to his biographer who met with him intimately for several years and by top court psychologist covering the case, singer Michael Jackson has it—as well as numerous other celebrities. According to Dorothy Lewis, colleague of Frank Putnam who pioneered this area, violent criminals, etc., have DID and/or a temporal lobe brain dysfunction. Anybody who, between the ages of two and eight, experienced significant trauma or abuse or even loss (for example, father dies, followed by mother seriously depressed, significant life upheavals, including sibling abuse) may have DID.

Movies like *Fight Club*, *Sybil*, *Secret Window*, and *Hide and Seek* dramatize severe DID—no coconsciousness and thick amnesia walls between personality parts or alters.

Personality disorders

Definition and symptoms: Personality disorders can only be diagnosed in adults, although the pattern usually appears in adolescents. They are rigid personality traits or patterns that do not change with situations. Often, they are people who stress out other people because of inappropriate ways of relating or emotional reactions or interpretations to the situations. The personality disorder impairs the person socially, occupationally, or in other ways of their life. There are about ten types (such as paranoid, schizoid, histrionic, avoidant, borderline, and narcissistic to be described below) listed in the *Diagnostic and Statistical Manual of Mental Disorders*, which is helping professional use.

Cause or etiology: During the first five years of life, a personality structure is formed based on the child's family environment—particularly during the first two to three years when they form an attachment with their parents based on whether their parents care for them properly and provide a secure home base. Abandonment, trauma, abuse, neglect, and even subtle forms of this reflect behavior. Whenever the parents' ego is more important than the child's well-being, maladaptive learning occurs, and the child develops an impaired personality or personality disorder.

Borderline personality disorder (BPD)

Definition and symptoms: A personality that is unstable in terms of interpersonal relating, self-image, emotion, and even perception of reality at times. The person with BPD has intense feelings of abandonment, is hypersensitive, and can go into rages when they feel that they are being abandoned. They may manipulate with self-mutilation or engage in suicidal threats or behaviors to avoid separation. Their relationships are intense and unstable. They view their significant others as either wonderful and overidealized or awful and devalued—black or white, no in-between. They are impulsive in at least two areas that are potentially destructive: overspending, eating disorders, substance abuse, sexual acting out, reckless driving, and so on. They tend to feel empty and depressed.

Cause or Etiology: During the first two to three years of life, the normal child develops a sense of self and trust in others and the world. The person who develops BPD does not have this stable personality foundation because he did not have a home life or relationship with his primary caretaker, usually the mother, that helped him feel secure. This could be related to a loss or abandonment by the mother figure, mothering by multiple caretakers, and/or inconsistent behavior by the primary caretaker. Nine-month-olds experience separation anxiety because when the mother leaves the room, the baby does not have the understanding that the mother will ever return. In the baby's mind, the mother no longer exists because the baby has not developed intellectually to be able to hold that thought in its mind that things exist when they are not in its sight. The person with BPD suffers from this same lack or impaired viewpoint, and that is why he cannot tolerate any little sign of rejection or abandonment. He uses the defense mechanism of splitting—perceiving everything as good or bad. He views himself as bad when independent and good when dependent. The majority of people with BPD are female, and they do tend to mellow out in their thirties or forties.

Treatment: Cognitive behavior therapy and dialectical behavior therapy to build the inner security that they never got and long-term support.

Narcissistic personality disorder (NPD) and closet narcissistic personality disorder

Definition and symptoms: Many people are familiar with exhibitionist NPD—the person who is grandiose, egotistical, selfish, self-serving, vain, jealous, competitive, power tripping, out for himself or herself, lacking empathy, and constantly seeking admiration and attention. What most people don't know is that there is a closet type of NPD.

Closet NPD has many of the same characteristics, yet they're expressed more subtly. The person gets a sense of grandiosity by rubbing shoulders with, flattering, or complimenting others and then basking in the reflected glow of their greatness. Such people are actually cold and lack empathy, although they can fake it. They're underassertive pleasers who feel good as long as they look good to others. They lack any real passions of their own because they need others to validate them. People with NPD may sometimes look like saints, but their interpersonal skills more often have a hit-and-run quality. For example, a man who has commitment issues is in a relationship and his live-in girlfriend goes out of town. Then he picks up another woman in a bar and goes to bed with her because he senses she's depressed and thinks one night of his attention will make her feel better (an interpersonal hit-and-run).

Narcissists are like addicts. They spend a lot of time and energy procuring their drug—attention and approval—getting high, recovering, and beginning the cycle over again. Yet their actions end up hurting others. To get their fix, they come across as someone caring, with a pleasing personality. Once they have your attention and approval, they move on to get a fix from someone else. If pleasing someone else means double-crossing you, they'll do it. It's like having a cleaning lady who steals from you. Actually, she has an antisocial personality disorder, is the narcissist crossing the legal lines, or is a best friend who spills your secrets in a distorted, mean-spirited way to others.

When a narcissist says something negative about you, she's revealing something about herself that won't make her look good, some insecurity she needs to project. The goal of the narcissist, even the pleasing closet type, is to feel good all the time by gaining approval. The closet narcissist can't admit that she may be wrong. She needs to make you feel she never intended to hurt you. If you do confront her, her reaction might be to say she's sorry you feel that way and appease you for the moment to get the approval fix. But if that doesn't work, she'll project out blame quickly to another "you" in some way.

That's why you may find yourself being constantly belittled in a relationship. For example, you may know a helpful person in your life who erodes your self-esteem, at the same time making himself look good, even better, because he's helping someone so unworthy. In the process, he makes you feel dependent and in need of his help, thereby ensuring his future fix. The simple equation is everything good is about the narcissist, and everything bad is about someone else. That's the splitting mechanism, how the narcissist discharges shame he accumulated at age two.

According to Erikson, a widely accepted understanding of the personality stages is that from ages two to three, children develop a sense of self and trust in the world. It occurs, or it's impaired. As you've seen in the discussion of DID in this chapter, a baby has no sense of integrated self. The crying baby doesn't know it's also the sleeping baby. Around age two, an authorial or observing self develops who begins to become self-aware. A child who learns to move away from her mother and play in her environment while maintaining a sense of security is a healthy child. When a toddler is encouraged to explore from a safe home base and the mother stands by, ready to provide love, support, comfort, soothing, help, and reassurance, the child learns that it's okay to break away from Mom. He can then become himself and love himself. But if Mom doesn't make herself available in a supporting role or just imposes her needs on her child, the child never learns to separate properly or develop a sense of self. This is called the rapprochement phase, when the toddler begins to be himself, trusting that the world, as based on his parent's unconditional love, will support his authentic passions, needs, and feelings.

Sometimes in narcissistic families where there has been sexual abuse, the parent who wasn't the abuser allowed it to happen or denies later that it happened and didn't protect the child at any time. For example, there was a recent out-of-court settlement because a mother refused to believe her daughter and protected her abusing husband. In another instance, a grandmother allowed her granddaughter to be chronically sexually abused while under her care. When asked why, she replied that she needed to fix everybody's dinner. She had a lot of people to attend to, and she blamed the mother for being a worrier and the four-year-old for being sexually seductive. In other words, the narcissist believes, "I'm a saint. I'm doing for others. You're all the bad ones. You confuse me by being worrisome. I was helping others. You're ungrateful. The child is to blame." No responsibility taken, but big damage done. That's the self-centered "I can't be bothered. I'm busy getting a fix" (approval for preparing dinner).

This particular narcissist would keep the family fat and disabled. They were her fix, and her cooking was their fix. It got so bad that one day when she was out shopping, her husband kept going to the kitchen, looking for her. When he came downstairs for the third time, his adult son tried to reassure him that mom was fine and probably running late. The husband replied that he was only looking for her to make him a grilled cheese sandwich. He was dependent on the narcissist, which brought him down to a lower level of narcissism (not concerned about his missing wife, just missing food). Disabled from his feelings, he lacked the willingness to carry out preparing his own food. He was unable to think about his wife apart from his dependent relationship upon her—disrupting his capacity to be concerned about her independently.

Even though not truly NPD, many people who are addictive in anyway—including the chemically dependents, codependents, and workaholics whose moral compass skewed—are being reduced to a narcissist level of functioning by their addictions. It's all about the addiction. What's convenient. What allows them their high. Once they release their addictions, they can interact at a nonnarcissistic level.

Another aspect of any dysfunction is that birds of a feather flock together. People with certain issues or personality problems or traumas are drawn to each other through the unconscious law of attraction. Like attracts like. Although there are no real victims, anyone who is with a narcissist is probably being manipulated by the narcissist—even though he may not realize it. Snared by the narcissist's belittling that causes him to feel unworthy, he does whatever is convenient for the narcissist—acting out the narcissism projection. By becoming the narcissist's subject, he's betrayed and betraying himself. This includes acting self-destructively. For example, a child with dyslexia goes to a special school and is progressing well when the narcissistic father insists that the child become a "real" man by going to military school. Now a teen and wanting to look macho to prove himself to his father and family, the child sacrifices his own well-being to assuage his father's ego.

About 1 percent of the population suffers from NPD. Teenagers typically go through a narcissistic phase; it doesn't mean they're going to end up with NPD. People with DID often have an NPD part, person or alter, which comes out or switch into at times. When people are heavily addicted, they may behave narcissistically. Systems can affect people to behave narcissistically too. See Zimbardo's new book, *The Lucifer Effect*.

Cause or etiology: Like all personality disorders, NPD is rooted in the first five years of life. The child who has NPD as an adult swas usually forced to create a "false self" to please a parent or other caretaker. Because the parent never displayed an interest in the child's well-being, the child never learned to act in his own self-interest. Repressing his real self becomes ingrained, and he comes to rely on his false self to interact with the world.

Here's an example: A little girl grows up in a small town, living with her parents in her grandfather's home. She's his pride and joy, and he lavishes gifts on her while her parents are busy working. But when her mother comes home, she's aloof. When the girl is five, her grandfather remarries and has a child of his own, so her family is forced to move out. When her grandfather never comes to visit her, she concludes that he was just using her. She uses the false self she created to please him to become a closet narcissist as an adult, and it usually works for her. She's generally well-liked and very popular, but she also dumps on others and neglects them when it suits her, like her once-doting grandfather, her narcissistic role model.

One day, a neighbor asks the grown-up girl to watch over the neighbor's house while she goes off to care for her sick mother. The woman agrees but promptly forgets her promise and even says, "I wouldn't notice if somebody came and actually picked up and took the house away." But the neighbor is none the wiser and thinks this woman is a good friend.

Narcissus-speak—the language of narcissism: Narcissism is explained in the Greek myth about Narcissus, a boy who tragically became enamored of his own reflection in a pool of water. He believed it was another person, the love of his life. He remained transfixed, unable to stop gazing at this own image.

Personality disorders usually begin to develop between ages two and three—set by age five or so. All of them, to some degree, contain narcissistic features. To speak the narcissist way, all you have to do is reverse everything unrealistic or offensive that a narcissist says. When the narcissist seems to express your viewpoint, he's really expressing his own, not empathizing. When he points out that you're doing something wrong, he means that he's doing something wrong.

To communicate with a narcissist, mentally reverse all the pronouns he uses and respond to your translation. If he says "I," he's referring to "you." If he says "you," he's actually speaking about himself. The closet narcissist appears to be empathic, feigning sympathy or other emotions, but really feels nothing. He'll do whatever it takes to make himself look good. Without an authentic sense of self, he's incapable of displaying real emotions. He has no inner experience to draw from.

Narcissists aren't unhappy; the people around them are when neglected or abused.

So if you're involved with a narcissist, narcissist-speak (Narcissus-speak) is a wonderful way to respond—to communicate without frustration, to set boundaries, and to avoid being wounded time and time again. When you respond to the reverse of what a narcissist says, he will often agree with you. Your viewpoint is the narcissist's viewpoint. Remember, he has no real ability to empathize. He's wearing a mirror that reflects back his own viewpoint, but he misperceives it as others' viewpoints. He can't even see other people behind the mirror, even know they're there.

Everyone projects at times, so narcissist-speak can be used whenever you need to help someone get a firmer grip on reality. To some degree, everyone has eight-track tapes replaying in their heads, distorting perceptions and the filter through which they see the world. While teenagers are going through their narcissist phase, narcissist-speak can come in useful in communicating with them—as well as open-ended mentoring comments.

Another technique for helping narcissists back off their grandiosity is to exaggerate their statements. Mirroring is what it is all about. When you reframe their I statement to "you" with empathy, you'll be accepted wholeheartedly by narcissists because your response indicates appreciation and deep understanding of them.

In fact, mirroring is the heart of therapy with personality disorders. It helps people gain perspective and release the inner wounds of childhood. By exaggerating what they say, the light in the mirror becomes so blinding even they themselves must adjust their perspective. For example, a narcissist who feels stupid may say, "Black people are stupid." His colleague responds, "Do we think we should lynch them all?" It's a basic exaggeration and obviously doesn't make the narcissist look good. So he refrains from making other racist comments.

You can't win an argument with a narcissist because his reality is too distorted. To be right, he'll lie outright. The narcissist I just mentioned stated that his favorite athlete had the most home runs. The next day, the colleague brought in the world-renowned sports almanac showing that another athlete held the record. The narcissist replied, "They never get their facts right!"

To come to terms with a narcissist, you have to be aware of and accept the narcissism. Ask her to come up with a solution but don't expect it to include your needs. After you consider the solution, say, "Okay, this covers all your wants. Now let's see if I can get one or two things." To look fair-minded, the narcissist will agree, and then you can insert yourself by way of admiring the narcissist.

It's best to not interact with a narcissist if at all possible. If you're already married to one, divorced—with children—from one, or blood relative to one, use these techniques to set boundaries and learn to speak their language so you're not frustrated or abused.

How do you function in a narcissist system, family organization, legal system, or society? By recognizing that the system serves its own agenda. Individuals are weak links and expendable. To survive, you need a highly differentiated sense of self. This begins with mindfulness—realizing that you're in a narcissistic system hell-bent to keep you dependent while someone else has all the power. Systems, however, are dependent on individuals for information and support.

Take the legal system, for example. The lawyer is dependent upon the client for information and follow-through on the lawyer's instructions. The client must maintain a healthy sense of self and speak honestly at all times—as well as use empathic narcissist-speak to unravel distortions and foster truth and justice. This empowers the narcissistic legal—litigatory—system to focus on the larger goal of good. Narcissist-speak is in no way harmful or disrespectful. It enhances the self-development and the growth for all, including the narcissist.

Narcissist-speak can be extended to the systems level, specifically to the legal—litigation—system, which by its adversarial nature is a narcissistic system. Attorneys essentially are asked to function or act as narcissists. Their viewpoint is the only right viewpoint. Their client is pure white as the driven snow. The opposing attorney's client is all dark and evil. Therefore, surprisingly, court is not about seeking truth or justice. It is about winning. Even winning through misrepresentations, lies, distortions to prove one's point and wind up on top—in the battle. This is why that it is best not to get embroiled in a legal battle (avoid narcissistic people and systems) and to mediate all legal differences if at all possible. If you are unfortunate to be embroiled in a legal battle, it is best to accept the narcissist—adversarial—positions of the lawyers and unravel the misleading communication simultaneously accepting that the narcissist will be unable to see beyond their viewpoint and balance reality or work toward truth and justice. The jury who is assuming normal communication is going on and is not translating the trial communication, and the judge who does understand that this is a narcissist theater will appreciate some help weeding out of this dysfunction. Remember that all lawyers are not narcissists. They are just asked to take this role by the system. Of course, being a narcissist helps facilitate this process wheel as systems or roles can affect people.

Lawyers need to function as social workers to encourage mediation in the legal arena. If you find yourself in the legal arena, slow down the communication process—pause, keep in mind your sense of self and truth at all times, and speak from this place of inner strength. At the current American societal level, we find narcissism operating in the war in Iraq. The civilians of Iraq who have never done anything to us, one can see, are victims (though we know there are no true victims) of societal narcissism. Our inflated sense of ourselves and our heightened fear has led us to act this out on innocent people.

By mirroring back to the individual or system the reality being projected, you help them own it, gain perspective, and get a real sense of self. As a listener, you're truly being empathic to the narcissist as well as staying true to your own self, which has the capacity for empathy. If you blindly or gullibly follow a narcissist, you run the risk of developing a mild form of posttraumatic stress disorder (PTSD), anxiety, and depression.

When this dark shadow appears in your life, follow these four steps of narcissist-speak (Narcissus-speak) to dispel the negative energy buried in you. Rather than getting PTSD, use reverse PTSD:

> P—Pause
> T—Translate in your head
> S—State the opposite and reveal the truth
> D—Detach

For example, if the narcissist says you're happy, she is saying she is happy.

Narcissists, because of their grandiose reality distortions to convey an image of perfection to themselves and others, speak of their own and others' wishes and fears as if they are real. Remember this when you translate what they say. A teen going through a narcissistic phase may take credit for something he didn't do, possibly to make a good impression on a new friend. Maybe it's something you wish he would do. When he says, "I always take out the trash," you say, "I wish you would always take out the trash." Another example is the narcissistic man who fears that if he tells his new girlfriend truthfully that he's only separated, not divorced, she'll reject him. If this narcissistic man is your friend, you might encourage him to be honest so he won't get caught in a lie later in the relationship and get into trouble. He takes your advice, comes clean with his girlfriend, and isn't rejected. But then he says to you, "You were wrong. I wasn't rejected." You remind him, "But you feared rejection. I advised you to be up-front, and it worked."

The person with NPD wears a box around his head, blocking his view. His head is surrounded by a trifold mirror, reflecting his own image and viewpoint. This is a defense mechanism. It is invisible. You don't know it, and he doesn't know it. The world and you are in his blind spot. He cannot see you.

Whenever what's said isn't consistent with reality and seems designed only to make the narcissist look good, usually at your expense (the projection of a negative onto others to maintain that "looking good" fix), it's your cue to translate what's been said into real terms. Don't take it to heart. Be of a higher heart. Send love, not fear. Recognize in your communication empathy for everyone.

Treatment: Long-term psychotherapy is best, but it's often difficult to get someone with NPD to seek it because the narcissist doesn't feel pain—he just inflicts it on others.

Famous narcissists and narcissistically wounded individuals: Many narcissists have used it to accomplish great things, including scientists and artists, but their personal relationships were often rocky because they exploited people.

Closet narcissists are often underassertive, pleasing types who prefer to associate with high achievers but who will sometimes slip and display surprising coldness and lack of empathy. Closet narcissists often escape detection because people tend to take them at face value and not know the underlying cause of their hit-and-run behavior.

Many achievers contribute to the world out of their narcissist wounds. As a child, if your parents displayed narcissism, you believed their subtle belittlement because you thought they were being honest with you. You tend to see yourself as your parents saw themselves. As a child, you didn't have the sophistication to distinguish truth from illusion. Instead, you believe it when they say you aren't good enough, and that belief becomes part of your superego or conscience.

Your shadow then is the narcissistic wound from your parent. As an adult, you carry this pain thinking it's your true self, but it's only your shadow self—the shadow that creates difficulties in your life. You develop defense mechanisms to protect yourself temporarily, but you can never use the law of attraction purely because of the unconscious negative energy that's projected. True change requires separating yourself from the pain your parent passed down to you.

Since you are a spiritual being who came into this world with some abandonment issues with God, you need your parents to reassure you that you are at earth school now and came from spirit. But if they themselves have been narcissistically wounded in any way, they can't guide you from spiritual form to earth form. They're not emotionally available to help you understand that God didn't abandon you but gave you a different form to express God. You need their unconditional love to help adjust. But instead, you absorb their narcissist projections, and it reinforces your sense of abandonment. Children who grow up like this think the world isn't safe and they are bad, unworthy souls who are never good enough, no matter what they achieve. These beliefs play out in suffering and in attracting unhealthy relationships, although they may achieve a great deal. And unless they receive insight usually from some form of psychological and spiritual healing, emotional pain and scars get passed down from one generation to the next.

Super high IQ

Definition and symptoms: Genius intelligence (150 IQ compared to the average person's IQ of 100) or even genius ability in certain areas of intelligence. Some have postulated that very high intelligence is a form of brain damage. The person may not be able to relate to others. They cannot filter out their own high-level ideas.

Treatment: Supportive psychotherapy and Mensa—an association for the gifted

Per Internet, famous people with a superior or above-high IQ: Ted Bundy (120?), Isaac Newton, Albert Einstein, Leonardo Da Vinci, Galileo, Nicholas Copernicus, and Charles Darwin

Famous people categories: Any reference to celebrities with disorders was obtained through the Internet famous people Google search engine and was not meant as definitive diagnosis. I personally have never met these people. This information is disseminated to the public by Google and was included to let people know that they are not alone.

> Everybody has normal life lessons or challenges. Which one of these twelve ego issues fits you? Lack of responsibility; overtalking, not listening; codependency or pacifying others; lack of humility or too much ego; communication problems; competitiveness or lack of cooperation; self-absorption or temper or impulsiveness; "can't see the forest for the trees;" loss or test of faith with fluctuating empathy; over-materialism; lack of forgiveness of self and others; and bottling up feelings or over-caretaking. Focus on growing in this area.

Disclaimer

The following are my original ideas and opinions based on well-accepted clinical knowledge and applying it to the broader concept of our world's ills. These ideas devise a parsimonious theory about what causes mankind's most difficult problems—aggression, conflict, and evil, if you will—in our world and how most simply they can be addressed and how these issues can be cured.

Cure the World's ills

Following is a theoretical framework or foundational information for you, the reader, to not only understand and benefit from knowledge to improve yourself, help others learn how to improve to become their best selves, and, more importantly, transform the world by transforming negativity/evil into good. By grasping this knowledge, we can advocate for mental health and medical and nongovernmental and governmental systems to relearn basic principles to improve the care of people.

The crucial goal is to get us to rethink and erase the screwed-up results of our misuse of our creative power and talent, namely our innate ability to create our lives through our own inner choice of positive thinking and positive self-talk. Google *Science of Mind*. Not to continue to ignorantly, innocently, inadvertently think damaging cognitions or spew negative self-talk thoughts, which are out picture and contaminate and damage our life. We tarnish our destiny through our own negative self-statements or inner self-talk.

Through negative thinking, we misuse our words. Our verb, our godlike faculties, is our free will and ability to cocreate our lives. Sometimes we underestimate our power through ignorance, through innocently misusing the power of our words and thinking, not realizing that our thoughts are like prayers, and through negative self-talk, we inadvertently contribute to the manufacture of mental and physical diseases and suffering of all kinds on earth!

According to the Bible, before Adam and Eve ate from The Tree of Knowledge of Good and Evil, incurring original sin, they were in paradise agelessly, blissfully enjoying the lush garden of Eden, flying and levitating luxuriously in their warm nakedness with their ultimate loving higher being. When suddenly, with the gulp of the fruit of Knowledge of Good and Evil open their awareness of the knowledge that there could be evil and realize the possibility of anti-paradise through negative thinking.

The not good, not perfect can occur at their request; they realize that not all good is possible as well as all good; in life could be bad and then they spew their first negative thought, "What will God think of us being nude?" They experienced their first negative emotion and shame even though, until now, they have lived a naked, blissful life in ignorance. God will now, all of sudden, be mad and upset at their nakedness!

With this simple negative thought and the fear that ensued, therefore, they fled, hiding themselves in shame! Hence, the original sin is simply knowing you can think negatively—not knowledge like God's ideas. Their discomfort with their nudity is the initial example of our power of free will to think negatively and thereby create negativity in ourselves and our earth. Our thoughts create the feeling. The feelings change how we relate and cause our behavior. The way we behave determines the outcome of our life situation. Look at the results we face in today's times from knowing we can think negatively!

Thus, the ultimate mission to help mankind is to return to its intended original state of positive thinking, the core of paradise from which we have run in shame far amok. Although now, in psychology, we have uncovered the vital need for positive thinking or positive self-talk—which we know as helping professionals and aspire to teach and promote as the most effective form of psychotherapy known as Cognitive Behavior Therapy (cognition equals thought). We have uncovered the value of positive thinking and self-talk, which is encapsulated in Cognitive Behavior Therapy, well known now as the most effective type of therapy utilized by most helping professionals or therapists or counselors.

As the most effective form of therapy, it works because cognitions (means thoughts) turn into life outcomes. Changing your thoughts that change your feelings, behaviors, and your life outcomes is how we create our destiny.

We are still infested with deep subliminal unconscious or subconscious underground layers of negative thoughts, muck, and mud that we need unstuck and thereby undo in our psyches, which will unloosen the chains and heal the pains in our world.

Following is how to uncover and unburden our fears and terror-driven false beliefs. FEAR is an acronym that means *False Evidence Appearing Real*. We have to hunt and track these down and expel them to return to the paradise we deserve, thereby unburdening and releasing unconscious triggered traumatic memories and erasing these crippling fallacies or delusions within our self-individual's false beliefs and collective belief systems or prejudices of groups, which hold us imprisoned in our current, sometimes miserable, human experience.

Through this illustrious tale, an Indian shaman explained this process, whereby we misuse our free will to create our lives and instead downgrade our lives and our human experience. A man was resting peacefully, sitting cross-legged in a beautiful forest, enjoying nature, when a thought popped into his head that he wished he had some food to eat because he was hungry. All of sudden, a luscious picnic appeared in front of him, and he gobbled it up, satisfied. Then he wished he had something to drink. What appeared? A goblet of his favorite juice, which he drank happily to the last drop. Then the man began to panic and thought negative thoughts, worried.

"How did this happen? Are the woods full of ghosts?" he feared.

Then, of course, true to form, the ghosts appeared. The man was so frightened instead of thanking the ghost for his delicious meal, he shook, trembling, negatively thinking that the ghost might eat him and kill him. Then, of course, given that our thoughts are prayers based on the power of this man's God-given free will to create his destiny through the power of his thought, his word—the ghost did just that as he predicted and gobbled him up! This is not a scary story—but a reality of how important it is to be positive! You are creating your life!

When you (the client) enter my office for the first time, you will have "a lot of fun paperwork" to fill out about yourself. I give tests because problems that impair lives and functioning have causes or roots in underlying mind, body, and spirit dysfunction, which, if ignored, not assessed, diagnosed, and understood, can make helping the person to be able to fix their problems futile because of the lack of identifying the root problems in the dysfunction. So it is vital to do proper diagnosing as well as relay these results to the client so we can work on these root causes of what brings the individual into therapy. Do not just focus on the precipitant, problems in living, or symptoms because the client's issues of daily problems are just the tip of the iceberg.

Moreover, these root problems in mental health issues that create conflict and aggression and destroy our peaceful existence can actually be boiled down to several simple diagnostic categories that are easily treatable. Once properly diagnosed, they fall into only several categories and can be easily and readily assessed in the first session or two. More people have these problems than you realize, which you will understand after you read this. They are addiction, including sex addiction, substance abuse, and chemical dependency, the spectrum of DID (Dissociative Disorders known as Complex PTSD) and the Bipolar type of depression), which is often seen and treated by doctors as anxiety and depression ineffectively seen as merely Unipolar depression because the Bipolar type requires different strategies and meds, and treating it as Unipolar depression is ineffective and often worsens it.

Likewise, Dissociative Disorders are often treated merely as Bipolar disorder, which is a chemical imbalance when DID is just a complicated relational, a more all-encompassing form of PTSD (C-PTSD) or Complex PTSD (Post Traumatic Stress Disorder) incurred through chronic traumatization during childhood. The spectrum of DID is an emotional disorder only effectively treated through talk therapy (Google Internal Family Systems therapy), not medication.

Not that medicating DID's acute symptom relief might not help out temporarily, but it won't cure the condition. Since the engorgement of Big Pharma, as they call psychopharmacology, the original concept of *split personality* diagnosed in the asylums by the founding psychiatrist Bleuler, who started up the original asylums of the mentally ill in the nineteenth century, was distorted, misunderstood, ignored, and converted into chemical imbalance disorder/psychotic disorders in the 1950s.

Certainly, taking high doses of tranquilizers called major tranquilizers or antipsychotics will numb one to the point that those inner dissociated parts of self—the inner voices—are quelled, and you won't switch or be triggered as easily into your modes, parts, and alters. They won't become active, "acting out" is reduced, and the inner disruptiveness is subdued. Still, it's just a Band-Aid approach that leaves the person labeled with a chronic mental illness called schizophrenia when better named DID spectrum—which is dissociative schizophrenia curable through IFS as well without dependence on medication that labels a person chronically mentally ill rather than facilitating real cure.

All this will be explained in the book *Not Fit for Human Consumption, Triggered Traumatic Memories, and the Violence Profile*. This is because the first therapy session or outpatient mental health visit is supposed to be an intake or clinical evaluation. For billing purposes for most mental health practitioners, the first session is even coded differently than the rest of the ensuing therapy sessions.

The first session is intended or supposed to be an in-depth clinical evaluation and history information-gathering session so the therapist can figure out the roots of the client's problems. Helping professionals are not supposed to just begin chatting with the client but instead originally are supposed to do an in-depth clinical evaluation of the client.

This I do by getting the client to complete a four-page fill-in-the-blanks, checklists, and general questionnaires about themselves and their background (all past and current legal problems, substance abuse, and medical psychological/psychiatric history to include a list of past and present symptoms mentally and physically, including mental and medical conditions, medication history, inpatient and outpatient history, as well as extended family's history, including their own psychiatric and substance abuse history and the client's childhood history, including traumas, losses, family dysfunctions, birth order, living situations, etc.), as well as the client's work educational and relationship history, status, and, of course, their current presenting complaints (symptoms, concerns, and goals they wish to get out of therapy, including details like how they are sleeping, which is very important to relieve anxiety and depression).

Much of this info is quicker to obtain through written answers and questionnaires, which in my first session include highly reliable and valid separate questionnaires and self-reports about dissociation symptoms and ADHD that are filled out the first session. I, as a therapist, follow up with my "thousand questions" to fill in needed details during the clinical interview, which can be short to a long time, depending on how much the client writes or how self-disclosing he or she is in their paperwork.

The second session begins with the work of therapy or counseling. Session two focuses on beginning therapy by first going over the results (which I have scored and addressed before the session). In addition, if the client desires and signs a formal release of information for me to share results with his or her doctor, I give diagnoses written in a letter with their help to aid their doctor with possible medications suggestions based on the clinical results as well as referral to their family medical doctor or PCP for the lab blood work where indicated such as to check their vitamin D and thyroid levels, which, if low, can be root causes of depression and fatigue, for example. Then and only then do we begin working on their presenting complaints and issues that precipitated their seeking therapy.

This all probably takes a little longer than some therapists who don't do the in-depth evaluation. I believe it is extremely important to understand the client's problems, needs, and guides of the treatment plan of how to help the client as they address their "problems in living" that motivated them to come and that they want to improve. The focus is on healing the mind, body, and spirit.

Possible test results related to our topic at hand to cure the world's ills are information gathering done in the first to the second session of good therapy, including assessing issues that will interfere with functioning and disrupt our paradise on earth. The main ones are addiction and substance abuse, and the main mental health disorders are Bipolar type depression (versus Unipolar depression) and Dissociative Identity Disorders spectrum (Complex PTSD), which impair an individual from being at their highest or best self. When caused and enabled by environmental dysfunctions, like family enabling, these disorders cause most of the problems on earth now from a broad picture perspective because all involve narcissism.

Lots of the other disorders in the DSM-5 are superficial behavioral descriptions of mental health problems, but the real evil, if you will, on earth actually stems from the root cause of these three main disorders: addiction, Bipolar Disorder, and spectrum DID. If one simply labels people with diagnoses like Cluster B Personality Disorders--immature acting out types, including Borderline Personality Disorder, Antisocial Personality Disorder, and Narcissistic Personality Disorder and less-known Histrionic Disorder, leave such people as often considered untreatable! Not to suggest blank Behavior Therapy (DBT) isn't very helpful but treating the root underlying complex PTSD spectrum (DID) is the cure.

When you treat the underlying root function, you can help them and yourself and others from their acting out! Parsimony is the key to all things—breaking things down to their simplest component or factors. Everyday interpersonal conflict up to serial killing can be eradicated and treated effectively by addressing the above diagnoses and stopping the enabling family or cultural group environmental problems or dysfunctions that feed into them.

What Are Drugs For?

Drugs come originally from plants and herbs, which scientists and others have converted into chemical medications or for recreational purposes. These plants and herbs are here on earth for us to partake of and enhance our abilities and levels of consciousness for us to understand and experience what is humanly possible in case we are not already functioning at that higher level of consciousness (look up Kabbalah Tree of Life). We are to try them to be able to learn and then let them go, not become addicted to them. Psychology and psychiatry are now studying the usage of psychedelics in this way as an "opening up" for clients to create the experience of self-love and better functioning.

The problem becomes when we don't get that we are capable of doing these experiences without drugs, and instead, people become reliant on or dependent on or addicted to drugs. They miss the point of the intention of our opportunity by exposing ourselves, learning about ourselves to using the experience as a vehicle to learn how to do it through natural methods to raise our conciousness.

The Four Main Culprits

The main types of mental disorders that cause aggression, negativity, and all kinds of evil, if you will, from everyday life interpersonal conflict, chronic outbursts, right up through extreme violence, including serial killing, are (1) Dissociative Identity Disorder spectrum or Complex PTSD, (2) Bipolar type of depression, (3) addictions, and (4) narcissism (although usually narcissistic tendencies, in my opinion, are only rarely full-blown NPD or Narcissistic Personality Disorder)—as these actually stem from some form of addiction, a term I am using loosely, and finally a central part or core of all addictions is narcissism. So addictions and narcissistic tendencies are part of all the other three main disorders. Some people have more than one or even all of these disorders in combination, especially chronically violent people.

The term *addiction* refers to one's preoccupation with acquiring or requiring, attaining, and recovering from some kind of "fix" as a lifestyle, therefore maintaining a selfish, unempathetic, callous way of relating interpersonally because narcissism is central to all addictions. This means they behave that way until recovery usually, and in the case of DID spectrum, there is usually a narcissistic part that pops out, although the whole person may not be narcissistic. In addition, the parts or modes or alters have walls between them which means they act narcissistically or egocentrically independently; they suffer from some amnesia and don't understand the big picture or even know other parts' or the host's personality, life needs, and perspective (lack of coconsciousness between parts; they come from their own single-minded egocentric perspective). The narcissistic mode, part or alter of DID spectrum and the Bipolar lifestyle of manically overcompensating render the individual functioning in a narcissistic manner at times even though their personality may not be NPD. This is not to say they deserve to be found not guilty by reason of insanity.

To reiterate, the four main culprits are (1) The DID narcissistic part and also the compartmentalized nature of parts or alters engineered that come out to do a specific job who are unaware of the big life picture, and a narcissistic part or alter is needed in 95 percent of DID spectrum in almost everyone on the spectrum, which will be explained. (2) Bipolar type of depression, (3) addictions, including sexual addiction and chemical dependency, abuse or binging types, and (4) narcissistic tendencies or even Narcissistic Personality Disorder (rare by itself)—a fixation with "looking good" at all times—and the latter two being present and causal in the two aforementioned disorders, DID spectrum and Bipolar depression.

In a nutshell, the core of each is narcissistic tendencies as a function of some form of addiction. It is the addiction that causes narcissism that causes the "acting out" selfish, callous, and unempathetic behaviors, which will be explained. Moreover, often people with anger management issues have several or all of these disorders combined, which go overlooked and untreated. Take Ted Bundy, the serial killer, for example, who generally appeared to be in manic effusive charm, was eventually thoroughly analyzed and was found to have the Bipolar type of depression. He certainly had narcissism and sexual addiction, maybe DID, given a traumatic family upbringing with an aggressive alcoholic father figure (grandfather).

It is up to the individual, the therapist, and others and agencies around such an individual to become aware of the symptoms of these disorders and get the person, when he or she is a child preferably, to get the correct diagnosis and treatment to cure them and thereby curb the aggression.

The Spectrum of Dissociative Identity Disorder (Complex-PTSD)

We now know that most disorders are on a spectrum. We don't think anymore that you are only an alcoholic if you are the homeless person laying on the street, unable to barely function, begging for coins for the next drink, trying not to succumb to alcohol withdrawal of tremors and hallucinations.

We understand plenty of people are on the spectrum of alcoholism. Functional alcoholics, who drink less, have less physical addiction and primarily have family problems because they are busy getting their fix and are less responsible or respectful to their mates and significant others and thus have a verbal conflict with them while denying and projecting their problems onto someone or something else. In other words, they are still alcoholics in the first phase of alcoholism dependence or binge drinking in which the hallmark feature is family problems, and they have yet to progress in their alcoholism to let it affect their work (such as poorer work performance, less motivation, or running late to work from being hungover), having legal issues like DUIs (more indicative of middle phase progressiveness of the disease of chemical dependency).

We also know autism is on a spectrum and plenty of people have more minimal symptoms—seem a bit "off" but aren't full-blown autistics like in the *Rain Man* movie, needing institutionalization or worse, maybe can't even speak or only flap their arms because the neurological impairment is severe. People on the mild end of autism used to be diagnosed with Asperger's syndrome and appeared normal except a bit socially "off." Now they are considered on the autistic spectrum.

We need to wake up, listen, and realize that Dissociative Identity Disorder is on a spectrum too. People who have experienced childhood chronic traumas or neglect often have DID—just milder forms of it, maybe not the full-blown Multiple Personality Disorder (as it was first called). The one in one hundred most severe type whose childhood traumas were so severe that the dissociation had to completely wipe out memories for the child to function without having a complete nervous breakdown. Most people's walls between parts or modes are thinner and allow some coconsciousness, whereas modes are so thick in severe DID that when they switch, they experience blackout form between the part of themselves called alters; at any level of the spectrum, one part of their brain is designated to hold memories that handle that particular job or life stressor (one client told me every time that he got a new job, he got a new part and now had the NAPA parts guy). People who receive extreme mistreatment as a child have such thick amnesia walls between parts, and they actually function as alters complete blackouts or amnesia of time where they switch parts and lack coconsciousness.

Most people aren't that bad off and have some coconsciousness or awareness, although they are not in control of the moment. This doesn't mean I advocate not guilty by reason of insanity. There is only one body or person responsible.

Usually, the life manager or host handles the appointments and daily life activities and is competent to show up nicely at the therapist's appointment to do life-functioning jobs. So he or she may appear quite together until they tell their therapist their horrible childhood history and confess to the severe symptoms they have—including getting a high score on the Dissociation Experiences Scale, confessing to amnesia of important life events, maybe not remembering parts or even years of childhood or life at all, as well as being able to see themselves do things as if watching themselves do something as if looking at another person and feeling they are more than one person, for a few examples of dissociative symptoms.

Dissociation is simply a defense mechanism we can use as children because we still have imaginations, and so we can self-hypnotize (go away in our minds when we realize we have only our mind to protect us, not any real protector in our life), so we begin to "go away," letting another part of our brain deal with a stressor—originally the traumas, but later, once we have learned how to dissociate, then any time, there is a new stressor in life like starting school because when the child first enters school, it is a stressor, so he or she adds a student part. Parts keep being created to handle every new life stressor. Please read *Not Fit for Human Consumption: Triggered Traumatic Memories and the Violence Profile* by this same author.

We are beginning to approach this spectrum understanding through the popularization and euphemizing of Complex PTSD and through the therapy called Internal Family Systems (which refers to our inner modes or parts that need healing). Simple PTSD is when a person experiences a trauma, say somebody is in a bus accident. If that person doesn't get over the trauma within a couple of months and is still experiencing nightmares, flashbacks, vigilance, and anxiety, causing them to avoid similar situations, such as driving in vehicles, they are diagnosed with Posttraumatic Stress Disorder.

Complex PTSD refers to when a young child, under the age of eight, experiences chronic, relational traumas so it develops a more all-encompassing complicated, more severe type of PTSD that affects their overall functioning and is not proceeded by good functioning brought down or disrupted by a later life traumatic event they can't seem to get a grip on. In this case, Complex PTSD or spectrum DID, as I call it because they are identical, the incidents happened to a person when a young child, many times in their home life, somehow so encompassed their whole living space, not just an outside isolated incident and the child believes no caretaker would protect them. They used their own imagination or self-hypnosis to do so, and this dissociation became their way of handling any new life stress, so essentially, all of their resources are compartmentalized into their parts, modes, or alters.

About 30 percent of my upper West-End office clients fall into this diagnosis, whereas colleagues of mine who work in the inner city where their clients were probably exposed to routine drive-bys and gunshots report a rate of 40 to 50 percent of their clients having it. Internal Family Systems therapy says everyone needs to return to their original inner health state of the self (the creative, compassionate self) but admit that their clients are the ones with chronic childhood trauma.

How do my colleagues and I assess it when other therapists miss it? We ask pertinent, relevant questions like, Do you have chronic memory issues? Do you find yourself acting like different people? Can you see yourself doing something and you're not in control? Do you hear inner voices (part), etc., telling you what to do or commenting on things you do? These are parts of self, not hallucinations.

People with DID at its most extreme form (like the homeless drunk in alcoholism or the institutionalized mute autistic in autism) are rare, yes, but should we not help the of those milder forms of it? Is everything black or white? Yes, I have had clients who had to look in the car trunk after a day out to discover they had been shopping at Walmart but also had some who knew they shopped but kept wondering why they found themselves on the way home, detouring to the airport, only to discover in therapy later that day that their teen part missed Mom, so they want to go try to get a plane to visit Mom. They were coconscious but blended with the teenage part out upfront or active.

Most people on the spectrum of DID have greater coconsciousness between their parts or modes that full blackout alters, like in the movie *Split*. They experience life with the same lack of control but have memories more like being ADHD forgetful; usually, before being assessed, they have been diagnosed with Bipolar (mood swings) and/or Borderline Personality Disorder (which people with DID all have and is a very accurate behavioral description of the DID spectrum). Not asking about DID symptoms during the first session is like a clinician never asking if the client drinks alcohol or does drugs. You can't get far in helping them without knowing these things about them.

Bipolar Depression

Let's start with the understanding that both Unipolar and Bipolar Disorder are just types of depression, and let's take the stigma off of Bipolar. Bipolar is just another form of depression and, in fact, one where the person with it has learned how to cope or overcompensate for their depression and is not stuck always in the depression with oversleeping, fatigue, lack of energy, being unable to get much done, socially withdrawn, and struggling to accomplish much because of serious depression. Unipolar depression needs more serotonin, and his or her PCP rightly prescribes them an SSRI (serotonin reuptake inhibitor) like Paxil, Luvox, Lexapro, Prozac, Zoloft, and their generic counterparts (or St. John's Wart, a supplement or tea that is a natural SSRI), then they perk up. Sometimes their thyroid or vitamin D level is low and, once found, can be treated rather than needing SSRI.

But back to the difference between Bipolar and Unipolar—the Bipolar person has learned how to raise their own serotonin and compensate for the depression chemical imbalance. By "eyeing" or spotting something shiny in their environment and then "putting on their running to chase it," becoming manic—this excitement causes them to turn on their own manic euphoric juices. Their own inner cocktail—a fix, if you will, for their depression—is temporary. Since impulsive, it often backfires.

First of all, what goes up, must come down. Soon after the manic frenzy, the euphoric brain neurotransmitters subside anyway, and the person is back with his or her chemical depression. Moreover, they "acted out" and often brought on negative consequences from their poorly thought frenzied actions. Typical manic behaviors include over-shopping, shoplifting, over-socializing, and over-sexing may cause marital infidelity, and poor financial behaviors like foolish business investments causing debt. The person who started out depressed now has situational reasons to be depressed. They may be exhausted from lack of sleep, overworking, overdoing, and overexerting, so after it, all are in worse shape too.

The ebullient charismatic Bipolar Ted Bundy goes unnoticed. Why? When I was in graduate school, we were taught that manic depression, as it was called back then, didn't even begin until middle age. Now we know the first significant episodes begin at the age of early twenties, and some people may even have it as children. The reason it went overlooked before is that Bipolar depression differs from Unipolar depression because the manic person looks and acts better and achieves more when in the high manic episode—on the go, working, schooling, charming others, and relating as a productive person.

They are on the go, so they appear productive. When they deflate into their withdrawn, depressed phase, other people just deal with this—or have to deal with their irritable outbursts. The irritability is the depression phase when the Bipolar person really wants you to away because they can hardly function and want to take to bed but blame you for their problems and doesn't admit their depression. They are in the hungover phase of their addiction, so to speak.

Likewise, another reason for Bipolar depression going undetected is that nobody bops into their PCP's or doctor's office, complaining, "Last week, I was on top of the world. I completed the month's work and got three girlfriends!" They may mention to their doctor a month later that they are depressed—the Dr. who assumes it is Unipolar depression, not asking if there have been any manic or hypomanic episodes or phases or symptoms at other times.

Then prescribed the SSRIs, which they don't need—as they already know how to shoot up their own positive mood neurotransmitters--this extra just complicates the problem, and the manic depressive cycle increases because the Bipolar lifestyle needs to be mood stabilized and medically treated differently as well as from a therapeutic standpoint of mood stabilization with talk therapy to reduce "acting out." Manic addiction therapy increases patience, assertiveness, and focus on a healthy balanced lifestyle regimen with regular sleep, exercise, and the correct meds for Bipolar prescribed, which would include one or two different type medications, an atypical antidepressant, not SSRI, rather mood stabilizing med combos like Lithium or Abilify with bupropion or Wellbutrin or Lamictal or Lamotrigine or Latuda by themselves. The Lamictal or Lamotrigine works wonders to reduce irritable outbursts per clients' families' reports.

Addictions and Narcissism

Let's start with the understanding that all people suffering from addictions, like sex addiction, chemical dependencies, Bipolar 1, and DID, behave like narcissists. All addicts are preoccupied with hunting for their fix, taking their fix, recovering from side effects of addiction, and then beginning the cycle of seeking their fix again. Real recovery has three phases, including (1) physical sobriety, (2) social sobriety, which means developing healthier relationships that don't negatively influence you to use, and (3) moral, psychological, and spiritual recovery. Any people in power need to be evaluated for these four culprits and get proper help before resuming their positions. Until they go into recovery, they are too busy, too preoccupied with their thrills to have time, energy, and wherewithal to have any concern for anybody else's feelings and needs; hence, they behave narcissistically, callously, unempathatically, and impatiently with others.

This narcissistic behavior is common to all types of addicts—those addicts whose fix is sexual addiction, lust dominance, those into alcohol and/or drugs, and those Bipolar individuals whose fix comes from their own euphoric inner cocktail realized through chasing something shiny and exciting by putting their running shoes on to chase it. The addictive lifestyle of the individuals suffering from the Bipolar type of depression who don't have to go to a bar for a drink but instead can release their own inner cocktail manic episode rush of dopamine, serenity, and adrenaline, and likewise, all or almost all on the DID spectrum have created a part to stand up of themselves, a narcissistic, selfish competitive protector of self. Who doesn't need a standup guy?

The problem with DID is that each part is compartmentalized and comes out when the need is triggered; in this case, if there is any interpersonal stress, the narcissist part pops out to do a job overcoming, not considering the host's broad life perspective and then lashes out at the enemy, which may be a family member, friend, coworker, etc. The narcissistic part or mode or alter of the person on the DID spectrum is preoccupied with endlessly fulfilling its job of selfishly getting his or her way by lashing out in a troublesome manner. I don't mean they all technically have Narcissistic Personality Disorder, which is a personality disorder starting around age three, where the child realizes they are not loved, so they feel abandoned and repress their real self to develop a false grandiose self to get constant approval, admiration, and special convenience to compensate.

It's safer that way than being yourself since they feel abandoned by their primary caretaker. People with NPD have to always be right and always be favored or their helium balloon of false self, the grandiose self, will deflate, leaving them lost, abandoned, and helpless. They use the defense mechanism of splitting, where the equation is everything good is about me, the self, and everything bad is outside; they self-project blame, and deny any wrongdoing.

Narcissistic tendencies are part of all four disorders that can lead to aggression and conflict, and this doesn't mean they are full-blown NPDs or even that once treated and cured, they will continue to behave narcissistically. Sociopaths or psychopaths once treated for Bipolar, DID addiction, and perhaps, if needed, in rare cases, NPD has curable narcissistic tendencies. They just act narcissistically—meaning out for themselves with no empathy for others. The addict is forever looking for his or her fix until they go into treatment recovery.

Finally, scientists have discovered that people with an excessive white matter in the prefrontal cortex demonstrate lying tendencies; we need research to discover quickly how to invent a device that registers this lying ability and have all that enter a courtroom wear one.

Neuropsychology indicates that excessive white matter in the prefrontal cortex means lying ability.

Guidelines for Healthy Relationships

1. Choose healthy people to be involved with—hands-on caretaking providers or empathetic listeners, not toxic people with whom you feel bad.
2. Marry well. Make sure you know the person does not have a major mental disorder. You need to have at least three love connections: (1) romantic chemistry, (2) best friend or parenting connection, and (3) religious or spiritual or life philosophy similarities.
3. Seek psychotherapy for mental problems that may interfere with satisfying relationships.
4. Seek couples counseling for chronic arguments and dissatisfactions—preferably before.
5. Have zero expectations. Your relationships are not the source of your happiness. You need to fulfill yourself.
6. Don't accept abusive behavior—whether mental, emotional, verbal, or physical. Walk away if the person becomes aggressive (say, "Excuse me, I've got to go to the bathroom"). Set boundaries. Don't participate in negativity.
7. Recognize that people who irritate you provide you with an opportunity to grow. When someone bothers you, this signals a button has been pushed and childhood pain has been triggered, which needs to be healed. You need to release the pain. No one can hurt you without your consent (see "inner child work"). In addition, we often project our shadow self—the dark side—onto others, which we need to face and heal (see "shadow work").
8. Recognize and release limiting human race consciousness belief that interferes with your freedom to express joyfully and relate healthily, such as unconscious beliefs that marriage is confining or that females are weak.
9. Practice healthy relating, such as good communication skills. Take time for openness and fun in your relationships. Take care of yourself so you have something to give to others.

Chapter 8

Be a Whole, Fulfilled Person

My goodness flows to me in a steady, unbroken, ever increasing stream of success, happiness, and abundance.

You are loving yourself, and you are ready to love your life
based on your core belief—I am important

As you work through your inner negativity and truly love and believe in yourself and maintain a core belief, "I am important," you are able to address your life, practically speaking, and make changes to live in a fulfilled manner. Most problems in living are from a lack of self-love or self-respect—negative thoughts about oneself. You won't approach your daily living in a caring way to yourself until you care about yourself.

Women particularly tend to discount themselves, their feelings, needs, and wants. A woman's self-concept often is overinclusive to include feelings and wants of significant family members. Gloria Steinem coined a phrase called empathy sickness, as women tend to focus on others' feelings and neglect their own. For example, mothers working full-time have little time for themselves—even the basics of healthy eating and sleeping, let alone time to take care of deeper emotional needs. These women take care of so many external commands that they find it hard to recognize their own needs and feelings at all. Once a woman's consciousness is raised to believe she is important, then she can start to make the life changes to make herself happy.

The following are guidelines on how to fulfill yourself. Every human being has some basic rights and needs that each is responsible for meeting in order to make oneself happy. Nobody else can make you happy. You have to invest the time and energy in yourself to meet your basic whole-person needs.

This involves weaning from addictions which have superficially pacified you or numbed your discontent so that you can discover your true essence, the healthy inner passions that you were meant to express and elevate you to being in a state of joy.

The whole person model of fulfillment

The whole person theory provides a model for understanding you and your needs better. Although this model was originated to help people recover from the pain of growing up in alcoholic families, it applies to anyone who comes from a dysfunctional family and needs to recover.

On the following pages, there are several charts—a circle describing a whole, fulfilled person; a circle of an unfulfilled person; and an empty circle to fill in with your own passions so you can enhance your own fulfillment.

LOVE YOURSELF, LOVE YOUR LIFE

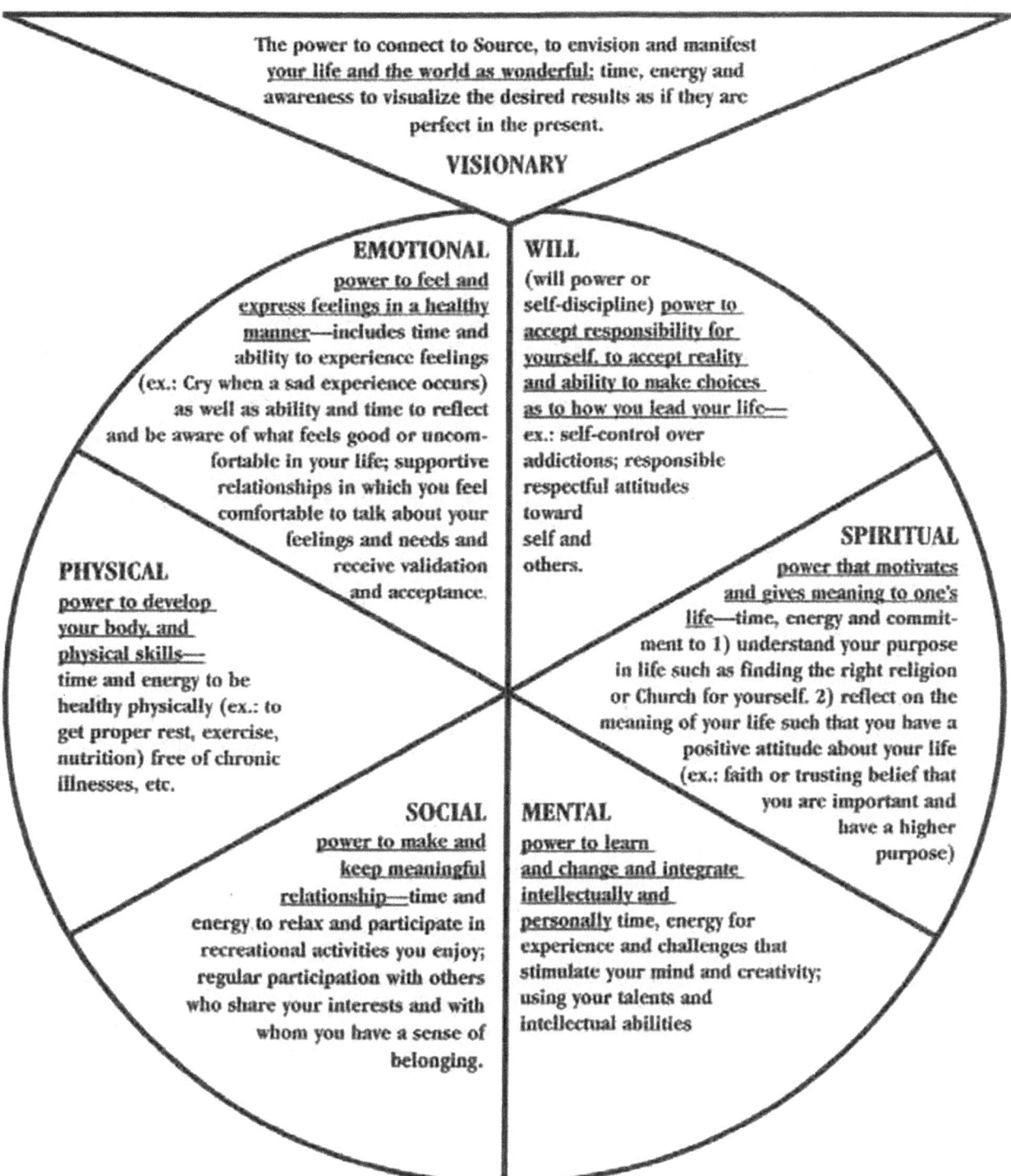

THE "WHOLE, FULFILLED PERSON" MODEL

From sources: Ancient philosophy and theology through to current psychology (example: *Another Chance—Hope and Health for the Alcoholic Family*, by Sharon Wegscheider).

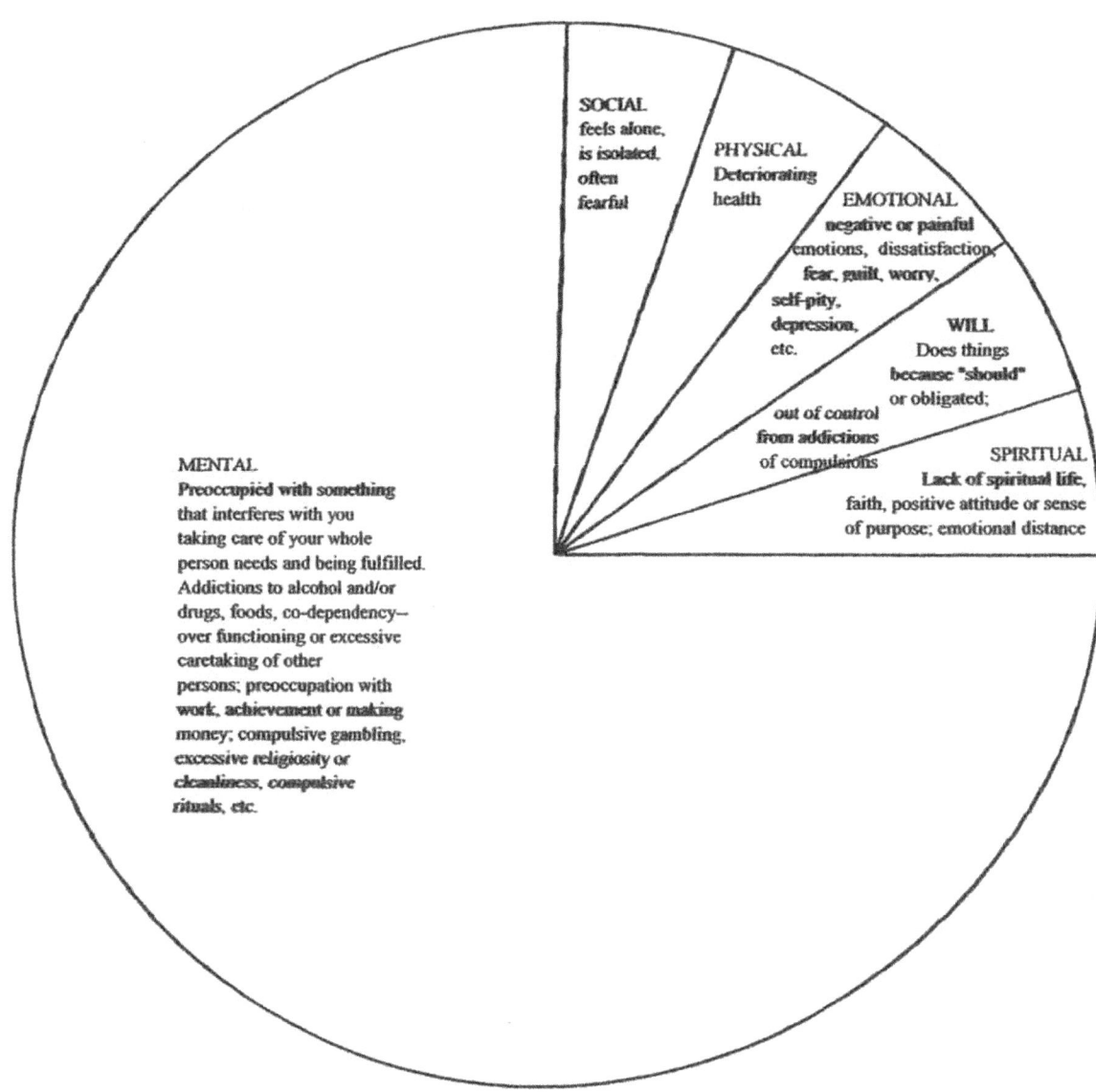

THE "UNFULFILLED" PERSON

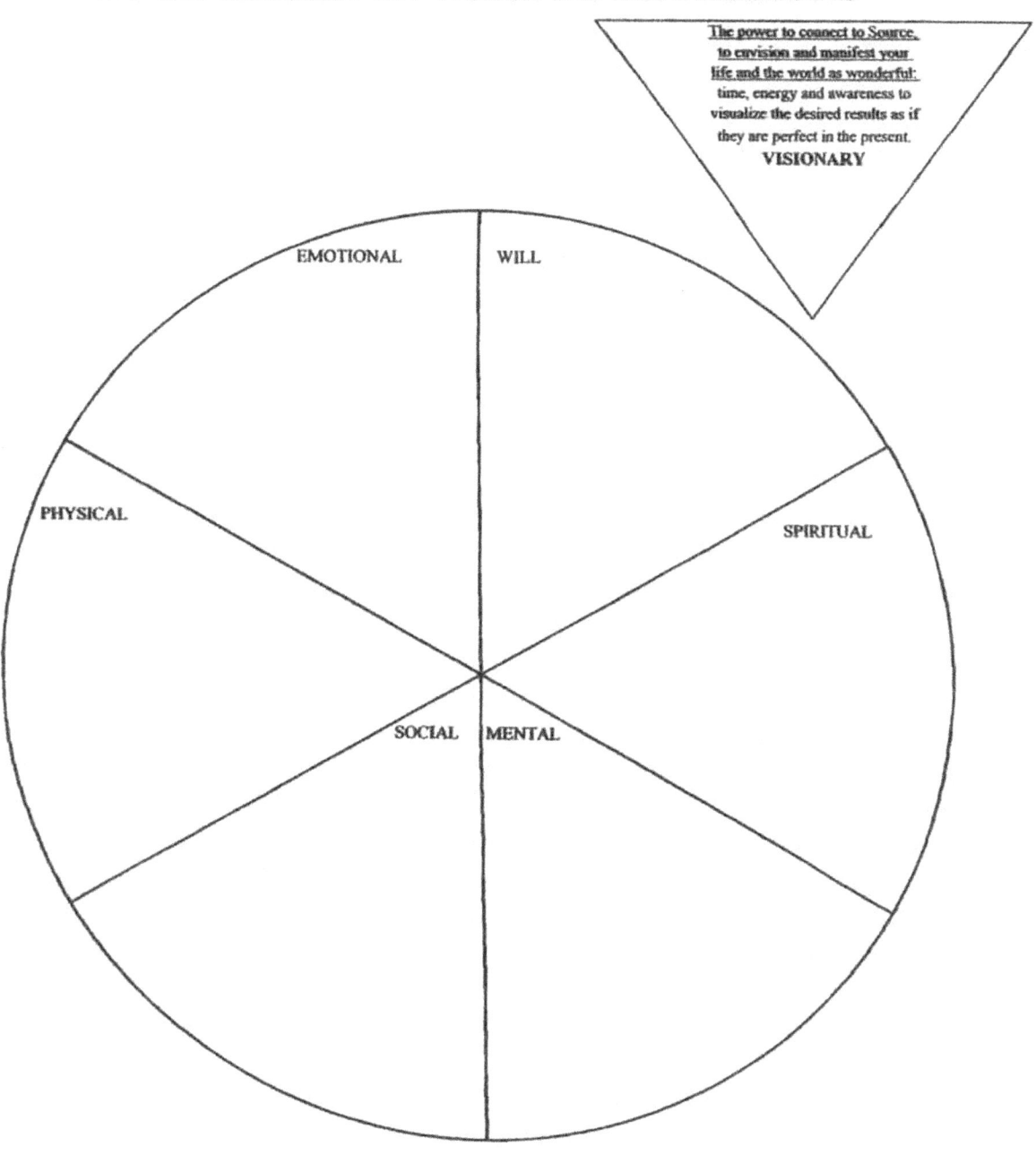

When you look at the circles of the whole, fulfilled person and an unfulfilled person, which are you most like? What needs are you neglecting? Look at the empty circle to begin to visually change yourself from an unfulfilled state to a whole, fulfilled state. Use a pencil to fill the pie slices with your own passions—what you could do in these areas to better satisfy yourself. Use the pencil because you may want to change and revise your plans in the future. The soul-searching you're doing from using focusing process can also help you uncover areas that you are neglecting in your life and how to better meet your needs. Think of past times when you felt a natural high. These experiences are clues to your passions that you may not be aware of.

Exercise: Consider how well you take care of yourself and your needs now:

Step 1: Look at the whole person diagram. Are you a whole person? Do you feel self-fulfilled? What areas are neglected in your life? Where do you need to devote more time and energy? Look over the unfulfilled person chart to see which negative experiences you relate to and need to improve on.

Step 2: Use the blank whole person circle to fill in activities or passions that would fulfill you in each of these areas. You identify these passions from current or potential interests you have, or you look back to moments of joy when you felt a natural high that you experienced to guide you to the activities or interests that can fulfill you now.

Old-school parenting

The importance of instilling self-esteem was not known or emphasized in the previous generation to the degree that it has become a parenting goal today. Many parents of the previous "scold and spank" generation were more concerned about raising us to become outwardly appearing functional adults. They trained us to be polite and get our homework and chores done. Did your parents ask regularly, "How are you feeling?" "Are you happy?" "What are your needs?" or "What can we do to help you get your needs met better emotionally?" If this did not happen or did not happen at the moment that you needed it (such as the example of the client who walked in on his parents having sex), then you probably did not learn about your rights and needs.

You experience self-fulfillment and life enjoyment when you are a "whole" person—when your lifestyle reflects that you value all of yourself and you meet your needs regularly. A whole person regularly has the time and energy to take care of himself or herself in the mental, physical, emotional, social, and spiritual areas. The whole person has the willpower for everyday functioning and responsibilities.

Dissatisfaction reflects a negative thought pattern. If your relationships are not satisfying, for example, you probably don't feel lovable. If you are physically unhealthy, you may not take time and energy for physical health, or you may believe heredity or what doctors tell you determine how healthy you are and therefore suffer the consequences. Your consciousness creates the neglect. You need to trace back to your unconscious belief system causing this neglect. Be guided to change your beliefs to more positive, self-enhancing ones to make the actual changes in your life to take care of yourself in the area that you have neglected.

Exercise: Think about the areas in your life you neglect. What negative thoughts do you have that are causing the neglect?

Addiction or dependency and coping versus self-care and self-actualizing

Many people have accepted rather intolerable, stressed-out life situations and feel chronically upset and out of control. Instead of feeling their feelings in order to change the situation, they become more and more preoccupied to *avoid* them.

"Dependent," "reactive," "externally focused," or "preoccupied"—these are words that describe a lifestyle of coping or struggling to be happy rather than loving oneself, "self-actualizing," and being truly happy. A preoccupation or excessive focus to derive happiness through an external source include work (workaholism), drugs or alcohol (chemical dependency), food (compulsive eating), relationships (codependency), gambling, hypersexuality, excessive religiosity, obsessive-compulsive rituals (example, overexercising, preoccupation with food in eating disorders, and fearing germs and putting a lot of energy into protecting oneself against them, for example, washing hands constantly), any soft addictions (like excessive TV viewing).

Dependency or addictiveness is a progressive emotional disease that has two parts.

First of all, the person engages in the "addictivity" (addictive activity) to feel good and needs more and more of it over time to get the same effect. Unless these tendencies are recognized and the person stops doing them—goes into recovery—the addictive behavior increases and worsens over time. The person's life gets engulfed more in addictive behavior—preoccupied with the addiction. When avoidance of feelings and neglect of the true self wins, increasingly negative life consequences occur, usually first affecting family needs and responsibilities, then progressing into work, financial, and possibly legal problems (such as a DWI or driving while intoxicated), and finally in health deterioration.

The second part of the disease, that the mind plays tricks on the self and others, blocks the person and his significant others from realizing that he is addicted. The defense mechanisms that we spoke of before, which are blind spots and our comfort zones—what are familiar to us—keep us coping, trying to fill our inner void with outside stuff rather than facing and healing ourselves. This also prevents us from realizing that we are preoccupied or addicted. We make excuses and rationalizations—project blame and deny and avoid that our misery is self-imposed. We pacify ourselves with the addictions to feel good temporarily—only to feel worse in the end as our life problems get more and more out of control.

Codependency is a type of addiction that originally meant enabling an alcoholic spouse or partner—overfunctioning for and walking on eggshells around them. Used in a broader sense, codependency now refers to any overfunctioning or overcaretaking in a relationship such that you neglect yourself. Codependency is a progressive disease stemming from negative childhood experiences and resulting in self-defeating personality. It leaves one an alien in his or her own life. Codependence seriously interferes with and deeply decreases quality of life and often promotes stress-related physical illness. Codependency creates pathological longing in the affected persons. In treadmill fashion, a person seeks to save and rescue the addict.

The codependent engages in addictive behavior—excessive caretaking, busyness, worrying, overachieving, overfunctioning—to fill an inner void, the lack of security and self-confidence and the sense of emptiness or depression. Ironically, she looks at the world through rose-colored glasses by using the defense mechanism of denial of problems. She tolerates bad situations, believing that they will improve or that they are not that bad to begin with. She may be addicted to the high she experiences when something good does happen following an abuse, such as when a battered wife experiences the high of a makeup period with her husband.

Many working mothers fit into this category of codependent. They overfunction in partnerships, taking on more responsibility for household chores and childcare. Yet they often feel inadequate or guilty because they are unable to live up to the superwoman expectation. They fear lack of approval by their significant others. Their low self-esteem prevents them from seeing how successful they are, out of touch with themselves, focusing on others' feelings and needs. They generally neglect physical, emotional, spiritual, social, and mental areas in their lives and have many chronic stress-related illnesses.

They may have fears, worries, and issues with closeness, trust, and control. They tend to believe that they have no one to depend on. They fear that they need to manage everything and be perfect in order to be loved. They are mentally preoccupied because all their energies—their focus—is on overachieving, overfunctioning, and overcontrolling to make everyone happy. They may even become addicted to the sensation of excitement because their lives are so busy and in constant crisis because they are trying to manage so much. Suffering and pitying themselves, they may feel like victims underneath.

No one explains to you that a newborn eats every two hours at first, sometimes on the hour if nursing, or that you will not sleep much consistently for several months—or longer. Nobody explains how much is involved in bathing, changing, feeding, and holding a baby. Arlene Rossen-Cardozo (*Sequencing*) discovered through thousands of interviews with women that women only have about ten hours a week of extra time beyond baby and household needs (this goes for caring for preschoolers too) before they become overwhelmed. Yet women attempt to work full-time after a six-week maternity leave. Men would not put up with this little amount of time for self to try to work and then meet all of a baby's needs. So why do women? Codependency?

Although both men and women can be addicted and codependent in some manner, more women than men probably have this form of dependency. If one is in a codependent relationship, then each is dependent on the other. The "rescuer," "fixer," caretaker needs their codependent for him or her to feel complete.

Male addictively takes a different form, machoism. Men are socialized to ignore, deny, and suppress their feminine sides—their feels, insecurities, and sensitivity. They are basically allowed to feel three things: boarded, sexual interest, and anger. In general, they are taught to appear strong. They are not encouraged to be whole, fulfilled people. They are taught to hold in their feelings. They are taught to be providers and to sacrifice their feelings and needs. Out of touch with their feelings, a boy or man is like a ship without a rudder and functions in a personally directionless, society-achiever mode. This is not to say that some men are sensitive to their and others' feelings. Society does try to encourage them to sacrifice themselves for achievement and to discourage their personal authenticity and expression.

Remember, when becoming a whole person, that you are and have unlimited possibilities to become whatever fulfills you, whatever your soul joys are. The whole person model of recovery can help you wean from your addictions and dependencies and understand your needs and rights and replace your addictions with passions that truly fulfill you.

The weaning process

We all desire happiness and strive for it even though we may not understand how to achieve it. We each have our own unique cocktail of brain chemicals—serotonin (positive mood), dopamine (alertness), and norepinephrine (adrenaline or rush)—that makes us feel happy.

People engage in addictive behaviors to stimulate the release of their own particular cocktail of brain chemicals to feel good, but what happens is that people habituate or adapt to stimuli such that it takes more and more of the same stimulus to get that high. With addiction comes withdrawal symptoms. Hence, recovery is a gradual weaning process. This is why the twelve-step support groups are essential support to alternative behaviors.

The whole person recovery model breaks this cycle and allows you to wean from addiction and progress to healthier ways of maintaining your body's natural high. The painful process of withdrawal as you recover from addiction or dependency is minimized when you replace the addictive activity with healthier passions truer to your needs and rights. The book, *Natural Prozac*, by Dr. Joel Robertson with Tom Munte, provides suggestions of activities, such as music and exercise. Crying is a great release.

Exercise: Compose a list of soothing or energizing things you like to engage in to substitute when you have cravings for your addiction. Breathe through the craving and substitute a healthier form of pleasuring yourself. Reduce the number of hours you spend in your addictive activity by replacing these with positive, soothing, and passionate pastimes. Write up a schedule carving out specific times that you will carry out your new mental, physical, emotional, spiritual, social, and volitional (willpower responsibilities) activities or passions so you view them and carry them out as self-care responsibilities equal to working, household chores, etc. Actually put them in your daily planner or BlackBerry.

According to *The Biology of Belief* by Bruce Lipton, a neurobiologist who has done extensive research in this field, brain chemistry is ultimately altered through change in belief. You need to believe that you are good and deserve good in order to manifest yourself as a whole, fulfilled person. Remember, you are what you believe. You can transform your life. You can live on a natural high of bliss.

To wean from an addiction, you must also break free from unhealthy family or peer systems—enablers, fellow addicts, and narcissists. This involves grief and loss. Substituting health support people—such as twelve-step programs, churches, or spiritual centers—makes this easier and is a necessary part of recovery.

You are loving yourself, and you are ready to love your life

Your joy guide

Prioritize your time and energy in the following way:

1. Do what you enjoy first in a well-rounded way. This includes doing for others when it brings you joy (i.e., caring for your children or a sick family member whom you love).
2. Do not do something that you do not enjoy just because it pleases someone else.
3. Do what you are responsible for doing that will ensure joy experiences in the future. (We do not enjoy taxes, but we do enjoy being free and out of jail!)

To elaborate:

1. Do for you what you need to do first before others' desires and responsibilities. This is a daily approach as to how you prioritize your day. For example, before you go on to something your husband wants you to do, do the things you need to do and then approach him, finding out what his needs are.
2. Make sure you do something for yourself each day that is a passion of a personal interest, no matter if others like it or not. For example, I shied away from line dance for a while, believing that nobody would like me if I was into country. I remembered the high feeling of joy following a brief phase of square dancing in elementary school's gym classes. I tried line dancing, and it turned out to be an adult passion for me and to be not only country but rather a combination of ballroom dancing, jazz, ballet, other dance forms, country hits, rock, and popular music. This led me to explore other forms of dance.
3. Sometimes joy comes from doing something unmemorable—that is, a responsibility which one has to carry out, or else trouble follows. For example, most people dislike the task of doing taxes yet enjoy the freedom from fines and jail that could occur if they did not fill out the forms and pay the money. Take time with your health, or your health will take time with you.
4. Finally, do not get confused about the joy of giving. When giving brings you joy (taking care of a sick relative and attending to others), then give and enjoy giving.
5. And as you drift to sleep at night, affirm all you've accomplished in the day and simply release anything that didn't get done to tomorrow. Go to sleep feeling good about yourself *and* wake up in the morning feeling good about yourself.

This is inspired by reverends Thelma and Dwight Smith:

Inspiration

At midnight,
I sit and write
'Til break of day
Calls, "Come play."

What give you to the human race
To make the world a better place?
Know your purpose is to be
These inner joys that set you free.

All who live have greatness to give.
For life ever inspires
When we act on soul, desires
Rise with the clouds of inspiration!

Fly with the wings of passion!
Free spirit to divinely express
And fulfill its missions, one with the best

Are some more willing than others?
Certainly, most mothers—
To take part in being grand,
Inspired through divine plan.

—A. Filosa, PsyD

You can do anything at any age! Free your mind of age consciousness and believe in yourself.

Did you know?

- The famous Grandma Moses began painting at age eighty and completed 1,500 paintings.
- Michael Angelo painted the Sistine Chapel at age seventy-one.
- Ben Franklin, at age sixteen, published his first newspaper column and, at eighty-one, penned the US Constitution.
- Bobby Fischer became a grandmaster chess player at age fifteen. Americans hailed Fischer as a Cold War hero when he won the 1972 World Chess Championship against Russian chess player Boris Spassky.
- Mozart wrote his first significant composition by age six.
- Golda Meir became the prime minister of Israel at the age of seventy.
- Margaret Thatcher became prime minister of England when she was fifty-three and remained for 11 years and 209 days.

Chapter 9

Raise the Human Race

What Matters

In the passing of years,
When the fancy car's gone,
When no neighbor's eye peers
At the lush lime green lawn
And grand house has grown worn,

Yet I'll shed no more tears.
What most matters in my earthly time phase—
How I care devotedly
For the wonderful children I raise.

What is sacred to me
Is the love light I beam on all humanity.

This world a better place I leave
Without regrets—no need to grieve.

—A. Filosa, PsyD

Part A—taking the "work" out of working mothers

I spend money with divine supervision freely and wisely. There is an abundance of prosperity in my life.

This section about women's issues is a *"must read" for men* as well as women because we are all influenced and limited by our unconscious collective—our human race consciousness—regarding gender. Although our attitudes may be unconscious or denied, femininity is associated with weakness and inferiority rather than deemed as the nurturing power and calming energy which can raise the human race to a critical mass level of unconditional love.

We need to become aware and free of limiting gender beliefs. Although women have made wonderful gains compared to a century ago when women were considered little more than men's property, women are still suffering. Women struggle as they learn to balance careers and family lives. Guidance is needed about how to have careers yet maintain sense of selves and fulfillment and satisfying family relationships. Burnout, divorce, and breakdown of the family are commonplace today. This section of the book is for women today who are struggling and trying to cope with too many demands—jobs, children, marriage, and home responsibilities—attempting to please others and to meet too many people's expectations.

This section is not, however, a how-to manual to teach women to tolerate the intolerable and to cope with too many pressures and stresses. Coping refers to the codependent pattern—the act of trying to manage or make the best of a stressful or difficult situation, rather than creating your life based on self-love and self-care. There are numerous books on the market encouraging women to develop their coping skills and organizational abilities to the level of superwomen. An example of this advice would be to delegate responsibilities to a husband (who may already be overwhelmed himself) or to advise the working mother to use up her weekends to make double batches of casseroles for the week's meals. The "superwoman phenomenon" expects too much of women and does not help them develop realistic expectations of themselves and encourage them to accept their own needs and feelings. Thus, this is not a book to teach women to be more efficient machines and to ignore their own feelings and needs, handle more stresses, and take on more and more situational demands. Efficiency is good; however, working more quickly and thinking harder is not the answer to women's current task of managing careers and home duties.

This is about women learning to love themselves, take themselves more seriously, and nurture themselves. Women's feelings need to be validated. Often, women's lives feel as if they are trying to tame an octopus with its many tentacles. The book supports that you are right; you feel tired, overwhelmed, and upset, not because you are weak, overemotional, hypochondriacal, or worrisome but because you are pushing yourself too hard.

This section of the book is to take some of the work out of the working mother and replace it with self-love. Ultimately, this comes from a focus on one's true self. The true self is deep within each of us. It is the survival instinct that guides us to do things because we need to—because the actions are right for us to help us survive. This is the opposite of being motivated solely to please others. Believing somebody (our employer, husband, parents, and children) or something else (society and finances) dictates what one should do. This approach involves developing self-esteem and the belief that your feelings, wants, and needs are important. This book is about developing a positive consciousness or attitude—a spirituality, if you will, that you are good and have a right to have your needs met. If you stop trying to please others and meet all life's demands, your world will not fall apart. Rather, there is more abundance of good waiting for you than you realize. Ultimately, your lifestyle (relationships and finances) will be better off because of a focus on self-care, rather than being ruined because of "selfishness."

Women and men must first to focus inwardly and uncover their true selves. It encourages them to change their life situations to suit their true selves. Feminists and nonfeminists agree with Gloria Steinhem, one of the foremost leaders of the women's movement, who has suggested in *The Revolution from Within* that the women's movement has progressed as far as it can in its present manner of focusing on changing external situations. Now the focus needs to be on women making changes "internally" to create their lives based on their true selves. This book describes a simple process by which women—and men—can come to understand themselves better and learn to use their feelings and needs to guide themselves to create self-fulfilling lives. This book provides a model for living a full, rewarding life based on realizing that you are a whole person and taking care of the many aspects or needs of yourself.

Specifically, the following are the guidelines on how to enjoy motherhood—to compensate for overworking.

Women have often suffered from being second-class citizens to men. Women have come a long way from less than a century ago when women were considered unfit to vote, to work, or to participate significantly in the "man's world"—the area beyond the home. Women today are still suffering as they struggle to balance career and motherhood. On the societal level, women are in the adjustment phase of learning to manage career, motherhood, and family life.

Many of our mothers did not work at all, or at least until the bulk of the childbearing years had passed. They could not serve as role models nor empathize with working mothers today without having had careers themselves. A job or career is like having another child in terms of emotional attachment and time involved.

In the final analysis, this serves as a guide for our daughters and future generations of women to find self-fulfillment, preserve their marriages, and raise healthy children during these increasingly stressful times of burnout, skyrocketing divorce rates, and the breakdown of the family. Many have already made the mistake of struggling too hard and trying to be supermoms and superwomen and have suffered the negative consequences of marital discord and out-of-control lives. Hopefully, the ideas in this book will help provide a better way.

My own poverty consciousness converted to prosperity consciousness—the outcome of which was for me to be able to go to part-time status, care for me, enjoy the mothering phase of my life, and now fulfill a dream to write this book and make a wider contribution to mankind than my private psychotherapy practice.

In other words, positive thinking allows you to transform your life. You may believe that you need to work full-time to have your basic needs met, but that is just an untrue, limiting belief. Begin to confirm that you have abundance and prosperity now and see how your life changes, as mine did.

Motherhood

> *Of all the rights of women, the greatest is to be a mother.*
>
> —Lin Yutang

A good mother is a fulfilled person, rested, happy, and able to be a good parent. She is patient, calm, and emotionally available for her children. This requires organizing your life to keep stress down and get enough help and rest to be able to take care of yourself and your children, to have fun for yourself and your family, and to take care of the basic whole person needs, such as physical exercise, sleep (eight hours), and time for creativity.

Normal personality development of children requires tremendous parental devotion. This is why most of us have come from dysfunctional families and have some problems in terms of our self-esteem and beliefs about what we deserve out of life.

Motherhood is often glamorized. We remember back to our childhood fantasy of playing mommy with baby dolls. Yet, in reality, motherhood can be quite stressful. We cannot just put away our babies like we could shelve our dolls. How do we minimize the stress when uninterrupted bathroom breaks seem like climbing Mount Everest? How do we make a dream come true?

Savor your mothering years—focus and care for you and your family's whole person needs

Motherhood can be living out our childhood fantasies of playing mommy to baby dolls! It can be a time of true joy, intense love, and closeness! When you have the time, energy, and support to savor your children's precious years—in other words, when you are not too overwhelmed by work and household responsibilities and when you arrange daily breaks during which you do what you enjoy and what meets your needs so you do not neglect yourself—the time you spend with your children can be (an almighty buzzword) "quality time." You can enjoy mothering as you pretended to as a young girl. The relationship with your children can be contented, quiet, and harmonious because you are relaxed and focused. You can use your visualization and positive thinking skills to create the family life you desire. You can avoid struggling and reacting to crises. After all, don't babies cry (and children too sometimes) to let you know that they need something? If you meet their needs and surround them in a thought world of love and security, the crying is minimized. Sounds fantastic? Remember that consciousness creates all.

Unfortunately, for many overworked mothers, children may be experienced as an exhaustive burden. To a working mother, children are a second full-time job facing you after your full-time workday outside of the home. People need to come home, take a break, and relax. However, this is very difficult for working mothers. Children are typically very needy and demanding at dinnertime (the "arsenic hour"). They have been separated from their parents all day and are often tired, hungry, and in need of TLC (tender, loving care). Remember that consciousness and the belief in peaceful, healthy, happy relationships can change all this. This will probably involve some actual life changes that you will be guided to make.

Arlene Rossen-Cardozo conducted interviews with thousands of mothers. She found that, for women to feel in control of their lives with enough time and energy for them and "mothering their children," women need to "sequence." "Sequencing" means having it all (career and motherhood)—but not all at once. In fact, she found out that when mothers of babies and preschool children exceed only about ten hours per week of time in terms of personal use (including work, exercise, and socializing), they become overwhelmed and stressed out. About twenty-five hours per week, including travel and preparation time, for work and other activities is comfortable for women of school-age children. This means that many women today are running their lives on "empty gas tanks"—pushing themselves into "overwhelm" and surviving on Prozac or other drugs.

Why decide to cut back work when you have children? You choose to be realistic. Realistically, you are going to be stressed out if you do not otherwise. You are going to stress out yourself and the people you love. The average couple talks only about thirty minutes a week. No wonder more than 50 percent of marriages end in divorce. With little communication, who can resolve problems, let alone enjoy each other's company? Often, small problems with children will smolder over time and develop into large disasters because they do not have time to deal with or even notice them. For example, a child's undetected learning disability leads to low self-esteem and eventually delinquency as the child's frustration increases because he cannot cope in the school environment. Mothers may suffer from chronic physical complaints—such as headaches, backaches, and stomach ailments—that stem from stress and overwork and the lack of time and energy to devote to rest, eating right, and taking care of themselves. These may eventually lead to chronic debilitating conditions, like diabetes or irritable bowel syndrome.

Exercise: Ask yourself these questions. If you answer yes to some of the following questions, you will want to consider sequencing—cutting back your work hours and other outside expectations to focus on the mothering phase of your life.

Regarding children:
1. Did you have a strong desire to become a mother, have a family, and care for your children?
2. Do you want to spend more time with your children?
3. Do you think you need to improve your relationship with your children?
4. Do your children have any special needs that cutting back at work would give you the time to help your children better?
5. Do you want to raise your children yourself, rather than give the responsibility to someone else? Do you want them to bond with you?
6. Do you not want to miss those special years with your children?

Regarding yourself and your needs:
7. Are you tired and physically sick frequently? In other words, do you think your health may be suffering because of stress?
8. Do you feel that you do not have enough time for yourself?
9. Do you feel that you are not able to take care of yourself as a whole person given your current life demands?
10. Do you feel overwhelmed or stressed out?
11. Do you think certain areas of your life are neglected and out of control?

Regarding marriage:
12. Is your marriage unfulfilling and in need of some effort (counseling, communication, and time for fun) to make it more satisfying?
13. Do you need time to spend enjoying your relationship with your husband (talking, intimacy, and having fun)?
14. Do you and your husband have a lot of complaints and arguments, or are you inconsiderate of each other?
    The answers to some of these may indicate a dysfunctional relationship as well.

Regarding external factors that may be keeping you from fulfilling your deeper needs or focusing on mothering:
15. Do you believe you are overly concerned with getting others' approval or pleasing others?
16. Do you feel you are not good enough in your parents' eyes? By doing too much, are you trying to overcompensate to feel better about yourself?
17. If you were to stay at home, do you believe you should do it the way your mother did? For example, do all the housework (even if you would rather not do it this way). Remember, your situation today is much different from your mother's time. Does your spouse insist that you work although you want to cut back? In other words, are you working to please your spouse or someone else?
18. Do you want to cut back but are scared?
19. Were you neglected or abused (emotionally, verbally, physically, or sexually) as a child?
20. Do you feel that you are not good enough if you are not achieving and working?

Good guilt, bad guilt, and raising secure children

There is only so much time in the day. You cannot do everything. We need to change our attitude that "mother" is just another name for guilt and worry. Working mothers often have more guilt and worry simply because they recognize their children's needs yet lack the time, energy, and mental faculties by the end of a long workday to take care of these needs. We all fear for our children in some way. We want to raise emotionally healthy and secure children with whom we have cooperative, respectful relationships. Parenting may be the most difficult job in existence. We are not given any formal training or education, yet we must assume the awesome responsibility of raising human beings.

Psychological research points out that the mother-child relationship during the first three years is crucial to developing the child's sense of self. This includes self-esteem and a sense of security and trust in the world. Thus, the early mother-child relationship is extremely important. Ideally, the infant will be emotionally fulfilled by his mother—primary caretaker's—love and nurturing. The nurturing experience during this critical period determines how full the child's cup of mother's love will be throughout his or her life. Will he or she feel secure with the full cup of mother's love to carry with him or her in his or her life endeavors to sustain through the trials and tribulations of life's journey? Or will he or she be hampered by an internal void or a cup that is empty? He or she must search throughout life for the love, approval, and attention from others and fill up the void with addictions because he or she did not receive them during the critical period. Will he or she be externally focused and needy because you could not focus on yours? Mothers need to be on guard about being stressed out, rushed, impatient, and regretful. Mothers set the stage for their children's security.

We all have the experience of being at school, work, or a social event and being unable to concentrate because we feel we left the stove burning or we misplaced something important. We spend our time wondering if we should return home to check and correct the situation. We cannot relax or enjoy what we are currently doing. This constant state of insecurity is the experience of the individual who has not gotten the sense of "mother at home, everything is okay" during the critical years. The person experiences chronic anxiety, insecurity, and worry and has difficulty concentrating, much like we felt when we feared when we left the stove burning or misplaced something important. They learn less and enjoy fewer things in their lives. People learn to bury or ignore the underlying insecurity and turn to addictions to numb the pain and fill the void.

Not only do young children need a parent at home but also older children, who continue to need the stable mothering figure and unconditional love to grow up emotionally healthily. Dr. Ross Campbell explains in his book, *How to Really Love Your Child*, that often children's behavior problems stem from lack of parental unconditional love *as experienced by the child*. Parents usually care about and love their children. However, this love may not be felt. Parents can communicate their love through appropriate physical contact, eye contact, and focused attention. Quality time is to the child not just some special treat but rather focused attention: when the parent relaxes and hangs out with the child and meets the child's needs from the child's viewpoint (while setting appropriate safety limits)—the parent visualizes the child as whole and perfect, the child plays, the parent sends vibes of love to the child, and confirms the child's joyful essence.

When a child behaves poorly, Dr. Campbell encourages the parent to wonder what emotional needs are going unmet. By thinking in a psychological, detective manner—using the Gendlin focusing process—a parent can figure out a child's underlying motive for acting up. Then the parent can meet the emotional needs directly to diminish the poor behavior. In other words, children express themselves through actions rather than words, and we, as parents, must read between the lines. Dr. Campbell gives an example of how his second son started acting up after his first son returned home from camp. During the time when the first son was away at camp, the second son was getting a lot more attention. He then began to act up. In a way, he was asking if he was still important. Instead of reprimanding his son for his behavior, Dr. Campbell talked his son to verbalize his underlying fear of lack of love, reassured him, and began to increase his focused attention on his son in order to help him feel secure.

Penelope Leach, PhD, a British psychologist and author of a number of parenting books, is outspoken against day care. For instance, she believes it is essential for babies to be with their mothers for the first two to three years of life. She explains that until an infant is about three months old, he has no sense of himself as a separate being. At that age, he begins to realize his caregiver is not in his control. This is very scary. He is unsure of his caregiver's constant devotion to meeting his needs. He feels helpless and fearful for his own survival. This is why an infant needs a one-to-one relationship with his caregiver. The consistency gives him a secure feeling, as if allowing him to reassure himself, "When I speak, you will acknowledge me. I am not powerless, not a nuisance or an object." This is the foundation of self-esteem and the belief that one is lovable and important, which is essential to creating a good life.

Consciousness does create. If you have made mistakes, know there are no mistakes; there is either success or learning to succeed. If you entertain the idea or belief that we are spirit and come to life with a soul and purpose, you also know that there is no reason for us as mothers to feel any guilt or blame. Children pull what they need from us. They can be very good at that, even under difficult situations. They also draw to themselves things that are right for their spiritual purpose, which could even include tragedies (by appearance), such as complete abandonment. You also know that consciousness changes everything, and when you are an adult, you can completely heal from any experiences you have had as a child or infant.

Maternal guilt is an emotion that needs to be erased. To evaluate one's guilt, Harriet Learner, PhD, advises to ask yourself two basic questions: (1) Are you doing something that is compromising your values that you know is wrong? (2) Are you breaking a promise or a commitment to someone? If you answer no to both questions, then your guilt is bad guilt and needs to be released and let go. If you are actually breaking a promise or violating a value, like stealing, then this is good guilt to guide you and remind you how to behave. Maternal guilt is almost all bad guilt.

Money issues

Many people unfortunately are addicted to money, work, or status. Particularly, middle-class citizens tend to revolve their lives around money. They believe the amount of money they have dictates what they can and cannot do. Women suffer a great deal of neglect when they try to work too much. Because of addiction to money and big-ticket (external status) items—like big houses and extravagant children's birthday parties—there is a fear that people will not have enough money to afford the nice things that everyone has. A woman can fear cutting back at work that she will not have any power over the money because she is "not really working."

Finances are not a reason to continue to work if you and your family are stressed out. Many women today work full-time and place their children with babysitters and day care. Dual-career couples, moving at breakneck speed, experience a lot of stress with no time to figure out how much the woman working is actually costing them financially. These overwhelmed dual-career couples, who attribute the stress to something else than the woman's working, would be shocked at how much the woman's work is actually costing them.

Any woman who is tired or sick, angry, and unhappy a lot should *calculate the cost of her working versus the amount of money she actually brings home*. This amount can be a dismaying shock. One woman I knew who worked six days a week as a hospital technician calculated that she only made $17 a week! Six days a week of work left her little time to spend with her family or to take care of herself. We calculated this by adding up the cost of gas to and from work, day care, babysitting costs, lunches, and other work-related costs, such as special work clothes. Then she subtracted that total from her net paycheck amount. We also included the more subtle costs of working too much. For example, she was so rushed that she bought fast food a lot. Thus, she could not keep her weight down and became obese, which she knew was related to chronic health conditions. This fast-food frenzy increased her food bill compared to healthier home cooking. Her day care preschooler was sick more frequently because he was exposed to more germs, which resulted in more doctor visits, more medicine, and more money going to health care.

Every working mother may not be able to whittle down their net pay minus expenses to $17 a week. I recently worked with a woman who did retail work and was making $100 a week after calculating expenses.

So our next step was to look at what areas in her budget she could reduce. After that, she realized she was making only $40 a week. Rather than working full-time for this $40, she let her job go, determined to figure out where she could get the extra $40. With an abundance of consciousness, she realized she had plenty of savings to cover this. She was able to pursue her dream of starting a small catering business, which easily made up the difference eventually.

When a lifestyle change is made and a woman reduces her work hours to take care of her family, the whole person needs are met and life joy increases. For example, this woman stopped pushing herself, and her chronic health conditions—like headaches, backaches, and stomachaches—subsided, and thus the medical bills were reduced. Once at home, she had more time for cooking, thereby saving money on restaurant food, which cost a lot and is highly caloric in comparison. She lost weight. There is time to think about expenses and improve the budget. The woman's relationship improved because she no longer feels tired, which reduced marital and family arguments, which could have led to the major expense of therapy and divorce—alimony and child support.

Although a person may not realize it, money worries are often an excuse to cover up personal concerns, such as the ones that have already been mentioned in previous sections of this book. Sometimes unconscious, emotional, psychological reasons or defense mechanisms underlie the overworking and overfunctioning and need to be addressed in order for the woman to reduce her work hours and be at home more. Some women who come from dysfunctional family backgrounds work to keep busy and avoid painful feelings. They may have felt criticized or put down and not good enough by their parents and thus overcompensate by trying to accomplish too much and look good. They do not slow down because they might have to experience unresolved grief or pain—or face a fear of intimacy.

The following are some reasons women overwork:

1. Self-esteem is based on work. Women equate the value of themselves with the job role. The solution, however, is not to continue to work full-time to prove one is worth something. Rather self-esteem needs to increase through counseling, women's support groups, and personal affirmation. Women can do what they want (even laying low at work and spending more time on selves and family) while *feeling* worthwhile.
2. Women are afraid to cut back at work because they won't have money. The solution is not to keep "plugging on" but to take the time to analyze and plan out your finances. First of all, are you really making that much money from your work when you consider all that you have to spend to support your absence from the home: day care fees, gas, eating out, professional clothes, not to mention subtler costs, like increased medical bills for the children from being in day care? Sometimes just cutting out things you don't need and won't even use—budgeting—is the real answer to this fear.
3. Women miss the intellectual and social stimulation they receive at work. Everyone (including mothers) has rights to get their whole person needs met. Everyone has the right to have breaks from their job, even from mothering with its continuous obligations. The satisfied woman today does not need to work full-time. She needs to arrange a daily break to take care of her whole person needs (e.g., exercise, have social outlets, participate in intellectual stimulating tasks, like workshops and reading). She is not totally responsible for the housework. She has babysitters, dad, relatives, teens, or nannies so she can continue to take care of herself. Aspire to not be bound to the housework like the woman of the fifties unless you enjoy it. Rather, pay for it and delegate or minimize the responsibility by asking her spouse, children, or other relatives or a teenager to help.

Part B—creating a lifestyle that allows you to care for yourself (and your family)

Practical guidelines during your life phase of motherhood

This section is about changing your lifestyle to take care of yourself during your mommy years. As you use the focusing technique to soul search and examine your needs and feelings, you make changes in your everyday life situations. You automatically become more assertive—knowing more what you want and being able then to express your feelings more confidently. You express your needs more clearly because you understand yourself better. You'll set limits more and assertively say no to things that do not feel comfortable for you, rather than giving in to please others or taking on too many responsibilities. You find yourself standing up for your rights, feelings, and needs more in your relationships. You are true to yourself and firm with others rather than giving into others' demands and expectations "selflessly" (without considering or respecting your own self, feelings, or needs). You recognize aggressive and intimidating tactics that significant others in your life may use (like putting blame on you or insulting you or denying or making excuses for disrespectful and irresponsible behavior toward you) to get you to let them have it their way.

As you focus inward and act on your feeling and needs, you intuitively make an overall lifestyle change so that your life is balanced and fulfilling. You work just enough to keep a standard of living you enjoy but not too much to be stressful; you have enough time to devote to your children, and the quality of their surrogate care is good enough that you do not worry about your children's needs being met well. You have the time, energy, and communication skills to foster a healthy marriage based on mutual respect. You have the time, energy, self-esteem, and support systems to live your life as a whole person. You believe you have rights and have the time and energy to meet your needs (mental, social, physical, spiritual, emotional, and will) in a fulfilled way. You are not engaging in addictive behaviors (you would not be preoccupied by getting your needs met through some external focus—work, gambling, alcohol, and caretaking others).

The following is a strategy to correct life situations so that you can change your lifestyle to take care of yourself and family and enjoy your mothering years:

1. First of all, think about how many hours per week you can realistically work and still take care of your needs and your family's needs satisfactorily and enjoyably. Write down what you need to do each week. Make out a tentative schedule for carrying out your responsibilities. Be sure to include time for sleep. The average woman needs eight hours nightly. Also, include a nap or rest time if you are a mother of little children because they tend to wake you at night and you need to compensate for the lost sleep. (Don't nap too long, or this will interfere with night sleep. Lay down quickly when you feel very tired and take a short power nap). When you have completed this somewhat-tedious-but-important schedule, you may be shocked at how little time you actually can devote to work! Face it—you have been pushing it, and many of the problems you have been experiencing (but blaming on other things) can probably be attributed to your overworking! Be brave and cut back your hours. Figure out how to switch jobs. Better still, become independent. For example, do freelance. Remember the figure of ten hours of work for mothers of preschoolers and twenty-five for mothers of school-age children (hours including work, preparation, travel time, and personal time). Whatever you do, be brave and make yourself the priority. Revolve around yourself and your needs and have faith that, as Jesus said, the kingdom of heaven is on earth and to paraphrase, "Ask, believing you already have it, and do not doubt and ye shall receive." (Whatever your religion, such beliefs are usually shared).

2. Ask yourself, "What are my reasons for being reluctant to cut back at work?" Confront them one by one—low self-esteem, fear of loss, or addiction to money and status. Go obtain whatever

support you need to heal your fears and concerns—spiritual counseling, psychotherapy, financial counseling to help with budgeting, and long talks with your husband—and then reduce your work hours and stress.

If you believe your need to work is more important than you are and the areas of your life which are suffering from your overworking, then stop reading here.

It makes sense financially to work full-time if the woman commands a great deal of money for her full-time services. Otherwise, costs for gas, lunches, and day care use up most of the wages anyway. Of course, if the mother has a mental or physical disorder, a nanny is also needed because it would be risky for her to be the primary caretaker alone.

It is very difficult for a woman to work full-time and raise children, particularly preschoolers, and not neglect something—herself, her husband, or her children's needs. It also requires incredible support systems and conditions (like money for a housekeeper and nanny) beyond the resources of many people. It is essential to have an employer who is flexible because mothers need to be absent from work to take care of sick children and other home emergencies.

3. Keep your hand in your career so you can keep your skills honed for when you wish to reenter your field. Collegial contacts can be maintained through social lunches. Skills can be maintained through professional reading and working part-time. Intellectual stimulation can be maintained through reading, workshops, and talking with others in the field. Social needs can be met by meeting with other mothers or other adults who share similar interests and hobbies.

The conditions of mothers who work full-time successfully are:

1. Mother traits:

   A. Robust health of the mother who also has a low sleep need.
   B. Mother has to really feel okay about letting somebody else be the primary caretaker of the children and in charge of her home. She should not feel guilty or depressed because she believes she is missing her children's early years and their relationship.

2. Excellent support systems:

   A. Full-time housekeeper and nanny for young children. An employee can sometimes be better than grandparents to care for the children while mothers work because grandparents are trying to wear two hats (grandparents are meant to love and spoil grandchildren)—not just take over the caretaking responsibility and meet their grandchildren's needs. However, somebody else has to take care of the home and children if the mother is not at home. One has to reason that for every hour a woman is out of the home, that is time taken away from some homemaking responsibility. Mothers of the fifties who did not work out of the home found childcare and homemaking to be a full-time job. A full-time nanny (or nanny and housekeeper) is obviously necessary when there are preschoolers. This is sometimes necessary for school-age children so someone is there for them when they get home from school. This gives the mother backup help when children are sick or on vacation.
   B. A part-time nanny for school-age children: Give the children a continued devoted person to help them grow into whole, fulfilled children while you're away. The attention given to a child's needs (social, emotional, physical, spiritual, and mental willpower) is the attention the

child as an adult will probably give to himself as an adult; the child is learning through his relationship with his or her caretakers how important his or her needs are.

C. Flexible, supportive husband who functions well in an egalitarian relationship with his wife and has good communication and listening skills. For example, he should be willing and able to split the home and childcare duties, such as:

1. Take off from work to meet children's needs during work hours, such as taking them to the doctor when they are sick.
2. Share home responsibilities. It's only fair for both spouses to have time for recreation and relaxation and taking care of personal needs. The wife should not be taking care of most of the home and child responsibilities with no time for herself while the husband has excessive time for hobbies. The number of hours for personal needs and responsibilities should be about the same for both spouses.

D. Flexible, supportive employer. Mothers have to have an employer willing to tolerate absences to take care of children. There are emergency situations, such as doctor's visits for illness and accidents or even a child forgetting his lunch. There are absences related to routine situations, like medical and dentist visits.

Because the above criteria may be beyond the current capability of the couple, the better option for most people is for the working mother to figure out the least number of hours she has to work to meet the family financial budget. Working outside the home (two to two and a half days a week, which fits the woman's family's schedule) with a housekeeper and nanny for the hours worked, a supportive boss, and a supportive husband can work well. Independent or freelance work on a less part-time basis (working from home) with good support systems is an option because the woman has fewer employer's demands to meet. She can work the number of hours and schedule her work hours to better meet her and her family's needs.

Full-time homemaking is also a manageable option. A woman might try sequencing—staying at home during the children's early years and gradually building up work hours as the physically exhausting demands of early child-rearing diminishes. Full-time mothering is probably best for younger women who do not have skills they need to continue to practice in the workplace because they are not bringing in much money anyway. These women can take educational courses and training, thereby getting intellectual stimulation as they mother. In the case of the younger woman (early twenties) who has not already developed a career, full-time mothering can then phase into a career or preparation (such as schooling and training) as the children grow older. Then the woman is prepared to get a job when she thinks the time is right and she can manage work and family well. When the life phase of the empty nest occurs (children leaving home), she is ready for an active, challenging career. During the various phases, she has not had to neglect herself or her family's needs.

Older, childless women (in late thirties and older) who have enjoyed the challenge of careers long enough and find their biological clocks ticking away can decide to enjoy the mothering phase and withdraw from the workforce completely with good money planning.

Women who have already developed professional and technical skills and want to work prior to the empty nest phase might try sequencing by keeping their hands in their careers to keep the skills and professional contacts. Limiting work hours to a minimum would be the rule. Do not burn yourself out taking on two full-time challenges (motherhood and career). Make a schedule. Write down your home and children responsibilities and put it in the form of a weekly schedule.

Exercise: Think about your whole person rights and put your needs down on your schedule how and when you will fulfill them during the week. Add these into your schedule. Here are some examples:

Health needs: Physical exercise three or four times a week. Eight hours of sleep nightly and rest or nap (at least thirty minutes) during the day if you need it or if you have very young children. Time for special health needs, such as if you have an illness or weakness.

Spiritual needs: Church or temple if you are religious. Daily spiritual practice, meditation, or prayer.

Socializing or recreation: Talking with your husband in a friendly manner daily at least one hour a week for problem-solving, two hours a week for social time with peers, and date with husband.

Emotional: Time every day for self-reflection and focusing inward on your needs, time to feel and express feeling, anger, fear, sadness, joy, or intellectual. At least two hours per week for creative pursuits or hobby.

Responsibilities: A certain number of hours to do laundry per week, two to three meals per day, childcare, then add up the hours—eighty plus, right?

Then write down what your children's whole person needs are and how you can meet them. Example, arrange routine such that they get enough sleep per night and arrange outside time for exercise and time necessary for you to cook nutritious foods for them.

Social: Playtime per week with peers.

Spiritual: Sunday school or religious education one hour per week, daily prayers, or spiritual practice.

Mental: School, nursery school, intellectual projects at home for young children not in school, depending on the child's developmental needs.

Emotional: Keeping your pace slow enough so you have time to be patient and to listen to and help your child feel wanted, express feelings and needs, and make choices so you can provide positive, focused attention.

Then write out a weekly schedule outlining when each of these activities occurs. You will probably be surprised to see that you have been trying to cram thirty-four hours of activities into a twenty-four-hour day. So be realistic. You cannot do it all. Write out a schedule that allows you to treat yourself and others respectfully and responsibly. Then strive to change your lifestyle. Get the household help you need. Talk to significant others, such as your spouse and other family members, to work out equality in your relationship so responsibilities are divided in a fair manner rather than you having to overfunction. Change jobs or cut back your hours to allow yourself to live a full life.

How to figure out a week's schedule to meet your and your family's needs

Step 1: Make your weekly schedule of chores and responsibilities. Write down what you do when you usually do it. Write in pencil in case, when you look at it later, you desire to make changes.

Step 2: Be sure to see that you are meeting your children's whole person (mental, emotional, physical, spiritual, and will) needs as part of your child-rearing responsibilities. Write in how and when you will meet your children's needs. By choosing to have children, this is your child-rearing job.

Step 3: After you have written your schedule, look it over. Consider your energy level. You do not want to try to do too much in one day and wear yourself out. Try to balance physically taxing and sedentary activities in a day. Make changes in your schedule if you see you are piling up too many chores in one day. Keep in mind the two-things-at-a-time rule. Don't multitask beyond two things at a time. For example, cook and watch children—not cook, watch children, and talk on the phone.

Step 4: Now think about your whole person needs. For example, regarding your physical needs, your schedules will need to allow you enough time for proper rest time (and nap possibly) each day. So look carefully over your schedule and leave appropriate time spaces for a break, proper rest, and exercise.

A. Copy the empty circle or draw one with approximate pie slices for the whole person categories labeled "mental," "physical," "spiritual," "emotional," "social," and "will."
B. Then write in several needs for each area, e.g., how you plan to fulfill yourself mentally, physically, spiritually, emotionally, socially, and will. At this time, you may need to use the focusing process. (What do I want? What feels bad? Why? What will make it truly better?) You may also want to think back over your life to remember what kinds of things you enjoyed in the past, and you may want to try those activities now. You may be so overwhelmed you cannot remember how to fulfill your needs. So think about yourself and what you enjoyed in less stressful times. Think about your fantasies and about what you might enjoy.
C. Now write in your organized weekly schedule how you will meet your whole person needs.

Regarding physical needs, remember to allow time for proper sleep (eight hours) and daytime rest, time to eat, and get exercise at least three times a week.

Regarding social, intellectual, and emotional stimulation, try to schedule a daily childcare break, a two-hour one, from the childcare each day, which you do something that you enjoy (be that social, like a woman's group meeting, something intellectually stimulating, like reading, and exercise if you enjoy it). Try to use at least a half hour for resting and focusing. Ask for help to make sure that you do get your free time. Negotiate an egalitarian relationship with your husband. He works outside the home; you work inside. The children are his responsibility too, not just yours. Share the childcare on weekends. Plan out how each of you can have personal time, time for rest and exercise. Point out that you are a person too! If you can't get help from your husband, hire a babysitter or mother's helper or even a young teenager to come to your house while you are there so you can have a break.

Regarding intellectual, especially when time is tight, as in the case with many full-time working mothers, women get much of their social and intellectual needs met in the workplace. Their friends are coworkers. They chat during breaks. Intellectual stimulation comes from the work challenge. Who has time for hobbies if you work full-time? Making a lifestyle change challenges us to fill the void the work once filled. At home, one has to use some ingenuity to get these social and intellectual needs met. Learn a new skill. Take a class. Do some soul-searching to determine what are truly fulfilling activities to meet your social and intellectual needs. This usually results in a choice of activities more fulfilling than what was available at the workplace. Think about and make a list of past activities that you enjoyed. Be brave and attend or even create groups that meet your needs. Groups are nice because you can usually depend on someone showing up, whereas individual mothers sometimes have to cancel due to sickness or other needs of children. Churches are often good for developing social ties. Find out which ones have memberships or peer group activities that interest you and meet at hours you can attend. Even start a group if you do not find one to your liking available. For example, if you belong to a church you like that does not have a women's circle, you can start one. Remember this is a process—a work in progress.

Regarding social relationships, think about all the current relationships you are in—with your spouse, other family members, and friends. Think about how you would like these relationships to be and what you would like more of through these relationships. Share these thoughts and feelings with these people to create more emotionally satisfying relationships.

True emotional fulfillment does not come from work status.

Regarding emotional, if you are unhappy, focus in on what is bothering you, take charge, and change the situation. Small changes can mean big differences in life satisfaction. Also, keep the boundaries. Don't depend on anyone to take care of you. (Do not expect to get exercise with children. They may not behave.) Do ask them for help with chores so you can have the extra time for exercise. In other words, you can't expect others to take care of your whole person needs, but you can adjust your responsibilities so that you have the time and energy to meet your own whole person needs.

The three keys to self-fulfillment while staying at home during the mothering phase are:

1. Scheduling daily breaks to take care of yourself.
2. Doing something enjoyable each day (getting your whole person needs met).
3. Being able to ask for help.
4. Proper sleep, diet, and exercise.

How can these be accomplished?

1. A daily rest or nap if you give your health and emotional well-being priority over achievement and getting chores done. Put your feet up and rest or nap while the little ones nap or engage in a quiet, safe activity, like playing in the playpen or watching TV. Try to arrange your children's schedule so they rest together. Be religious about resting while they rest. Take the phones off the hook or turn on the answering machine. Ignore all else. If you feel you really have too much work to do, lie down and plan out your chores and mull over difficult problems. At least your body can rest, and you may find your mind will doze off.
2. Schedule a daily pleasurable activity to meet your needs means you have to arrange childcare. This could mean your nanny and housekeeper time is used not only for work but a few hours for your own personal needs and chores. Hire a teenage babysitter to come a couple afternoons a week. Arrange with a relative for the children to visit once a week. Work out with your husband for him to be responsible for the children a couple of hours a week and part of the weekend. Use this time for your meeting whole person needs, not chores. Being able to ask for help is often the crux of self-care. With children, you could be working all your waking—and sleeping—hours.
3. Keep in mind that research has shown that a person can only do two things well at once. If you start to feel overwhelmed, think about what you are trying to do. Stop and cut back to two things at a time. For example, are you trying to entertain and talk with your children while fixing dinner? (How many children? Three!) Put at least two of the children where they are safe and occupied independently (playpen or artwork). This way, you are cooking and talking to one child only at the same time. According to this rule, if the phone rings (cooking and phone calls are two things, remember?), you would need to occupy the other child in an independent endeavor as well during the phone call. The two-things-at-a-time rule can apply to major life responsibilities as well. For example, child-rearing and taking care of oneself are two things. You need to get help to take over the tasks in one area if you take on more than two life major endeavors. Full-time work would necessitate a nanny and housekeeper to take care of the child-rearing area. Nobody is going to be able to take care of you except you.

Having a part-time nanny and housekeeper or mother's helper in your home can be less expensive than placing your children in day care. This is particularly true if you have more than one child to pay for and when you consider subtle costs, such as that children in day care are sick more frequently, which means increased medical expenses.

A nanny and housekeeper or mother's helper may, in addition to caring for the children, do laundry, dishes, and other light household maintenance, which reduces your stress level. This helps keep your health better and makes you less likely to resort to quick fixes to cope, like fast food, which costs more than home cooking. Help in the house generally gives you more support, such as time to think about how you want to run your life, which should cut down on overspending or spending money impulsively to cover feelings of dissatisfaction.

The woman who makes the decision to work minimally or not at all during these mothering years needs to realize she is mothering. She is not just a mother, her role, or her job. Rather, she is a person who is doing the job of mothering. She remains a whole person with social, intellectual, spiritual, physical, and emotional needs. She has a right to try to get these needs met even though children's needs and wants may be constant (as much as twenty-four hours a day, seven days a week).

She needs to plan out childcare help so she can take care of her needs regularly. She needs to take the time to arrange time away from the children through her husband and sitters. As a general rule, she needs to arrange at least a one-hour (two if possible) break daily to do something pleasurable that meet her whole person needs (example, resting, exercise for physical health, reading, intellectual stimulation, socializing, taking time to focus, attend support groups or counseling to get needs met, praying, meditating, or some kind of spiritual practice).

She needs to schedule daily naps or rest times to compensate for the physical demands of mothering and nighttime losses of sleep. Allowing oneself to get too tired results in a lack of patience and nurturance, which is the main reason you have decided to be at home. At any type of work, the worker gets breaks. Mothering should be treated no differently.

The woman who makes a lifestyle change to be at home needs to realize she will be experiencing numerous losses of social, emotional, and intellectual stimulation that she got at work. She may be lonely and bored at first. The reason many women do not want to quit work is because at least at work you can talk and socialize with adults during breaks. The tasks are often intellectually challenging. Adults recognize your efforts. At home, the adult stimulation and support is missing at first. Creating this is the goal of the woman during the first year at home.

Remember when you care for yourself, you are actually better at caring for others. Talk to yourself positively. Don't call yourself names, like "selfish."

How to make the lifestyle change

1. First, you must change poverty consciousness to prosperity or abundance consciousness. Make up affirmations to yourself that reflect belief in you and your life's goodness and that you are provided for at all times.
2. Say these affirmations regularly.
3. Analyze your income and expenses, as in the above example, including subtle costs, like the toll overworking is costing you in ill health (doctor visits and prescriptions). Figure out how much money you are actually netting per week. Deduct nonessential expenses that you are willing to give up. Be open to help to compensate for any leftover expense.
4. Moms, be brave and cut back or even quit your job. Trust that your ideas can be realized. You can savor your mothering years and fulfill your own and your family's whole person needs.
5. Compliment yourself for choosing to change.

Creating a schedule reflecting your new lifestyle of self-love

> You may have been getting many needs met at your job—for example, socializing with coworkers, getting emotional support, and obtaining mental stimulation from the work activities. Now you will have to create activities that will fulfill you at home—true-to-self passions.
>
> Step 1: Draw whole person circles for yourself and children. Fill in the blank with passions that you intend to pursue like you did in the whole person model exercise. Draw one up for your children as well.
> Step 2: Write out your weekly schedule (Monday to Sunday). Insert the actual times you plan to carry out your responsibilities, including laundry and grocery shopping. Notice where you have free time spaces and insert your whole person passions onto
> your agenda as if they were any other responsibility on the list. Actually, schedule the times that you would perform these activities. Remember this is a process. Many mothers initially feel overwhelmed by this exercise. They assume they have to meet all their whole person needs right away. This is for you—not to add additional stress or demands. Gradually add activities that reflect your passions at a pace that works for you.
> Tip: I tend to run late all the time so I set my clock ten minutes fast to ensure that I will be on time when I go somewhere. When I look at the clock, I forget it is ten minutes fast, and it gets me going. In other words, put some breathing room into your schedule. For example, when one of the children act up, you have time to take care of them—and yourself!

Chapter 10

Shine the Light

This little light of mine. I'm going to let it shine. Let it shine! Let it shine! Let it shine!

—famous song of our childhood

The real key to transform your life is to recognize that we, and the entire universe, are all light energy or beings—divine sparks of the white light energy that comes from one source. We know this from many scientific fields, including the cutting-edge physics information regarding the zero-point field and the observer effect—the power of intention creates reality—the ultimate source all love. When you reach a vibration of love for yourself and others and raise your children to truly care for themselves, you raise the human race to reach a critical mass of love and understanding so we can achieve brotherhood and harmony.

Groups of scientists and great thinkers all over the world are working on the revolutionary concept now. White light is a combination of all colors of the spectrum. This light spectrum will be utilized in medicine for diagnosis and treatment. This white light discovery of energy will help us transcend our race (human race) consciousness—the limiting beliefs we have regarding differences in terms of race, gender, nationality, religion, and all superficial characteristics—because we will realize that we are all one—love, light, and laughter. Choose to use your energy and power and shine your light to create heaven on earth.

Recently, I traveled with a group. The power of intention was made empirically clear through our digital camera photos. White circles of lights not visible to the naked eye—manifestations called orbs—appeared. If you question whether orbs are merely photographic artifacts, like dust or smudge on the lens, why were they showing up consistently on everybody's cameras? Later, I investigated—read up on this phenomenon on the Internet, which disputes convincingly any material causes—in any event, if the power of intent increases photographic smudges, then it is still a demonstration, right?

What are orbs? They look like white lit-up decorative Christmas spheres. They are speculated to be light beings, souls angels, ethereal energy imprints, nature spirits, or quantum physics encoding of messages to help us remember who we are. We do not know. What we do know is they appear in pictures taken with digital cameras. What we found out is they increase in appearance in response to the power of intention, prayer, worship, and ceremony. On this spiritual retreat, we visited sites to raise consciousness regarding respect for feminine energy in our world. Our positive consciousness preceded us—a few orbs were noted on our preliminary photos, which then led us to try an experiment to see what would happen if we sent these orbs love and light. To our amazement, all the different digital photos revealed that, through shining our light, the orbs proliferated like a single flower whose pollen has been carried to bloom and create an abundant meadow of wildflowers. I wish I could show you another powerful photo, which to protect privacy rights I cannot include in the book. After planting in the ground a special gift she had brought, one group member held her arms high in a victory V shape. The photo revealed a large orb tucked between her hands like a big beach ball!

Check out these before and after photos (see the next page) and take the orb challenge yourself. Aim your camera toward the light for more clear results. Choose to shine your light everywhere and create heaven on earth.

We are all one—love, light, and laughter!

Homework for the rest of your life

Ways to transform

1. Use thought stopping of negative thought and replace it with positive self-talk at the moment religiously (excuse the pun).
2. Learn to visualize and engage in whatever daily spiritual practice connects you to your source. Envision your life and your world as good—the way you desire it.
3. Keep a gratitude journal. Do count your blessings.
4. Surround yourself with positive-minded people.
5. Focus on the good in yourself and your world and know that through seeing yourself and others as whole and perfect, this will manifest in your life. Whatever you put your attention on grows.
6. Read and attend classes and workshops related to the power of thoughts that will help you learn more about how to transform yourself, to love yourself, and to love life. Extra resources were mentioned in the references section, and there are many more sources.
7. Find a cognitively knowledgeable, enlightened psychotherapist, such as a licensed clinical psychologist, who focuses on positive self-talk and understands the power of intention.
8. Affirm daily, as needed, "I am good, and I have, and I deserve all good" and "I release all fear, and I accept only the joy of the moment and the harmony, peace, and love of my experiences and relationships." Add your own affirmations on a piece of paper.

Glossary

Adult Child of an Alcoholic (ACOA). A person who, while growing up, had a parent or guardian who had an alcohol problem. Many people do not realize their parent had a problem. People with alcohol problems tend to hide it well. This is why it is called a family disease. Ever heard of the analogy of the pink elephant in the living room? The whole family ignores the problem. The children have been trained to think they, or something else, are to blame for the afflicted parent's irresponsible, disrespectful, and erratic behavior. This is similar also to the story of "The Emperor's New Clothes" when the whole kingdom was conned into thinking the tailors made the king beautiful garments when he was really naked.

Another reason people don't realize that their parents may have an alcohol problem is that alcoholism is a progressive disease, and people tend to associate alcoholism with the late phase only—when the alcoholic is drinking early in the day, every day, and obviously drunk, passing out, exhibiting total dysfunction. Most people think that if they only drink a couple of times a month, they are not alcoholics.

In actuality, alcoholism has four phases, beginning with problem drinking during which the person with the alcohol problem may be only drinking a couple of drinks a couple times a week, regularly looking forward to relaxing with alcohol. In this problem-drinking phase, the person is psychologically dependent whereas as the disease progresses, he or she has become physically addicted and cannot stop drinking without experiencing withdrawal symptoms, which are at their worst—tremors and hallucinations—at the late phase. That person is about five years from death through some kind of organ failure related to alcohol poisoning of the body. Prior to the final phase, the first three phases could last anywhere from five to thirty-five years because the person is less physically addicted—experiences less severe withdrawal—and therefore can stop when they experience enough flack or pressure from their environment—for example, DWI (driving while intoxicated), spouse, family, or employer pressure. The alcoholic stops temporarily whereby fooling himself and everyone that he does not have an alcohol problem. Yet the problem progresses. Eventually, he gradually resumes drinking, and the life consequences get more severe as the drinking increases over time. The hallmarks of the phases are:

Phase 1: Problem drinking, even drinking a couple of drinks a couple of times a week on a regular basis with the expectation of relaxation—escapism.
Phase 2: Family conflict, verbal aggression, and irresponsibility.
Phase 3: Job, legal (DWI), and financial problems.
Phase 4: As stated earlier, constant drinking, all the above problems. Late phase leads to death from some organ failure.

Active Listening. An aspect of communication whereby, contrary to how we usually have been taught to talk, the receiver of the message doesn't interrupt with his or her own viewpoint. The listener keeps quiet or reflects back to the talker or sender of the message the sender's own thoughts, feelings, and needs to show concern and to make sure he understands what is being said. In a respectful communication process, the roles then reverse, and the other person has a chance to express and be heard. The goal is win-win negotiation whereby both parties' view and needs are now out on the table, and some form of compromise or mutually satisfying solution can be decided.

Addiction. Any mental preoccupation of a person's energy and time that interferes with the person being responsible, respectful, and caring to self and to others. Addictions can be hard or soft. An example of a soft addiction would be when a husband comes home and watches TV all evening while the house falls down around him or his wife is overwhelmed, overworked, and enraged and the children are ignored. Hard addictions are more familiar to us—like alcohol or drug use (including recreational and prescription drugs). A compulsive eater with diabetes is another example. A sex addict committing adultery is another. Sometimes, addictions, like workalcoholism or codependency (overly caring and overfunctioning for others, like family members), look good on the surface and do provide superficial benefits to the person or others. But the person and his or her family's real deeper needs are neglected—for example, health deteriorates, relationship satisfaction declines, and so on.

Affirmation. Positive statements you make to yourself—inspiring messages that uplift you emotionally and guide you to think positively about yourself and your life. For example, "I am good, and I have and deserve good things in my life."

Alcoholism. A person can be an alcoholic and not drink at all or only drink a couple of drinks a month. See also **Adult Children of Alcoholics (ACOA)** for the description of the disease and its stages.

Anger. You may wonder why I have included such an obvious word. Many people think of anger or its variants (annoyance, irritation, or rage) as an emotion to be reckoned with. Actually, it is a superficial defense mechanism to clue us in that we need to check in with ourselves to discover the genuine emotions—fear and sadness—that we need to address. Anger is the red flag or signal that something is not going well for us internally emotionally to ask ourselves the questions, "What's below? Am I sad or scared [or some form of these—hurt, disappointed, rejected, or anxious, nervous, worried]?"

Assertiveness. Healthy form of communication whereby one person shares I messages about herself, and the other person actively listens (feeds back what the person said), and the roles reverse—with the goal being open, honest, intimate, and sharing about oneself, one's needs, one's background, and so on so that both parties can truly get to know and understand each other and proceed to negotiate solutions to their interpersonal or personal problem that are mutually satisfying.

Catharsis. Venting and releasing of true emotions—sadness, grief, fear, or terror—through safe ways that are nonharmful to self or others, such as crying, talking emotionally about, or physically releasing the stress, such as taking an old tennis racket to some old phone books and pounding on them while revisiting in your mind some negative experience. (You can talk out loud. Just be sure nobody is around to wonder what you are doing or interfere with your releasing.)

Cognition. The heavy technical term which psychologists—and other talk-therapy-type helping professionals—use to mean one's thoughts, particularly one's statements about oneself and one's world.

Cognitive. About thoughts or inner thinking, particularly self-statements—what one thinks or says about oneself and one's world, positively or negatively.

Cognitive Therapy or Cognitive Behavior Therapy. Psychotherapy based on helping the client change his negative, put-down, disillusioning thought patterns to positive self-enhancing thoughts that help him believe in himself and believe that positive life outcomes are in store and that he or she has the control to *create* his or her life. Research has proven this to work, including to change brain chemistry without drugs—for example, to increase serotonin in the brain and thereby diminish depression without antidepressants.

Consciousness. Your thoughts, your beliefs, any internal talking or thinking or words you use to express to yourself. All humans have this inner dialogue going on inside themselves. Ironically, consciousness, as used in this case, is partly unconscious and below your conscious awareness—namely, the beliefs or attitudes that you hold that you do not admit to yourself because they would be too painful in some way to acknowledge to yourself and are deeply blocked out or buried, yet it still affects your attitude about yourself and your world and your life.

Collective Unconscious or Race or Human Race Consciousness. Thoughts or beliefs that we, as a group of humans, believe. Although we may not be aware of them or admit we buy into them, they still affect how we run our lives. For example, that people with alcoholism will get worse; that people who are married should do everything together; that Americans should have two cars, a house, and two children; and so on. These beliefs limit our freedom.

Chemical Dependency. Dependency or preoccupation of time and energy with alcohol and/or drugs of some sort, which can be recreational, like marijuana, cocaine, methamphetamine, heroin, or prescription drugs that have addictive capacity, like the benzodiazepines (Xanax, Valium, Klonopin, etc.) or narcotics (painkillers, like Percocet, Talwins, and Darvocet) to the detriment of taking care of oneself and others responsibly. Drug dependency follows a similar course to alcoholism. See also **Adult Children of Alcoholics (ACOA).**

Coping. Trying to make the best of an uncomfortable, stressful situation—a quick fix—rather than changing something to make your life truly better; a helpful life strategy good only to a point and shouldn't be overused. The real goal is to figure out how to get beyond existing to meet basic survival and safety needs so you can truly express yourself in a self-actualized manner and pursue your true inner passions and creativity, be the person you were meant to be, and be able to express and feel joy.

Codependency. Overcaretaking, overfunctioning—enabling people who aren't taking responsibility for their lives because they have some addiction which zaps their energy, time, willpower, and faculties preoccupying them. Codependency results in neglecting one's own needs—with negative life consequence, such as deteriorating health, unhappiness, and social isolation.

Defense Mechanism. Blind spots preventing one seeing and understanding what is going on with themselves, much like the blind spot in a car. It can be dangerous if you don't check your blind spots—you miss important information. You can crash into a life problem without realizing why—namely, you did something inappropriate, like running into a car next to you because you forgot to check your blind spot out your side window and a car was there in the lane when you tried to move into it. With psychological blind spots, you conflict with people because of your own invisible blinders to the reality of the situation. Therapists and very supportive people in your life can help you see your blind spots. *You need to face your blind spots and let them go to be able to improve your life.*

Dissociation. A primitive defense mechanism used a lot more frequently than most people, including therapists, realize. A young child begins the habit of mentally going away from emotionally upsetting or damaging experiences, like sexual, physical, verbal, or mental abuse of a chronic nature, neglect, or poverty. The child puts amnesia walls around the experiences and develops either inner identities or mood states around the experience that can be triggered to come out by seemingly inconsequential events. For example, a woman raped near an elevator may be triggered to reexperience her terror in the form of a confusing panic attack when she goes near any elevator. She doesn't know why she suddenly can't breathe and feels like she is going to die. That part of her brain that holds the memory of the rape or the feeling does. (See chapter 7, mental disorders, for more information.)

Focusing, Focusing Inward, or the Focusing Process. By Gendlin, PhD. A specific step-by-step process or procedure one can use whereby you start with whatever is bothering you and break it down to its most bothersome reason and then cure it by coming up with a solution that truly feels right for you and makes you feel relieved and better in your body (see chapter 2). Your body doesn't lie.

Grief. A personal internal process you go through when you experience a loss of any kind that is significant to you—not limited to losing a loved one—and can also refer to losing one's innocence as a child through some abuse or neglect or even loss of an object, such as a ring that had sentimental value to you.

Grief Work. The process of mourning—allowing yourself to feel your painful feelings and release them in a five-phase process:

1. Denial, shock, and disbelief.
2. Bargaining that the person or thing will return if you do something good.
3. Anger or guilt, which is anger turned inward—the phase where many people get stuck and stop the process.
4. Sadness so severe it feels like you are going crazy and which bubbles up like an ocean wave and demands immediate release through crying.
5. Acceptance, the light at the end of the tunnel, whereby you experience relief from pain and remember warm memories of the person and feel the person in your heart or spiritual connection and know you've learned and grown from the experience.

Helping Professional. Person whose job it is to help people in some way—used here to primarily refer to those who provide psychotherapy or talk therapy to help people feel better and get over their life stressors or problems. These include licensed clinical psychologists, licensed clinical social workers, and licensed professional counselors. Licensed clinical psychologists have doctorates, compared to the master's level training of the other two. They also can perform testing or evaluations that may be necessary to initially understand your problems better, such as ADD and ADHD evaluations. Psychologists are sometimes confused with psychiatrists who are medical doctors whose practices to prescribing drugs, such as antidepressant, antianxiety, or antipsychotics for the symptom relief of mental problems, whereas the psychologist is trained to counsel the person to figure out how to change his life for the better.

I Message. Talk about self, feelings, needs, style, what works for you, and how you were raised. Do not mention the other person or even say "you." Objective: let the other person understand you. If they care about you, after they think about it, you will see change in their behavior versus having to point out they are doing it wrong now in "you message" form—which is how we have been erroneously taught to communicate which, however, blocks communication by making others defensive.

Metaphysics. Related to quantum theory in physics, which explains that invisible physical laws impact or influence our physical reality—a worldview that allows you to create your life the way you want it to be based on information about your spirit and how it works.

New Thought. A religious philosophy very similar to cognitive psychotherapy and supported by research on the observer effect which explains the law underlying cognitive therapy—the philosophy that teaches that our thoughts, our consciousness, and our beliefs create our lives and the world in a self-fulfilling prophecy manner.

Observer Effect. The influence that living beings have through the power of their thoughts and intentions on physical reality—mind over matter. The power of focused attention and intentionality—the observer effect—has a tremendous amount of research support.

Prayer Treatment. A procedure for praying presented by New Thought which is different than traditional prayer (whereby the person beseeches an old man in the sky to meet one's needs). Rather, prayer treatment involves making a personal connection with God, allowing God to flow through you by specifying your desires (putting out your word), making positive self-statements to create a positive self-fulfilling prophecy. It has five steps:

1) Recognize your higher power. Connect with God by calling out God's name—for example, God, one source, divine spirit creating and fulfilling our heart's desire.
2) Unify with your higher power. Feel a personal relationship or oneness with God.
3) Claim now. State your specific desires as if they are already reality, with knowledge that God is providing all for you—for example, "I am abundant and prosperous."
4) Give thanks as if it has already happened as well as count all your blessings. Put in present tense.
5) Release it. Let it go and have no doubt that God will fulfill your need.

Race (Human Race) Consciousness. Stereotypes we hold about race, gender, health, institutions (like marriage), and life in general that limit behavior and our ability to visualize and achieve our potential. See **collective unconscious**.

Reframing (Reframe). Put a positive spin on it—see the good or the silver lining in the cloud. For example, a child's temper tantrum can be seen as an annoying hassle or as a clue to what the child needs. Children express their feelings through action, not through talking like adults do. By reframing temper as a way of asking for attention to meet an underlying need, the parent can help the child figure out why he or she is emotionally upset and what can make it better.

Role Play. A psychological or interpersonal exercise, role-playing is taking formal turns with yourself or with a real or imagined person to achieve a higher level of satisfaction within your relationship with someone else, or within yourself, to reduce inner conflict or release some inner emotional pain. For example, your therapist might ask you to role-play what you would like to say to someone about something bothering you and request you to actually imagine the other person and what they might say back so you can experience how the conversation might go and so you can develop a good plan for carrying out the real scenario. In another vein, the therapist might ask you to play both sides of yourself about an internal conflict you have to see if you can resolve it. Like writing a list on paper clarifies what you have to do, role-playing gives you structure to clarify and resolve internal personality conflicts or conflicts between individuals.

Self-Actualization. Time and energy to do what you really want that brings you joy and allows you to make your fullest contribution to the world to express creatively and fully your gifts and talents.

Science of Mind. Has nothing to do with Scientology, except that most religions do hold some common beliefs. A New Thought religion that reveals that our beliefs, our consciousness, and our thoughts create reality (cognitive therapy, only with the metaphysical or spiritual underpinnings). Science of Mind explains the spiritual laws, like physics explains physical laws, like gravity.

Shatter Analysis. The name I've coined for the clinical model I use to help people because it transforms a person—shatters inner negativity that a client holds about himself and the world. A person comes in broken, like a broken windowpane. And rather than simply patching the broken window, the therapist removes the broken pane and replaces it with the person's truth, passions, and joys to help transform the personality into an authentic individualized pattern, like a stained-glass mosaic that truly expresses the individual's unique beauty and perfection.

Synchronicity. Meaningful events which occur simultaneously that many people would just call coincidences or accidents and which perceptive people with higher abstract reasoning or people that understand metaphysics would comprehend as the world working in an orderly manner to bring more order, harmony, and flow to life—a skill most people can cultivate once they understand and can use it for their betterment. For example, some things are meant to be or not, and life pulls you in a direction or signals you. For example, numerous people tell you the same thing or something pushes you in a direction different from your planned course because it was meant to work out that way. For example, a man is prevented from meeting with a potential business partner because of traffic delays. He finds out later that this businessman was a criminal.

Source. Higher power as you perceive or God by all its many names. The all-good, all-powerful source and all-wise and loving force that creates and provides for all—of which all is made. Once you tap into the source, you have unlimited power to create for your own and others' good.

Spirituality. Being aware you have a spiritual core—namely, that you are more than just a material body, that you are a form of light energy, and that you have a spirit body that is connected with the source.

Spiritual Law. Related to the cutting-edge new branch of physics (quantum theory, the Copenhagen interpretation, and observer effect) that explains that we are powerful energy and how to use this energy to love ourselves and love our lives and create a wonderful world.

Trauma. Bad stuff that has happened to you, including verbal, mental, emotional, or sexual abuse, losses, neglects, life disappointments, and so on. They continue to affect you emotionally—even though you may not be aware of it—and which cause you to think negatively about yourself, others, and the world and, therefore, cause you to think and do things that are self-destructive or counterproductive often without realizing why.

Truth. You, the truth of you, who you real are, your deepest needs and capacities.

Unconscious. What you are unaware of about yourself, which includes beliefs or attitude, the foundation of your self-esteem—which you need to become aware so you can release any negative thinking that could be causing you to behave counterproductively or self-destructively, which can prevent you from expressing your true joys and potential and fulfilling yours needs completely.

Vibes. Your energy and your intention impacting on reality. You know what this means. What you don't know is that—face it—this is just a catchy word for telepathy, psychokinesis, and other psychic phenomena. What you really mean when you go psychic is that you are really going physic. By "physic," we mean utilizing the latest knowledge in physics that we and the universe are all light energy and that our consciousness energy affects physical reality. You are using the energy laws that quantum physics is now investigating and proposing when you send vibes or feel vibes. If someone picks up on your vibes or you pick up on vibes, you are tuning into someone's inner workings of their mind, their thoughts, and their inside energy. How many times have you been thinking of something and the other person verbalizes and comes out with it? "Vibes" is the slang term for the spiritual law explaining how this happened.

Word. Refers to "speaking your word" or making positive self-statement or expressing your power of intention to create the outcome in your world you'd like to receive. It refers to a metaphysical or spiritual law, like gravity or electricity is in physics, which is rapidly becoming another law in physics. It means when you connect with the source to manifest your desire. Best example is when Jesus Christ raised the dead or changed water to wine by connecting with God and believing God to give him the power and flow through him to create a physical manifestation in our world.

Whole Person. Fulfilled person who has time and energy for meeting one's mental, emotional, physical, social needs, and life responsibilities and who comes from their spiritual core to them so accomplishment is effortless and lasting.

Win-Win Negotiation. The procedure whereby a mutually satisfying solution to a people problem or conflict occurs based on respect for all parties' needs.

Zero-Point Field. We and the universe are hollow microtubules of light comprising a mutable pulsating light field. In essence, we are truly light beings. At the subatomic particle level, there is field of random activity of infinite possibilities called the zero-point field (ZPF), which the observer effect—the power of intention—causes to crystallize or freeze into a set reality.

REFERENCES AND RESOURCES

Amen, Daniel G. *Healing ADD: The Breakthrough Program That Allows You to See and Heal the 6 Types of ADD*. New York, NY: The Berkley Publishing Group, 2001.

Azar, Beth. "A Case for Angry Men and Happy Women." *Monitor on Psychology*. American Psychological Association, April 2007: 18–19.

Baumann, T. Lee. *God at the Speed of Light: The Melding of Science and Spirituality*. Virginia Beach, VA: ARE Press, 2001.

Beattie, Melody. *Beyond Codependency*. Center City, MN: Hazelden Foundation, 1989.

Beattie, Melody. *Codependent No More*. New York, NY: Hazelden Foundation, 1987.

Bockian, Neil R., Valerie Poor, and Nora Elizabeth Villagran. *New Hope for People with Borderline Personality Disorder*. New York, NY: Three Rivers Press, 2002.

Borg, Marcus, Jack Kornfield, and Ray Riegert. *Jesus and Buddha: The Parallel Sayings*. Berkeley, CA: Ulysses Press, 1997.

Broder, Michael. *The Art of Staying Together*. New York, NY: Hyperion, 1993.

Campbell, Ross. *How to Really Love Your Child*. New York, NY: New American Library, Penguin Books, 1977.

Cardozo, Arlene Rossen. *Sequencing: The Groundbreaking Book on Having It All but Not All at Once*. New York, NY: Collier Books, Macmillan Publishing Company, 1986.

Colgrove, Melba, Harold H. Bloomfield, and Peter McWilliams. *How to Survive the Loss of a Love*. Allen Park, MI: Mary Books, 2001.

Crandall, Patsy. "The Pain of Co-Dependency." *Virginia Baptist Hospitals Mental/Health/Substance Abuse News Digest* 3, no. 20 (May 1990).

De Laszio, Vicki Staub, ed. *The Basic Writings of C. G. Jung*. New York, NY: Random House, 1959.

Deangelis, T. "APA Task Force Report Decries Culture's Sexualization of Girls." *Monitor on Psychology*. American Psychological Association, April, 2007: 51.

Dossey, Larry. *Healing Words*. New York, NY: HarperCollins Publishers, 1993.

Ellis, Albert and Irving M. Becker. *A Guide to Personal Happiness*. North Hollywood, CA: Wilshire Book Company, 1982.

Erikson, E. H. In R. M. Liebert, R. W. Poulos, and G. D. Strauss. *Developmental Psychology*. Englewood Cliffs, NJ: Prentiss-Hall, Inc., 1974.

Fillmore, Charles. *The Twelve Powers of Man*. Lee's Summit, MO: Unity School of Christianity, 1930.

Foundation for Inner Peace. *A Course in Miracles*. Tiburon, CA: Foundation for Inner Peace, 1975, 1985.

Freeman, James Dillet. *The Story of Unity*. Unity Village, MI: Unity House, 2000 (soft copy, 2007).

Gendlin, Eugene T. *Focusing*. New York: Phantom Books, US and Canada, 1981.

Gibran, Kahill. *The Prophet*. New York: Alfred A. Knopf, Inc., 1923.

Gray, John. *Men Are from Mars, Women Are from Venus*. New York, NY: HarperCollins, 1992.

Gray, John. *What Your Mother Couldn't Tell You and Your Father Didn't Know*. New York, NY: HarperCollins Publishers, Inc., 1994.

Hallowell, Edward M. and John J. Ratey. *Driven to Distraction*. New York, NY: Pantheon Books, 1994.

Hartmann, Thom. *Complete Guide to ADHD*. Grass Valley, CA: Underwood Books, 2000.

Hartmann, Thom. *Healing ADD*. Grass Valley, CA: Underwood Books, 1990.

Hay, Louise L. *Heal Your Body: The Mental Causes for Physical Illness and the Metaphysical Way to Overcome Them*. Carlsbad, CA: Hay House, Inc., 1982.

Hay, Louise L. *The Power Is Within You*. Carson, CA: Hay House, Inc., 1998.

Hoffman, Elizabeth Hanson. *Recovery from Smoking*. Center City, MN: Hazelden, 1991.

Holmes, Ernest Shurtleff. *Science of Mind*. New York, NY: Jeremy P. Tarcher/Putnam, 1938.

Holy Bible, The.

Internet. Google search by E. Hepler for famous people per categories of mental disorder.

Jampolsky, Gerald G. *Love Is Letting Go of Fear*. Berkeley, CA: Celestial Arts Publishing, 1979.

Keyes Jr., Ken. *Handbook to Higher Consciousness*. Coos Bay, OR: Love Line Books, 1973.

Larsen, Earnie and Carol Larsen Hegarty. *Days of Healing, Days of Joy*. New York, NY: Harper and Row, Publishers, Inc., 1987.

Lawlis, Frank. *The ADD Answer*. New York, NY: Penguin Group (USA), Inc., 2004.

Leach, Penelope. *Children First: What Our Society Must Do—and Is Not Doing—for Our Children Today*. New York, NY: Alfred Knopf, Inc., 1994.

Lee, A. J. *Cørrelations*. Mechanicsville, VA: Circle Eyed, 2005.

Lerner, Harriet Goldhor. *The Dance of Intimacy: A Woman's Guide to Courageous Acts of Change in Key Relationships*. New York, NY: Harper and Row, 1989.

Lerner, Harriet. *The Dance of Fear*. New York, NY: HarperCollins Publishers, Inc., 2004.

Lerner, Harriet. *The Dance of Anger: A Woman's Guide to Changing the Patterns of Intimate Relationships*. New York, NY: Harper and Row, Publishers, Inc., 1985.

Lipton, Bruce H. *The Biology of Belief: Unleashing the Power of Consciousness, Matter and Miracles*. Santa Rosa, CA: Mountain of Love/Elite Books, 2005.

Masterson, James. *Closet Narcissistic Disorder: The Masterson Approach. In R. Klien MD. The Newbridge Assessment and Treatment of Psychological Disorders*, A Video Series. New York, New York: Newbridge Communications, Inc., 1995.

McTaggart, Lynne. *The Field*. New York, NY: HarperCollins Publishers, 2001.

McTaggart, Lynne. *The Intention Experiment*. New York, NY: Simon and Schuster, Inc., 2007.

Newman, Mildred and Bernard Berkowitz. *How to Be Your Own Best Friend*. New York, NY: Ballantine Books, 1971.

Peale, Norman Vincent. *The Power of Positive Thinking*. New York: Prentice Hall Press, 1987.

Porter, Carolyn. *A Woman's Path to Wholeness*. Woodstock, GA: Empower Productions, 2001.

Price, John Randolph. *Empowerment: You Can Do, Be and Have All Things*. Carlsbad, CA and Sidney, AU: Hayhouse, 1992.

Putnam, Frank W. *Diagnosis and Treatment of Multiple Personality Disorder*. New York, NY: The Guilford Press, 1989.

Putnam, Frank W. *Dissociation in Children and Adolescents*. New York, NY: The Guilford Press, 1997.

Ray, Sondra. *Loving Relationships*. Berkeley, CA: Celestial Arts Publishing, 1980.

Robertson, Joel and Tom Monte. *Natural Prozac, Learning Release Your Body's Own Antidepressants*. New York, NY: Harper Collins Publishers, 1997.

Shinn, Florence Scovel. *Your Word Is Your Wand: A Sequel to the Game of Life and How to Play It*. Marina del Rey, CA: DeVorss Publications, 1928.

Sills, Judith. *Biting the Apple*. USA: Penguin Books, Viking, 1996.

Smith, Huston. *The Religions of Man*. New York, NY: Harper and Row, 1965.

Steinem, Gloria. *Revolution from Within*. Boston, MA: Little, Brown and Co., 1992.

Strohl, Lydia. "Why Doctors Now Believe Faith Heals." *Reader's Digest* (May 2001): 108115.

Sue, Derald Wing, Christina M. Capodilupo, Gina C. Torino, Jennifer M. Bucceri, Aisha M. B. Holder, Kevin L. Nadal, and Marta Esquilin. "Racial Microaggressions in Everyday Life." *Monitor on Psychology*. American Psychological Association, May–June 2007: 271.

Sylvest, Vernon M. *The Formula*. Fairfield, IA: Sunstar Publishing, Ltd., 1996.

Tavris, Carol. *Anger, The Misunderstood Emotion*. New York: Simon and Schuster, 1982.

Walker, Herschel. *Breaking Free My Life with Dissociative Identity Disorder*. New York, NY: Simon and Schuster, 2008.

Walsch, Neale Donald. *Conversations with God: An Uncommon Dialogue*. New York, NY: G. P. Putnam's Sons, 1994.

Wegscheider, Sharon. *Another Chance: Hope and Health for the Alcoholic Family*. Palo Alto, CA: Science and Behavior Books, Inc., 1981.

Wickett, Michael, Ed Bernd Jr., Jose Luis Romero, and JoNell Monaco Lytle. *The Silva UltraMind ESP System*. Laredo, TX: Nightingale Conant.

Yutang, Lin. Quotations from Internet.

Zimbardo, Philip G. *Shyness*. USA: Da Capo Press, 1989.

Zukav, Gary and Linda Francis. *The Heart of the Soul*. New York, NY: Simon and Schuster Source, 2001.

Zukav, Gary. *The Seat of the Soul*. New York: Simon and Schuster, 1989.

Information for the Helping Professional—
The Clinical Psychotherapeutic Model

I coined the term "shatter analysis" to describe this eclectic clinical model for multiple reasons. The therapeutic goal is to shatter the negative self, the negative self-talk, the negative core beliefs and to transform the client's self to vibrate at a joyous, whole new way of being—to create a wonderful life based on unconditional love of the self and one's world. The process is similar to working with stained-glass art. Like a cracked window, the client comes into psychotherapy broken. This model, like working with stained glass, removes the broken pane and replaces it with the person's joys and passions—his shiny, colorful, unique pieces—is then transformed into a perfect individualized pattern that truly expresses his individual beauty and perfection.

Initially, psychotherapy focuses on rapport building and helps the person problem-solve to resolve current life stressors to put out the brush fires or quell the crisis and stabilize the individual's life. This model, however, not only helps the client get out of the alligator pit but helps him stay out of the alligator pit. The person's core negative beliefs that limit their transformations are shattered so they can become the perfect crystallized sparks of divinity—the truth of themselves, their true purpose and joys.

As a licensed clinical psychologist, I have worked successfully for decades with clients using this clinical model that I have developed that integrates the major schools of thought or theoretical orientations of the human behavior sciences as well as major concepts from philosophy, theology, and spirituality. These are supported by empirical research in sciences, quantum physics, neurobiology, psychology, and medicine.

Chapter 1: cognitive behavioral therapy: cognition or consciousness creates a self-fulfilling prophecy

Chapter 2: humanistic-existential phenomenological approach: focusing, a structured interview technique to resolve problems in living

Chapter 3: psychodynamics, attachment theory, Gestalt therapy, and inner child work: insight-oriented work to heal past emotional wounds underlying current maladaptive coping strategies and disorders

Chapter 4: client role induction: information to educate clients and the public to encourage usage of psychotherapy, support groups, and other resources

Chapter 5: metaphysical or spiritual underpinnings of psychotherapy: the paradigm shift, which explains why therapy works and how true change occurs—the bridge between traditional psychology and metaphysics, the cutting-edge branch, quantum physics

Chapter 6: communication and assertiveness: skills building

Chapter 7: relationship issues: healing through relationships and healthy relationship principles for developing good support systems and partnerships. Also, information for the helping professional include medical model diagnoses so people can adjust their expectations about themselves and others as well as know when to seek professional help

Chapter 8: whole person model of recovery: addiction theory and recovery therapy

Chapter 9: family and child therapy foundation premises: stereotypes or collective unconscious beliefs that need to be addressed in order for family and couples' therapy to be effective. Addresses and transcends consciousness limitations regarding femininity and masculinity, parenting and children's needs, and more

Chapter 10: shine the light

The first three chapters provide a sequential approach to doing psychotherapy. Materials from the other chapters are introduced to the client at the teachable moment, often with handouts, included in this book.
My intention is to reach people at many levels:

* Teach the individual self-help concepts and tools so one can heal, be happy and fulfilled, dramatically improve life, and reduce suffering.
* Educate the public about psychology and other resources to aid them to be more informed consumers and to role induct clients into the therapy process so they are more willing to enter, appreciate, and benefit from it.
* Contribute to the field of human behavioral sciences and especially clinical psychology by providing a psychotherapy primer, text, and workbook, although written in laymen's language as a self-help book with entertaining stories, examples, poems, and a workbook format with instructions, exercises, and homework. Provide a clinical model that fledgling and experienced therapists can use to work out their blind spots or issues so that they can provide better care to their clients as well as learn useful psychotherapeutic theories and techniques in an integrated format.
* Introduce and encourage a paradigm shift—formally known as thinking outside the box, recognizing the prison door is open—that will help raise our human consciousness, particularly enlighten fellow helping professionals understand and incorporate the spiritual underpinnings as to why cognitive therapy works, namely, that we are made of light energy that follows certain laws and that if we utilize it, then we can reach a critical mass of divinity, individually and collectively.

Scientists and great minds around the world are understanding and investigating that we and the universe are composed of light energy. In my opinion, in the not-too-distant future, medical assessment, diagnosis, and treatment will involve analyzing the patient's light spectrum. Clinical psychology and helping professions need to get on board.

INDEX

abandonment 10, 16, 23, 25, 28, 92, 111, 112, 117, 144
abreacting (catharsis) 30, 78, 158
acceptance 6, 12, 14, 30, 37, 65, 66, 160
action 6
active listening skills and empathy 84
acupressure points 31
addictions or dependencies 104
   chemical dependency 104, 133
   codependency 36
   compulsive eating 105
Adult Children of Alcoholics (ACOA) 36, 157, 158, 159
affirmations 6, 14, 43, 50, 54, 56, 88, 98, 152, 156
aggressive communication 82, 83, 84
agoraphobia 107
Al-Anon 3, 36
Alcoholics Anonymous (AA) 14, 36, 104
alcoholism 104, 157, 158, 159
   Adult Children of Alcoholics and Al-Anon 3, 26, 36, 104
   coping versus self-care and self-actualization 139
   defense mechanisms in 7
   phases of 104
   twelve-step support groups for 36
   whole person model of fulfillment 128
alters 7, 109, 110, 111, 120, 122, 123, 124
alters defined. *See also* dissociative identity disorder (DID)
Amen, Daniel 163
anger defined by, iceberg analogy
   venting as expression of 28
anger defined, by iceberg analogy 18
   as a feeling versus as a behavior 160
   as a guide to clarifying yourself 19
   as a signal or red flag 18, 158
   exercises for viii
   homework for 11, 14, 22, 31, 87, 88, 96, 105, 132, 156, 168
   using as a guide to clarifying yourself 19
   ways to cool down or chill 86
Anger, The Misunderstood Emotion (Tarvis) 19, 165
anxiety disorders 107
   definition and symptoms 107
   famous people with 104
   treatment for 107
   types of 108
Aristotle 60
Asperger's disorder 106
assertive communication 81, 83, 88
assertiveness 82, 83, 158
attachment theory 31, 167
attention deficit disorder (ADD) 26, 103, 106, 160, 164
attention deficit hyperactivity disorder (ADHD) 105, 106, 107, 160, 164
   associated features of 106
   cause or etiology of 106
   definitions and symptoms of 105
   famous people with 106
   related disorders 106
   treatment for 107
attitudes 1, 2, 6, 8, 9, 15, 34, 43, 50, 55, 66, 95, 139, 159
auditory processing disorders 106
authorial-self 110
autism 106
awareness vii, 6, 7
basic emotion 16
Biology of Belief, The (Lipton) 135, 164
Bipolar disorders 107
   Bipolar I 107
   Bipolar II 107
   cause or etiology of 106
   definition and symptoms of 107
   dissociative identity disorder and 7
   famous people with 108
birth trauma 97
blind spots 7
borderline personality disorder (BPD) 109, 110, 112

born-again Christians 63
  fundamentalist 49, 62
  New Age Thought 49, 60
  Protestant 61, 62, 63, 64
Breaking Free (Walker) 111, 165
Broder, Michael 97, 163
Buddha 62, 63, 65, 163
Buddhist 61, 62, 63, 65, 71
Campbell, Ross 143, 163
Cardozo, Arlene Rossen 134, 141, 163
caretaking provider 102, 127
catharsis of fear and insecurity 78, 158
chemical dependency 104, 133, 159
childhood trauma 15, 25, 123, 124, 176
childhood trauma, healing. *See also* inner child, healing
childhood trauma, healing from. *See also* inner child, healing
child molesters 110
  focused attention and 110, 160
  raising, using old-school parenting 132
Christianity 64, 163
Christian Science 71
closet narcissistic personality disorder
  See also narcissistic personality disorder (NPD) 112
coconsciousness 110, 111
codependency 36, 133, 158, 159
Codependents Anonymous (CODA) 36
cognition 6, 34, 54, 158, 167
cognitive dissonance, theory of 15
communication 19, 35, 81, 83, 85, 91, 98, 99, 100, 102, 116, 117, 127, 141, 142, 146, 148, 157, 158, 160
  categories of 82
  efforts in, boundaries created to support 83
  empathy and active listening skills 84
  exercise in 141
  I messages versus you messages 158
  principles, summary of 91
  sending out vibe of love and desire (crown chakra) 85
  visualization used in 141
  win-win negotiations in 85, 88, 91, 98, 158
compulsive eating 104, 133
Conversations with God (Walsch) 54, 165
coping with anger and anxiety
  versus self-care and self-actualizing 132, 159
Coping with anger and anxiety 86
  defined 86
couples' relationships 97
  communication in 98
  couples' therapy for 99

  divine harmony in 98
  human race consciousness regarding 100
  long-lasting, qualities of 97
  love connections in 99, 103, 127
  marital myths and 100
  masculine and feminine energy in 100
Crescenzo, Luciano De 44
crown chakra 85
crying 27, 28, 30, 110, 113, 134, 141, 158, 160
Dance of Anger, The (Lerner) 18, 81, 164
Daniel, Amen 106
DBT 121
defense mechanisms 7, 8, 9, 10, 11, 12, 16, 19, 26, 92, 110, 112, 116, 117, 123, 126, 133, 145, 158, 159
  denial 9, 11, 30, 106, 133
  identification with a lost object 10
  immature defenses 10
  introjection 10
  minimization 10
  projection 10
  projective identification 10
  rationalization 10
  repression 11
denial
  defense mechanisms 160
dependencies 104, 134
depression 2, 7, 30, 36, 50, 54, 66, 82, 106, 107, 108, 109, 110, 116, 133, 158
  cause of 109
  cognitive therapy for 158
  definition and symptoms of 158
  famous people with 111
  in dissociative identity disorder 110
  treatment for 109
  types of 109
dialectical behavior therapy 112
DID 121
dissociation 30, 110, 159
dissociative evaluations scale 111
dissociative identity disorder (DID) 7, 110
  associated features 110
  cause or etiology of 110
  definition and symptoms of 110
  famous people with 111
  treatment for 111
Dissociative identity disorder (DID) 109
Driven to Distraction (Hallowell) 107, 163
dysfunctional family 7, 20, 26, 36, 92, 101, 128, 145
dyslexia 106, 114
dysthymia 108

Einstein, Albert 44, 106, 117
electricity vii, 48, 71, 162
Emerson, Ralph Waldo 6, 37, 109
emotional freedom therapy (EFT) 30, 31, 107
Emotions Anonymous (EA) 36
empathetic or empathetic listener 102
empathy and active listening skills 84
empathy sickness 128
Employee Assistance Program (EAP) 36
empowerment 13
   of thinking or thoughts in personal awakening 56
   of thoughts, in self-fulfilling prophecy 1
   of words 49
Erikson, E. H 113
exercises vii, viii, 50, 81, 168
   for coping with anger and anxiety 11
   for defense mechanisms 11
   for feelings and emotions 16
   for focusing 19
   for healthy communication 91
   for inner child work 97
   for love connection 127
   for movement 36
   for process of change 6
   for self-fulfilling prophecy 6, 15, 23, 43, 71, 140, 160, 167
   for sending out vibe of love and desire 85
   for sequencing 141
   for thought stopping 12, 56, 60, 156
   for transforming or transformation 14
   for whole, fulfilled person 18, 91, 104, 128
   for win-win negotiations 85
eye movement desensitization reprocessing (EMDR) 30
false self 114
family, dysfunctional 7, 20, 26, 92, 101, 128, 145
   as guides to understanding and loving yourself 28, 95, 128, 135
   defense mechanisms to cope with 7
   family of origin 101, 110
   fear as basic emotion 16
   feelings 7
   feelings chart 16
   focusing inward as guide to self 20, 22, 25, 83, 149, 159
   of abandonment 10, 16, 23, 25, 26, 92, 112, 117
   releasing 78
   self-esteem problems and 101
   twelve-step support groups for 36
   whole person model of fulfillment 128
   working women and 133

Field, The (McTaggart) 55, 164
Fillmore, Charles 67
Fillmore, Myrtles 72
Fischer, Bobby 137
focused attention 55, 143, 149, 160
focusing 7, 18, 19, 20
   focusing inward 149
   focusing-inward technique 24
   focusing process, Gendlin's 143
Focusing 20, 22, 24, 107, 159, 163
Focusing (Gendlin) 20, 22, 24, 143
Franklin, Ben 137
Gendlin, Eugene T 20, 22, 24, 159, 163
generalized anxiety disorder 107
genius intelligence 117
Gibran, Kahil 38
God 30, 37, 38, 43, 44, 45, 48, 49, 50, 54, 61, 62, 63, 66, 67, 72, 73, 117, 160, 161
   as universal source of love 43, 44, 62, 63, 64, 73
   oneness with vii, 37, 44, 49, 63, 64, 66, 67, 73, 95, 97, 161
Graham, Billy 62
Grandma Moses 137
gratitude v, 73, 156
Gray, John 25, 87, 100
grief 10, 11, 16, 23, 26, 30, 32, 34, 97, 107, 111, 135, 145, 158
grief work 30, 160
Hallowell, Edward (Ned) 106, 163
Hartmann, Thom 106
Hay, Louise 6, 50, 54, 55, 56
Heal Your Life (Hay) 6, 50, 54, 56
helping professional psychologists
   social workers 116, 160
higher power 37, 42, 43, 44, 50, 60, 61, 62, 63, 64, 65, 66, 72, 93, 96, 98, 161. *See* God; *See* God
homework 11, 14, 22, 44, 87, 88, 96, 105, 132, 156, 168
   for anger 11
   for spirituality 44
   for training thinking or thoughts 19
   for transforming or transformation 14
homework anger defined, by iceberg analogy
   homework for 44
How to Really Love Your Child (Campbell) 143, 163
human race consciousness 100, 139, 159
hyperactive type 106
hypnosis 30
identification with a lost object 10
I messages 82, 83, 84, 88, 91

immature defenses 10
inattentive type without hyperactivity (ADD) 106
inner child, healing exercises for
    transactional analysis 28
inner child, inner exercise for
    healing from past trauma 32
insecurity, releasing 78, 158
Inspiration (Filosa) 136
intellectualization 40
introjection 10
intuition 53, 55, 60, 72, 74, 77
Islam 62, 68
    five pillars of 68
Jackson, Michael 111
Jesus and Buddha, The Parallel Sayings (Marcus, Kornfield, Jack, Riegert, and Ray) 65, 163
Jesus Christ 49, 63, 67, 71, 162
journal or journaling viii, 79, 102, 156
joy guide 135
Judaism 61, 62, 64, 67
Jung, Carl 78, 95
Koran 62
Lacy Speaks Her Truth (Filosa) 89
Lawlis, Frank 106
law of attraction 54, 56, 95, 114, 117. *See also* observer effect
Leach, Penelope 143
learned helplessness 34
Lerner, Harriet 18, 81
Lewis, Dorothy 111
light energy viii, 6, 55, 56, 63, 73, 154, 162, 168
Lipton, Robert 55
love as basic emotion 16
    connections in couples' relationships 97
    God as universal source of 43
    in healing inner child 95, 96, 127
    sending out vibes of 56, 73, 79, 91
Love Letters (Gray) 87
Lucifer Effect, The (Zimbardo) 114
major depression 108
masculine energy 100, 101
McGraw, Phil 97
McTaggart, Lynne 55
Meir, Golda 137
Men Are from Mars, Women Are from Venus (Gray) 25, 100
men, male addictivity in 133
Mensa 117
metaphysics defined
    metaphysical theory and 60

synchronicity and 73
Michelangelo 109, 137
minimization 10, 106
mirroring 115, 116
moody type 106
movement (exercise) 36
Munte, Tom 134
narcissism 113, 114, 115, 116, 117, 121, 122, 126, 176
narcissistic personality disorder (NPD) 112, 114, 116
Narcissus-speak 114, 116
Narcotics Anonymous (NA) 36, 104
Natural Prozac (Robertson and Munte) 134
negative thinking 2, 7, 8, 9, 12, 16, 54, 72, 109, 162
neurotransmitters 106, 108
New Thought 43, 58, 71, 72, 73, 160, 161
observer effect 6, 55, 56, 71, 154, 160, 162
obsessive-compulsive disorder (OCD) 18, 107, 133
Oneness (Filosa) 46
One Source (Filosa) 48
Open Up to Help (Unity prayer) 33
orbs 154
Overeaters Anonymous (OA) 36
overfocused type. *See also* attention deficit hyperactivity disorder (ADHD)
panic disorder 107
parenting 29, 99, 127, 132, 143, 167
parenting codependency in 158, 159
    old-school, whole, fulfilled person and 132
passive-aggressive 84
passive-aggressive communication 82, 83
passive communication 82, 83, 84, 106
pedophiles 110
personality disorders 111, 114, 115
    borderline personality disorder 109, 110, 111
    cause and etiology of 114
    definitions and symptoms of 114
    mirroring used for 116
pervasive developmental delay 106
physics cognitive therapy and 6
    intuition and 55
    quantum 44, 54, 55, 66, 154, 160, 162, 167
Poems by Filosa 5, 41, 47, 48, 53, 59, 70, 77, 89, 136, 138
    Guidance 75
    Inspiration 136
    Oneness 46
    One Source 48
    Revelation 39
    To See the Sea 69
    View 4

 What Matters 138
 Words 58
positive thinking vii, 6, 15, 43, 50, 54, 55, 56, 60, 66, 72, 91, 109, 140, 141
postpartum depression. *See also* depression
posttraumatic stress disorder (PTSD) 31, 107, 116
prayer 42, 43, 46, 49, 50, 53, 65, 66, 67, 68, 73, 75, 85, 149, 154, 160
precognitive dreams 79
problem-solving dreams 79, 80
projection 9, 11, 14, 19, 92, 106, 114, 117
projective identification 10
Prophet, The (Gibran) 38
psychic. *See* physics; *See* physics; *See* physics; *See* physics; *See* physics
psychodynamic therapy 32
psychotherapist 31, 34, 35, 96, 102, 109, 156
psychotherapy 111, 117, 140, 147, 158, 160, 167, 168
 attachment theory used in 31
 during motherhood 146
 emotional freedom therapy 30
 Employee Assistance Program offered for 36
 explained 6
 eye movement desensitization reprocessing 30
 for addictions and dependencies 134
 for anxiety disorders 107
 for attention deficit hyperactivity disorder 26
 for dissociative identity disorder 109
 for healing inner child 167
 for healthy communication 91
 for narcissistic personality disorder 112
 for super high IQ 117
 function of 38
 hypnosis 31
 movement used in 36
 opening up to 73
 psychodynamic therapy 32
 releasing homework used in 14
 twelve-step support groups used in 11
Putnam, Frank 111
rapprochement phase 113
rationalization 10, 133
reframing 87, 161
relationships, healthy 92
 caretaking provider in 102
relaxation techniques 107
releasing of fear and insecurity 158
religion vii, 38, 43, 45, 60, 62, 63, 64, 67, 71, 146, 154
repression 10, 11
reverse posttraumatic stress disorder (PTSD) 116

Revolution from Within, The 140
Ritalin 106
Robertson, Joel 134
role play 29, 96, 161
sadness 16, 18, 19, 23, 27, 30, 91, 107, 149, 160. *See also* grief
Saint Augustine 61
Science of Mind 71, 161
Scientology 43, 71, 161
Seat of the Soul (Zukav) 13, 54
Secret, The (video documentary) v, 54
self-actualizing 132
self-esteem 2, 6, 21, 33, 34, 35, 50, 81, 106, 108, 109, 113, 132, 133, 139, 140, 141, 143, 144, 145, 146, 162
self-fulfilling prophecy 1, 6, 15, 23, 43, 71, 160, 167
sequencing 134, 141, 148
Sequencing (Cardozo) 134
Sex and Love Addicts Anonymous (SLAA) 36
shadow 38, 92, 95, 96, 97, 116, 117, 127
Shakespeare, William 81
Silva UltraMind ESP program 74
situational depression 109
somatoform disorder 110
source. *See* God
speaking your truth 49, 67, 91, 114
spiritual law vii, 49, 54, 60, 65, 66, 71, 72, 161, 162
sponsoring thoughts 6, 54
Steinem, Gloria 128
stonewalling, *also* known as gaslighting 98
stress management 107
super high IQ 117
superwoman phenomenon 139
Tarvis, Carol 19
Thatcher, Margaret 137
thinking 13, 49, 55, 71, 72
thought creates 50, 71, 72
thoughts 13, 16, 36, 54, 66, 67, 71, 72, 89. *See* thinking
To See the Sea (Filosa) 69
toxic people 102
transactional analysis 28
transformation 50, 167
transforming 14
trauma 7, 9, 11, 12, 15, 25, 27, 28, 30, 32
triangular breathing 88
truth 14
twelve-step programs 104, 135
Unity prayer 50
Unity religion 67
vibes 56, 73, 79, 91, 97, 143, 162

View (Filosa) 4
visual processing disorders 106
Walker, Herschel 111
Walsch, Neal Donald 54
What the Bleep Do We Know!? (movie) 56
What Your Mother Didn't Tell You and Your Father Didn't Know (Gray) 87
whole, fulfilled person vii
whole person model of fulfillment 128
win-win negotiations 85, 98
wish fulfillment 78, 80
women 11, 22, 62, 69, 97, 101, 139, 140
  codependent 114, 133, 134, 139
  feminine energy of 100, 154
  money issues for working women 144
words as key to empowerment 13, 50
world religions 37, 49, 60, 61, 64, 65, 66
world religions common threads tying together 61
You Can Heal Your Life and Heal Your Body (Hay) 50, 54, 56
you messages 82, 84
Your Word Is Your Wand (Shinn) 50, 54, 92
Yutang, Lin 140
zero-point field 55, 66, 154, 162
Zimbardo, Philip G. 114
Zukav, Gary 13, 50, 54

About the Author

Dr. A. P. Filosa, Psy. D., also known as aka Anne F. Creekmore, Psy.D. is a highly accomplished Licensed Clinical Psychologist based in Richmond, Virginia. Her exceptional achievements have garnered recognition and honors, including membership in the Phi Beta Phi Honor Society and multiple features in Who's Who in American Women. She was honored as the Top Doctor Licensed Clinical Psychologist in Virginia in 2017 and subsequently received the prestigious titles of Virginia Psychologist of the Year in 2019 and 2021, as well as Virginia Clinical Psychologist of the Year in 2021.

Dr. Creekmore is a distinguished alumna of Virginia Commonwealth University, where she graduated with Honors. At a remarkably young age of twenty-six, she attained her doctorate in clinical psychology through the esteemed Virginia Consortium of Professional Psychology, which was co-sponsored by the College of William and Mary, Eastern Virginia Medical School, Old Dominion University, and Norfolk State University.

As a prolific author, Dr. Creekmore has enlightened readers with her insightful books, such as "Love Yourself, Love Your Life," "Wisdoms and Ways of Abundance," "Find Mr. Right (or Mrs. Right): The Perfect Ten," and "Not Fit for Human Consumption: Triggered Traumatic Memories and the Violence Profile." Her latest work delves even deeper into the assessment and treatment of disordered behavior that wreaks havoc in our world, providing breakthrough information and understanding.

Dr. Creekmore's journey goes far beyond her professional expertise. As a devoted parent of two and a metaphysician, she leads a life that brims with meaning, granting her unique perspectives shaped by personal triumphs and even profound traumas. From these extraordinary experiences, she has forged a transformative theory of psychotherapy known as shatter or shadow analysis. This groundbreaking approach, firmly rooted in the profound principles of the law of attraction, unlocks the door to understanding various psychotherapeutic methods. It empowers individuals from all walks of life, granting them invaluable skills to enrich their own mental well-being.

With remarkable clarity and compassion, Dr. Creekmore presents the essence of shatter analysis in her masterpiece, "Love Yourself, Love Your Life." Its pages overflow with accessible language, crafted to reach a wide range of readers, ensuring its profound benefits are within the grasp of all seeking them. Through her tireless work, she champions mental health breakthroughs with the transformative power to reshape our world. Drawing upon four decades of clinical experience and practice, her wisdom and insights shine as a beacon of hope and change.

Dr. Creekmore's advocacy extends far beyond the confines of her therapy room. With a burning passion, she calls for a paradigm shift in our collective approach to mental well-being. Her voice reverberates with the urgency and potential to alter the fabric of our society. Rooted in a deep wellspring of wisdom, she combines her extensive knowledge with unwavering empathy, breathing life into her healing mission.

"Love Yourself, Love Your Life" represents the culmination of thirty-five years of diligent study in psychology, philosophy, theology, and spirituality, complemented by extensive psychotherapeutic experience with individuals from all walks of life and diverse perspectives. Dr. Creekmore has worked in diverse settings, including residential and inpatient facilities, the Department of Corrections, and outpatient private practice. Her clinical expertise encompasses various areas, such as relationship issues, family systems, abuse, grief and trauma resolution, stress-related illnesses, Attention Deficit Hyperactivity Disorder (ADHD), anxiety, depression, spiritual counseling and energy work, unipolar and Bipolar Depression, Complex PTSD (or the Dissociative Identity Disorder Spectrum stemming from early childhood trauma), substance abuse, and narcissism.

Dr. Creekmore sheds light on the destructive consequences that arise when multiple disorders, such as Complex PTSD, Bipolar depression, substance abuse, and narcissism, go untreated (referred to as comorbidity). She has also uncovered the language of narcissists, which she calls Narcissus Speak. Dr. Creekmore provides valuable insights on how to communicate and negotiate with narcissists effectively. Furthermore, she emphasizes the importance of mental health professionals conducting thorough assessments and displaying a genuine curiosity to identify these disorders in young individuals. By intervening early and providing appropriate treatment, professionals can effectively help prevent the manifestation of havoc during adolescence and adulthood.

Dr. Creekmore offers a comprehensive range of services, including clinical evaluations and psychotherapy for individuals, couples, and families. She is also skilled in hypnosis and provides recordings in MP3 and CD formats that cover topics such as anxiety, depression, addiction, sleep disorders, and imbalances in dissociative disorders. Additionally, she delivers educational lectures titled "Understanding Conflict and Violence" to further educate and empower her audience.

Countless individuals have embraced self-love and transformed their lives by working directly with Dr. Creekmore, and now her book, "Love Yourself, Love Your Life," is a powerful tool for those seeking personal growth and fulfillment.

Dr. Anne P. Filosa Creekmore, Psy. D. serves as a guiding light, reminding us all that challenges are not problems but rather opportunities for personal growth.

Some of Dr. Creekmore's numerous awards:

Who's Who of American Women 1993-1994-Current
Phi Kappa Phi Honor Society Lifetime Membership
Top Doctor 2017 Top licensed Psychologist
2019 Virginia Psychologist of the Year Top 100 Registry
2021 Virginia Clinical Psychologist of the Year Top 100 Registry
Top 100 Doctors 2023 Lifetime Achievement Recipients
Pinnacle Professional Member

www.ingramcontent.com/pod-product-compliance
Lightning Source LLC
Chambersburg PA
CBHW060949170426
43201CB00026B/2427